The Fraudsters

How Con Artists Steal Your Money

The Fraudsters

How Con Artists Steal Your Money

Eamon Dillon

MERLIN
PUBLISHING

First published in 2008 by
Merlin Publishing
Newmarket Hall, Cork Street,
Dublin 8, Ireland
Tel: +353 1 4535866
Fax: +353 1 4535930
publishing@merlin.ie
www.merlinwolfhound.com

ISBN 978-1-903582-82-4

A CIP catalogue record for this book is available from the British Library.

10 9 8 7 6 5 4 3 2 1

Typeset by Artwerk Ltd
Cover Design by Graham Thew Design
Cover image courtesy of Comstock Images
Printed and bound by CPI Cox & Wyman, Britain

Contents

Acknowledgements

First and foremost I want to thank Ann Marie for being an absolute bedrock of support and a font of wisdom. Without her this book would never have been written.

There are others, as is usual in this line of work, who can't be thanked in public but to whom I owe a debt of gratitude.

I want to also express my gratitude to my supportive colleagues at the *Sunday World* who are always ready with advice and encouragement, in particular Des Ekin, Eddie Rowley and Sarah Hamilton. Photographers Liam O'Connor and Padraig O'Reilly are fantastic colleagues and provided very valuable assistance. The *Sunday World* is a unique environment for which Editor Colm MacGinty and Managing Director Gerry Lennon can take full credit. Because of that this book has been written. Our managing editor Neil Leslie and news editor John Donlon deserve a huge thank you for letting the authors among the newsroom staff work on their favourite subjects. Owen Breslin, again provided invaluable assistance in sorting out the photo section. Lawyer Kieran Kelly is second to none in his legal advice and thanks are due for his vital role in helping this project to its conclusion.

Thanks are also due to the hard-working staff at Merlin Publishing, Aoife Barrett, Chenile Keogh, Laura Synnott, Julie Dobson, Tony Hayes, and to Graham Thew, Don Harper and Martin McCall.

Introduction

"Exercise caution in your business affairs, for the world is full of trickery. But let this not blind you to what virtue there is; many persons strive for high ideals, and everywhere life is full of heroism."

From *The Desiderata* by Max Ehrmann, 1927

This book is about people who steal money. The characters in the following pages are thieves. Just because they don't snatch a handbag or threaten a victim with a blood-filled syringe doesn't make them any less venal. Being a con-artist is a tawdry affair, there's nothing glamorous or heroic about it. While the label *con-artist* implies some sort of worthwhile talent, it basically comes down to being able to lie and cheat. The word con, which comes from confidence-trickster, has come to mean a fraud, a scam or a rip-off. The first known usage of the term 'confidence man' was in 1849 when it was used by newspapers during the trial of William Thompson in New York. He chatted with strangers, eventually asking if they had the confidence to lend him their watches, which he would then walk off with. If there is an art to being a fraudster it is the ability to treat all potential victims with utter contempt.

Con-artists are thieves who rely on pretending to be someone they're not. They appeal to both the highest and lowest human emotions to lure their unwitting victims into their web of deceit. Fraudsters will feign being in love, pretend to be a friend, a police officer or just about anything to win the confidence of their victim. It is an inherently anti-social crime, even more so than the type of petty offences to which the term is usually applied. Unlike drunks urinating in gardens, or late-night vomiting teenagers, fraud has developed the potential to subvert the qualified trust on which civilised society is based. Every day people make split-second decisions based on the person they see in front of them. When money is handed over to someone in a shop the assumption is made that because they are standing behind the till and wearing the uniform they are working for the shop. It would be entirely unexpected if the shop assistant pocketed the money and walked out. The unspoken trust that exists between strangers allows society to function with relative ease. The social contract is held together by a sense of what is right or wrong. Untroubled by that morality, fraudsters exploit those social conventions to steal money, by using and abusing that trust.

Con-artists look like ordinary people. If anything they probably appear more successful and trustworthy than the average person. The ideal con-job is one where the victim never even knows they have been targeted. They may even thank the fraudster who walks away with their money. The best fraud ever carried out will never be known. By definition the finest con-artists are still out there, pretending to be the person everyone else thinks them to be. They could be a head of state, a top chief executive or a multi-millionaire self-help guru. Truth and lies are easily mixed together to create a tapestry of a fake reality, that becomes increasingly difficult to unpick. Fraud never appears to be black and white and clever con-jobs are always poised to maximise the potential for confusion should the need arise.

People still love a story about a clever fraudster. There's a sense of *schadenfreud* in knowing that someone else got caught out. If the victim fell for a trick because of their greed or lust then it is easy to take the moral high-ground and laugh at the poetic justice of it all. But people like the idea that someone clever enough can outwit the system, that they can use their wit to beat the odds. That's fine until the next time you're the victim. It's reflected in the movie depictions of con-artists. Leonardo Di Caprio played Frank Abagnale in *Catch Me if You Can*. Based on a true story, it's impossible not to like the character of Frank Abagnale as he is portrayed. He comes across as a loveable, troubled kid, who uses the financial system and people's gullibility to act out his own fantasy of being a worthwhile and important person. The film barely scratches the surface of the effects such frauds can have on the people who are out-witted. Even in the grittier *The Grifters* in which a dying John Cusack meets his estranged mother played by Anjelica Huston, con-artistry can be interpreted as being some worthwhile form of wisdom to pass on to the next generation.

The reality is different. It can even be sinister. Organised crime is heavily involved in fraud. They are well placed to ensure the various factors needed for success come together. Reluctant participants or victims can be subjected to intimidation to ensure that the scam reaches its final conclusion. Professional criminals have easier access to fake documents and are able to draw on experienced criminals. They also have the resources to steal or bribe their way to getting inside knowledge. Insiders working for call centres, credit card companies, banks or insurance companies can be compromised or cajoled – one way or another. Such scams don't have to rely on skill to successfully avoid the forces of law and order. If the police get on their trail, the junior members of the racket are simply sacrificed and they in turn are too scared to point the finger at the true organisers. Funds raised through insurance fraud, card skimming, counterfeiting and mortgage fraud are known to have been used to raise capital for more serious criminal activities such as drug dealing. They have also been a source of funding for paramilitary and terror groups all over the world.

Many individuals involved in fraud can also display signs of anti-social personality traits, some to the point of being psychopathic. Dr John Bogue, a forensic clinical psychologist based in NUI Galway, characterises a person with a psychopathic personality as being perfectly equipped to be a con-artist: "They can present a very plausible, calm demeanour and façade. People with psychopathic personality disorder typically are charming, they're manipulative, glib, cunning, with superior, albeit often superficial, conversational skills. They are smooth talkers with velvet-tongues. However, they are also social predators, they are callous and they have very low anticipatory anxiety levels which makes them very good for committing certain crimes as they are not unduly inhibited by fear or rumination of consequences. A consistent research finding is that psychopaths have no such qualms because they don't learn from previous experiences. When they are caught, the punishment or adverse consequences are not taken on board. They are not effectively internalised."

These individuals are not as unusual as we would like to think. Dr Bogue explains that everyone to some extent possesses adaptive psychopathic traits: "If you have mildly psychopathic traits it can arguably make you a more successful person. It would be better for you to have some traits than none at all. If you had none at all you would probably have yielded opportunities throughout your career to other people that would be to your detriment." It may seem a little unfair, but many of the characteristics listed by Dr Bogue as being part of a psychopathic personality could be applied to successful politicians, business people and athletes.

The real difference boils down to the fact that a fraudster will work hard to avoid hard work. In terms of a psychopathic personality it amounts to a belief that they are owed a good living by the rest of the world. "There's a sense of personal entitlement that overrides everything. It's narcissistic and grandiose in many ways: 'Why should I work? That's for little people.' That sense of entitlement would probably propel a lot of people to engage in white collar fraud and get rich quick schemes," according to Dr Bogue.

Fraud is not a victimless crime. It can have a devastating impact on a victim's psychological well-being. The idea is to build up trust with someone and then to manoeuvre them into the best position in which to abuse it. Quite often those victims will be the most vulnerable members of society, such as elderly people without younger family members nearby to rely on for advice. Becoming the victim of a scam can have long-lasting negative effects for these people. It can create anxiety and an unnecessary fear of crime. There are also those people whose sense of altruism is abused by con-artists. The perfect example is the unsolicited email from a con-artist purporting to be wealthy and religious looking for a like-minded soul to help distribute their substantial wealth. It can have a personal cost to victims that far outweighs any damage to their bank balance.

Another cost of fraud is the amounts financial companies admit are being stolen every year. Banks and credit card companies can be economical with the truth when it comes to acknowledging that they are the victims of con-artists. For at least a full decade, during the 1990s, they failed to inform customers that fraudsters could easily glean enough details from cash machines to empty an account. Over the years, the increasing level of fraud, however, has forced banks to confront the fraudsters with new security measures. They have changed ATM technology to make it harder for the scam artists. Bank customers are also now well aware of the possibility of fraud while using an ATM so in Ireland and most European countries debit and credit cards now come with a micro-chip. This has narrowed down the scope for fraud.

The widespread use of fake money drafts has also forced banks to issue warnings to customers. In the past they were accepted as being as good as cash, now customers are told that it can take a few days before such drafts are actually cleared. Just like ordinary victims of fraud, financial institutions don't like to admit being tricked out of money. After all, they are supposed to be smarter when it comes to minding cash. On the other hand, insurance companies are probably guilty of over-stating the extent of fraud to justify increased premiums and therefore increased profits. Just like acts of frauds, the cost of fraud is difficult to pin down.

Every now and then a particularly audacious fraud will make the news, whereas the mundane reality is that fraud and theft continues every day of the week. Fraud and con-jobs are an age-old problem. One way or another people have been tricked out of their wealth and riches throughout history. Lying and cheating is part and parcel of the human condition. The type of individuals and even the scams detailed in this book have been around a long time. For example in the 1800s,

Scottish con-artist Gregor MacGregor tried to attract investment and settlers to the non-existent country of Poyais. Fortunately, unlike those who bought their tickets for Poyais, most people are unaware of the true extent of fraud for the simple reason that the vast majority of people rarely end up being the target of fraud. While fraud is widespread and endemic, it is just a small fraction of the overall economy. The chances of becoming a victim to fraud are reasonably low. By applying common sense and keeping a close eye on bank and credit card accounts those chances decrease even further. Hopefully readers of this book will be a little better armed to avoid falling for the tricks and to recognise a potential scam before going too far.

Eamon Dillon
September 2008

ONE

The Charmers

The best con-jobs are simple ones. The victim is found and a carrot is dangled in front of them. The lure can be anything from the promise of sex, cash, racing tips or even a cheap supply of shirts. On paper such a fraud looks straight-forward enough, but it takes skill and nerve to carry off a confidence trick. After all, the victim has to be lulled into the right frame of mind before the fraudster can spring the trap and get the money. It is about exploiting a person's greed, gullibility or fear.

All good con-artists and liars have an instinctive understanding of basic human psychology and know how far they can push someone to get them to part with their cash or property. It can also take someone who is utterly devoid of the usual sense of right and wrong. They have no understanding of how their actions can affect other people. Psychologists describe such people as high-functioning sociopaths. Typically they appear perfectly normal, but in reality have little affinity to people who surround them and with whom they interact. From an early age they learn how to mimic normal behaviour to avoid the wrong sort of attention and to attract the right kind. For them the usual moral constraints don't apply. Even the prospect of being caught and challenged about their behaviour carries none of the mortification or humiliation a person would normally be expected to experience. This complete lack of fear of consequences goes some way to explaining why some serial fraudsters continue the same con trick, over and over again, despite the high probability they will be caught out and punished. This is also the type of fraudster who is perfectly poised to take on a fictitious role or the identity of another person. They change identities the way other people change coats. It is possible that even the fraudster may believe, at least for a while, that they really are the invented persona.

Con-artists who have a gift for charming people come across as entirely plausible. The vast majority of people don't spot such a fraudster until it is too late. When a powerful lure is thrown into the mix, a person's natural scepticism is eroded even further. Fraudsters don't have facial tics nor do they nervously peer over their shoulder. They look like very ordinary people or, even worse, like just the right sort of person needed at that moment in time.

The lean, fit-looking man who casually walked into the pub, looked like just the sort of person who would fit in with the regular customers. Who could tell if he was a genuine chap or a serial con-man just out of jail looking for his next victim? With his charming Irish brogue and easy-going manner he made good company for his fellow drinkers. The patrons in the English country pub were well-used to members of the horse-racing fraternity, but this guy really knew his stuff about the Sport of Kings. He introduced himself as Dean, a professional jockey. The race fans knew of Dean Gallagher as a top Irish jockey who made a good living in the top ranks of the sport. It was a real pleasure to have him mixing with the regulars. He was generous with his information as well. A little bit of inside information from the racing game can go a long way.

The next day, two of Dean's tips came up trumps, providing a nice little earner for anyone who had followed his advice and placed a bet with the bookie. The pub's usual customers were delighted to befriend the famous hurdle jockey. More nuggets of information like that would turn drinking in the Douglas Bar in Normanton into a profitable and pleasant pastime. Landlady Lorraine Doran said: "He gave them some tips, they wanted money and they invited him to come back to Derby because he said he wouldn't be racing the rest of the week. It was very, very believable that he was Dean Gallagher."

One evening, shortly after his fortuitous appearance in the boozer, Dean was back again, spending a few hours chatting amicably with drinkers at the bar. Then, just after closing time, 'Dean' abruptly left. He disappeared into the night and so did STG£2,500 of the pub's takings.

"I went down the cellar, and was down there 15 to 20 minutes at the most, to do the beer order but I came back up and there was no sign of this man and the money had gone missing," said Lorraine.

It didn't take the Herts Constabulary long to come up with the name of a suspect they wanted to interview and it wasn't Dean Gallagher. The police quickly discovered that Terry Kirby, a 37-year-old Irishman, would certainly have been able to help them with their enquiries if they could locate him. The Douglas Bar was the latest in a long and impressive list of targets taken in by the plausible fraudster.

Kirby became a professional con-man and criminal not long after his racing career failed. He was part of a hard-working respectable family and grew up in the town of Newbridge, Co Kildare. It is an area steeped in the traditions of horse-racing and gambling. He gained some experience from racing stables on the nearby Curragh racecourse, before travelling to England as a teenager in 1983. He hoped that over there he could follow the same path of success already blazed by several Irish jockeys but he was never going to make the cut as a professional rider. Kirby, however, knew horses and how to talk about the sport. Coupled with peoples' fascination for an 'inside' tip, he realised that he had an in-built hook that made him a perfect confidence trickster. His caper in Derby in July 2007 was the most recent in a very long string of con-jobs that all followed a similar pattern. The Kildare man is gifted with an easy manner and an ability to chat up people from almost any background. In one job, in the summer of 2001, a tourist from the United States found Kirby's charms irresistible. Robin Ward met Kirby in a Galway city pub where the failed jockey again introduced himself as successful jump jockey Dean Gallagher. Robin had just arrived in Ireland and was staying in a city tourist hostel. They agreed to meet the next day and Kirby then accompanied her on a tour around Connemara. Ten days after they first met, Kirby offered to refill the petrol tank of the Nissan Almera she had rented before it was returned to the company. She never saw Kirby or the €20,000 car again. Unfortunately for Ms Ward she hadn't taken out theft insurance when hiring the car and the company later deducted €14,000 from her credit card. When the car was eventually recovered she was reimbursed the money but still had to pay the €3,500 rental bill Kirby had run up while he was behind the wheel.

That wasn't the end of his spree during the summer of 2001. Using the stolen car, he drove to west Clare where he targeted another foreign tourist. This time he stole €600 and credit cards from a Japanese tourist at a hostel. Kirby then drove across Ireland to a racing stable in County Carlow. He would have known the best time to approach was when the stable staff and jockeys were riding out the horses. Having disposed of the tourist's Nissan Almera, he targeted the car of a professional jockey, stealing his wallet, before driving back to the west. On the way he lifted another wallet from a parked car in Loughrea. He used the cards to buy petrol and cashed a forged cheque for €250 in a pub.

Two months after disappearing with Robin Ward's rental car, Gardaí in Galway caught up with Kirby. He immediately admitted the string of thefts and frauds. It then emerged that he had already amassed 35 convictions in Ireland and the UK since he left home as a teenager. At the subsequent criminal trial in October 2002 it was said that Kirby had become involved in crime in the UK and developed both gambling and cocaine problems. He had just been released from prison when he met the unfortunate Robin Ward. At Galway District Criminal Court, Judge John Garavan sent him right back, imposing a 22-month sentence.

Despite his considerable skill and ability to win the confidence of his victims, Kirby operates without any long-term strategy. He almost always poses as a professional from the horse-racing fraternity, using his background to good effect. Once a racing tip proves right, his victims immediately feel a degree of gratitude towards him and the good tip reinforces the persona Kirby has chosen to adopt. Although he merely moves from one opportunist theft or con to the next, Kirby uses clever ruses to maximise the returns. In criminal terms it elevates him above the status of a mere snatch thief or a pick-pocket. Kirby's strategy of sticking to a simple *modus operandi* that works for him possibly explains how over the years he has managed to hoodwink some top names in the racing industry, as well as other professionals with years of business experience. An Irish music promoter would be expected to know all the pitfalls and the potential for grubby trickery in an industry generously populated by dubious operators. Yet even with his experience one such showbiz manager fell victim to Kirby's standard con-trick. One December night in 2003 Kirby turned up at the sold out concert of Australian folk singer Tommy Emmanuel in Galway. He persuaded the promoter that he had driven all the way from Kildare to get to the concert and succeeded in getting himself in the door. Later, he spoke to the agent and the singer. He introduced himself as jockey Conor Dwyer and duly tipped two horses for the next day's racing. By happy coincidence, Kirby told the pair he would be in Cork the next day where Emmanuel was again on stage. Both horses came in winners so Kirby was a welcome figure when he turned up at the hotel while the sound check was going on. During a break he went to the hotel reception desk looking for the key to the singer's room on the pretext of getting a piece of equipment. The receptionist, clearly thinking he was part of the singer's entourage, gave Kirby the key. In the room the fraudster found the proceeds from the preceding nights' concerts and coolly helped himself to several thousand euros. It was a simple theft, made entirely possible by Kirby's plausible manner.

Professional racing is not an easy sport even for those at the top. To get there takes a long process of apprenticeship that involves tough physical work, long hours and poor wages. There is also the constant threat of injuries, broken bones, as well as the burden of careful dieting. Even the best prepared and most skilful jockey can fall victim to bad luck. The hard nature of the sport means that there is a fraternal bond between members of the racing community, even between rivals. By posing as a jockey, Kirby exploits the unspoken honour system that exists between the professionals who know that a career ending injury could be just around the corner. Kirby has also been clever in his choice of jockeys identities. For instance Dean Gallagher is originally from Kildare but was based in France for part of his career. Another favourite fake persona used by Kirby is Graham Lee. In reality Lee is a native of Galway who won the Aintree Grand National, but who would not be a particularly well-known face in his home county.

The classic example of Kirby in action was in January 2004 when English racehorse owner and company director Bill Adams had the misfortune to encounter the con-artist in an Oxfordshire pub. At least seven or eight people in a crowded pub introduced the Irishman to him as jump jockey Graham Lee. Kirby was able to put on his usual convincing performance and Adams had no reason to believe he was anyone other than the Galway man. Being involved in the sport as an owner, Adams believed that 'Lee's' appearance in the area, between racing commitments, was connected with negotiations to join a new trainer. Then one Friday night Kirby turned up at his door claiming that he had engine trouble with his Mercedes and asked Adams if he knew anyone who could lend him or hire him a car.

"I thought he was Graham Lee. He had given me two tips which both won. So I said he could use my car, thinking he would go up to the local hotel where he was staying, sort his car out and come back," Adams said in a newspaper interview.

Three days later there was no sign of Kirby or the 3.2 Executive XJ Jaguar he had borrowed. It was only when Adams contacted the real Graham Lee on Monday morning that he realised he had been conned.

In early 2007 the Turf Club, the body that governs racing in Ireland, took the unprecedented step of issuing a warning through their text messaging system to its members. It stated that a fraudster known to pose as a professional jockey had recently returned to Ireland. In fact Kirby had just been released from jail in Ireland after serving time for a string of thefts and frauds. Among his offences was befriending a stag party in Kilkenny city, who he later relieved of all their cash and wallets. Although Kirby had kept his head down for a while in the UK, he soon came back to Ireland. He inveigled his way into the confidence of staff at County Kerry's only racing stables, by again posing as Dean Gallagher in February 2007. This time he stole a 4x4 jeep from a racehorse owner he had met following a meeting at Thurles. The man generously allowed 'Dean Gallagher' to stay in his house for three nights and even invited him to take one of his horses for a gallop. The subsequent theft of the owner's Land Cruiser prompted the unusual warning from the Turf Club to its members.

Not long after his next theft, in April 2007, Kirby ended up back behind bars in the UK. He was spotted by jockeys at Sandown racecourse driving a car he had stolen from one of their colleagues. He had simply driven into the yard of trainer Richards Philips in a Peugeot 106, parked the car and got into the BMW belonging to Philips. He had then driven away as if it was a perfectly normal thing to do. The Horseracing Regulatory Agency in the UK followed the Irish Turf Club's lead by publishing a picture of Kirby in July 2007, describing him as a fraudster known to have impersonated jockeys at every racecourse in Britain, as well as the Douglas bar in Normanton.

For Dean Gallagher, the jockey Kirby seems to favour as his alter-ego, the fraudster's career has been a real problem. He told the *Racing Post*: "It's driving me mad, and I have got to do something about it. It's my name that is getting dragged through the mud, and he could be damaging my reputation."

In March 2007, Gallagher had been told how Kirby had booked into a Newmarket hotel under his name and had used a bank card bearing his name: "He paid cash, but he was seen in the town with a Lloyds TSB credit card in my name, although as far as I know he hasn't used any of my money. The guy was also going 'round pubs in Newmarket, claiming to be me, although when somebody who knows me pulled him up, he changed his story and said he was Terry Kirby."

Considering his long list of criminal convictions, self-confessed gambling and drug problems, Kirby obviously found life as Dean Gallagher better than his own.

Property developer and self-promoting business guru Donald Trump wrote: "As long as you're going to be thinking anyway, think big." Terry Kirby is obviously well able to think big things for himself, as he moves between jail and opportunist con-jobs. Compared to one American fraudster, however, the bogus jockey is strictly small time. While posing as a professional jockey, Kirby's tips gave people the tantalising prospect of making some extra beer money with inside information from racing stables. Ralph Cucciniello, however, was holding out the chance to change people's lives for the better.

The 55-year-old New Jersey man has spent a lot of time with lawyers over the course of his career. Physically he was at a different end of the spectrum when compared to Kirby. Short, fat with a pinched face and a head full of grey hair, Cucciniello is no oil-painting. But his operation wasn't based on good looks. Thanks to his legal experience, he had little problem in convincing clients that he was indeed a lawyer. With an

office cubicle and an email address at Yale's Law School
library in Connecticut, there was no reason to doubt
that he was the law academic that he claimed to be.
Cucciniello told people he worked in a clinic that
specialised in immigration law. He would tell potential
clients that he had recently discovered a loophole,
through the Department of Homeland Security, which
could be used to help well-heeled immigrants to
regularise their status. Claiming to have found such a
loophole gave him power over illegal immigrants' lives.
He was offering them the possibility of escape from the
constant nagging fear that everything could abruptly
change forever with deportation. Since the September
11, 2001 attacks on the World Trade Center, US policy
towards illegal immigrants has become even more
draconian. If caught, there is no chance to say goodbye
to loved ones. There is no stay of execution to tie up the
usual loose ends of life. Within days, even hours, an
illegal immigrant can be sitting handcuffed on a plane
home, banished from ever returning to their career,
friends and even family. Cucciniello was telling people
that he had a magic wand that would make that fear go
away and bring an end to a life hiding from officialdom.
He was holding out a chance for illegal immigrants to
get a green card and to step out of the shadows. The
work being done by Cucciniello at the Yale Immigration
Law Clinic seemed to be a dream come true. Just as
Kirby seemed to offer a chance to beat the bookie,
Cucciniello had a way to beat the US immigration
system.

It was a powerful and irresistible lure that tempted
many Irish immigrants to take a gamble with this
immigration lawyer. Some clients made contact
through causal friends among drinkers in Irish bars. It
seemed to be worth risking a few thousand dollars and

Cucciniello was a very smooth operator. The deal clincher for everyone was Cucciniello's apparent easy access and affiliation to Yale Law School. He played the part of an attorney with perfect poise. Security guards at the law school library knew Cucciniello by name and he was waved through with his clients. Cucciniello knew his way around the place. Despite tighter security since the library was bombed in 2004, he went unchallenged accompanied by Irish immigrants with bags of cash.

Among the illegal Irish, Cucciniello had discovered a pool of potential victims who were the perfect patsies. They all had something to hide from the authorities and were willing to pay cash to keep their American dream alive. He told different people different stories, but was equally convincing in every variation. One illegal immigrant was told that Cucciniello knew an immigration judge whose daughter he had helped to get into law school. Another was told that the idea from the clinic came from a university dean of Chinese ancestry who wanted to help immigrants. The scam was built up in careful steps to give the potential victim confidence. Cucciniello organised for his clients to have medical check-ups which he said were part of the process. Everything seemed official. There was also always a plausible explanation about the status of their case as it wound its way through the labyrinth bureaucracy. He even told people that it was perfectly safe for them to travel in and out of the United States while their case was being processed. Cucciniello even bought some of his victims discounted airline tickets through Yale's travel service. One group of Irish people were treated to a trip to Las Vegas to watch a boxing match. As well as being hit for Cucciniello's usual $5,000 fee, this group were also persuaded to invest

$20,000 into a new company. Not long afterwards they were told their investment had already made $8,000. News quickly spread, by word of mouth, through the tight-knit circle of illegal Irish immigrants about this bright assistant at one of the United States' most prestigious Ivy League universities.

One Irish woman, a Belfast native, living in New York had already had the bitter experience of being taken in by a fraudster who promised green cards to illegal immigrants. A con-woman called Christine Owad had suckered hundreds of immigrants into paying her cash, by persuading them she was an expert in immigrant law. Despite being conned once before, the Belfast woman still felt it was worth taking a chance. She paid Cucciniello his $5,000 fee after visiting him at his office at Yale Law School in Connecticut. As ever, he remained supremely convincing. He lived in an apartment in Connecticut that belonged to Yale Law Professor Steven Duke. Cucciniello had been working for Duke carrying out some volunteer research for the professor. Duke was working on a legal appeal against mobster Martin Taccetta's murder conviction.

By early 2006 suspicions were beginning to grow about Cucciniello's activities and the Belfast woman became concerned. A rumour spread that one of Cucciniello's Irish clients had been arrested by immigration officials, despite his professed high-level government contacts. The Belfast woman contacted Cork-born private investigator Olwyn Triggs who had been involved in investigating the Christine Owad case. Triggs had emigrated from Ireland to New York at the age of 17 and spent the next 14 years working as a detective in the city. She talks in a rapid-fire delivery, with a mixture of a New York and an Irish accent.

"I met with one of his initial victims. He would use

people in groups and get them by saying he only had space for one more and then would call and ask can you get two more people in. There was one Irish girl he had a lot of dealings with. She turned him onto a lot of people," explained Triggs.

"There was a case in New York city, Christine Owad, two years previously. She had 700 victims in a very similar scam, in a parallel scam. I believe that he didn't know Owad, but he [Cucciniello] read up about her because he did tell some of the victims her problem was that she was too nice. He was aware of who she was. That case was very close to home because some of my very good friends were involved with her. She was working around the neighbourhood where I lived, so I started looking into her and found out she had a rap sheet just as long as his. She had done this before so we contacted the prosecutors and she was arrested. Because of that a lot people knew I had been involved in that case. One of the victims called me when she was involved with Cucciniello and told me 'You know, I think I'm being taken again.' There were double victims in both these cases."

It didn't take Triggs long to discover the real truth about Cucciniello. She discovered pretty quickly that all his legal experience was from the wrong side of the desk. He had an arrest record going back as far as 1975 on fraud charges. Over the course of his sordid criminal career he had taken on various guises such as a television producer, a psychologist and a nursing home operator. In 1991, he was sentenced to 30 years in jail for scamming several elderly people. In 1996 he was again sentenced to 30 years in jail after being convicted of defrauding several people in a $250,000 business scheme. He even married one of his victims and ripped off his mother-in-law for several hundred thousand dollars.

"He is a career criminal; his entire life he has done this. He married one of his victims at one point. He used to point out the house they were building together while he was fleecing her mother of this money," said Triggs.

To add insult to injury for Cucciniello's victims it emerged that he was an informant working for the Federal Bureau of Investigation. As a result he never served a day behind bars. A former lawyer for Cucciniello said he was a valued government asset. It later emerged that Cucciniello had actually been part of a federal witness protection program before he took on the bogus persona of a Yale law professor.

"He never did any time in these cases. He pled out in every one of his cases. He always had dirt on somebody else. His lawyer said that he saved the life of a federal agent and that's why he got off. I believe he turned State's evidence against somebody else, that he had some dirt on somebody. He's just a sneak, a pure scumbag," according to Triggs.

Triggs decided it was time for Cucciniello to get a taste of his own medicine. She posed as a potential new client, desperate for his legal advice and help to get a green card. "He'd start out by saying this conversation is privileged and protected almost like what an attorney would say. He'd give that same cover, 'you know anything you say can't be used by any federal or state agencies.' He would have this whole speech, he would say that in every single conversation and would say it really fast like he was used to saying it to every one of his victims. I guess he thought somehow he was above the law."

Cops in New York City were interested in acting on the information the private eye had on Cucciniello. They asked Triggs and the Belfast woman to persuade him to meet them in the city. Once they got him to New York he could be arrested.

"I had several conversations on the phone with him. He told me to come to Connecticut and to Yale and he gave me directions how to get there," said Triggs.

Instead she got him to drive to New York where the police were waiting for him to be lured into their jurisdiction. Wearing a hidden microphone and camera, Triggs was only too happy to set the trap and be the bait. "In order to get him down from Connecticut to New York we had to pretend there was more money coming in from a new victim. So I sat in a coffee shop with her in Greenwich Village. The police waiting for him, locked down the block, so once he pulled up they had him right away. We were both wired up with audio equipment and we have him with her saying 'get in the car'."

Triggs would have played out the scenario to the end to find out as much as she could about Cucciniello, but they had been warned by the NYPD not to get into his car. The city cops didn't want to lose the chance of making the collar if he drove out of their jurisdiction.

"I would have gone all the way to Connecticut with him if I was allowed but they wouldn't allow that because they wanted to nab him in New York. Once he showed, they arrested him."

Her impression of Cucciniello was that he was a convincing liar. Armed with her professional experience she could see that there were plenty of tell-tale signs that should have convinced people not to get involved with him.

"To be honest with you, it was a little bit obvious for me from day one. He was too friendly with his victims. He met some of these people 20 or 30 times. The girl from Belfast he would pick up from the train when she would go there. For me that should have been a little bit of red flag. He had a different vehicle every time he showed up; he always had a rented car," explained Triggs.

While the warning signs were there for people to have noticed, figuring out who is a con-artist and who is for real is a lot easier in hindsight. The key to Cucciniello's fraud was the false promise of hope that he held out and his apparently bona fida connection to Yale Law School.

"He's very, very good. I like to think he wasn't so good that he didn't get caught. I don't want to give him any praise, but looking back at all the cases over the years I worked where there were scam artists, he was quite good. A lot of extremely intelligent people were taken by him. We all like to think: 'I wouldn't be caught like that, I wouldn't be that stupid.' Everyone pretty much got wrapped up in the idea that there was a way out, there was a loophole," said Triggs.

Cucciniello was bailed shortly after his arrest for fraud in New York. His freedom was short-lived when he was arrested again in June 28, 2007 at the Marriott Residence Hotel in Rhode Island, this time by agents from the Federal Bureau of Investigation. The FBI had taken up the investigation after the NYPD had started the running on the case. Cucciniello had been living at the Marriott Hotel for several weeks after his initial arrest in New York, but had made no attempt to disappear with his ill-gotten gains. He had abandoned his apartment in New Haven, Connecticut where he had lived for the previous three years, playing out the role of a law professor. The apartment was part of the property owned by the real law professor, Steven Duke. When the cops arrested him in Rhode Island he was wearing a Yale University t-shirt. He waived his rights to an extradition hearing and was sent back to Connecticut for trial in a federal court.

The fraudster's attire had changed when he arrived from jail into the New Haven court house just days after his Rhode Island arrest. He wore a red jump suit and was handcuffed. Bail was set at a hefty $3.5 million. Unable to raise the bail deposit, Cucciniello stayed behind bars until January 2008, when he appeared at the Superior Court in New Haven. He entered a plea, under the Alford Doctrine in which a defendant doesn't admit guilt but concedes that the State has enough evidence to convict him. He pleaded to several counts of larceny in the first and second degree, one count of racketeering and three counts of impersonating an attorney.

Superior Court Judge Richard A. Damiani gave Cucciniello a choice. Convinced that Cucciniello had hidden at least part of his ill-gotten gains, the judge offered him seven months to pay back $300,000 to his victims. In that case the judge would sentence Cucciniello to 20 years to be suspended after serving 12 years. Otherwise Judge Damiani said he would impose a 30 year sentence, to be suspended after 20 years served. For the 56-year-old con-man this was effectively a life sentence. "If you fall short, I won't make any adjustments. It's an all or nothing situation. The bottom line is we are going to have restitution," said the judge.

The judge, like Olwyn Triggs, was also intrigued by what Cucciniello had done with the cash he scammed. She is convinced that he possibly squirreled away millions of dollars in off-shore bank accounts.

"There has to be somebody else involved in this. I don't think he could have done it all by himself. He couldn't have hidden the money himself; it's probably in someone else's name, not his family members to the best of my knowledge. I'd say it's in an off-shore account, but they don't know. We don't know if he put it up his nose with a bunch of hookers every day. He's quite an unattractive man. He just might have gone to Vegas a lot and partied with some women; we just don't know. If there was a budget that's what I'd go after, but I've spent the last six months of my life 24 hours a day on this."

"A lot of laws have changed in the last few years so it's impossible to start checking at a private level and there's no budget for it anyway. This has been a pro-bono case for me from the beginning. I know the State's attorneys have looked into where the money is. I very much feel it is buried somewhere and that he has a partner. They [the police] don't actively pursue it the way we would like them to, like in the movies where they check every bank account in Bermuda. There's probably a million dollars or millions somewhere. No one was tracking this guy until all this came to light."

As yet Cucciniello has not paid back any money to his victims.

An Irishman named Brian Donnelly was responsible for bringing a lot of people into the scam. He set up a television company with the professional fraudster. Donnelly, however, claims to have been an innocent pawn who was also scammed by Cucciniello. Triggs has a different opinion: "I very much think he is guilty from the beginning, because he did set up Offshore Productions, his company, with Ralph. He claims he was scammed himself for more money than anybody else. Ralph took out credit cards in his name and he's left with that bill. They brought him in for questioning several times. Some States thought he was guilty, others didn't. I don't think they pursued him very much."

There is also the human cost to Cucciniello's cruel deception. What had seemed to be his generosity in organising discounted airline tickets was in fact a way to keep track of, and hold an element of control over, his victims. "There were a lot of people who were tremendously hurt. One girl miscarried a baby. People were deported or caught at the border. We think he possibly turned them in because they were getting wise to his scam so he prevented them from coming back to the country or sent them out by paying for a plane ticket."

"The whole thing was hyped up with hope. It was all to do with hope and the promise of the green card. A lot of people were well within their 90 days and they intended staying legal and going back home and trying to come back here on vacation. He convinced them to overstay and they are the most bitter victims because they had weddings, Christmas with mother next year, and they wanted to go home for that. They were going to stay within the laws of the United States immigration but didn't because of him."

"There was one woman who was in Connecticut who had a nine-year-old son and he [Cucciniello] would tell the child 'Don't worry you'll see your Grandma real soon.' The kid had been raised by the grandmother in Ecuador. It was really sad for these people because they really believed he was from Yale University because he looked like a lawyer and acted and spoke like a lawyer," she said.

Triggs also believes that there were a lot more than the 110 victims she discovered. "I would not be surprised if there were hundreds more. We only actively pursued the Irish community and I had calls from South America and a lot of Latin American countries and possibly Polish. I didn't reach out because I didn't want to deal with the press when it came to this case at all. It's possible there are a lot more victims. He knew these people wouldn't come forward. There are hundreds of them out there still. They don't want to get involved. They figure it's worth the five grand to let it go and not have anyone know where they live."

The pain and emotional damage inflicted by the likes of Cucciniello and Terry Kirby is rarely acknowledged in the fictional versions of con-artists or grifters as they are known in the United States. Leonardo Di Caprio's role as Frank Abagnale in *Catch Me If You Can* captures the sneaking admiration that people have for a con-artist who can outwit corporations, greedy rich people or other criminals. The reality is very different – less Robin Hood and more robbing banks. The sense of violation people experience, after their trust has been abused, is something that many people can find very difficult to cope with. No one likes being lied to, but it's made worse when the lies are believed. The human cost of fraud can't be measured by accountants and numbers. The anti-social and criminal behaviour of con-artists also has the potential to corrupt the bonds of trust that exist in civilised communities. One serial fraudster who has shown his true dark criminal nature is Scottish con-man John Cronin. As well as being a cheat, liar and a thief, he is a sexual predator. He embodies the sinister side of the idea people have of a con-artist being a likeable rogue, living on his wits to stay a step ahead of greedy creditors and unsympathetic police.

Born in Tranent, Scotland, on July 18, 1971 John Cronin spent his early years between East Lothian, Limerick and the US, where his father Michael served in the military. Cronin was always on the move. His Limerick-born father had left his home in Limerick at 17 and joined the army in the US. He and Jeanette, a young woman from Scotland, met and married there. In 1970, they settled in Tranent and John was born soon afterwards. They lived for brief periods in Ireland, Tranent, the US, and again in Tranent. Young Cronin went from school to school. From an early age he began to exhibit behavioural problems. He had trouble fitting in anywhere. The first real indicators of emotional and behavioural instability came when he was five years old. He had been sent to a private school but his parents were asked to remove him after he urinated on the floor and attacked teachers. The pattern continued as he got older. He went through numerous Catholic primary schools, special educational and psychiatric centres, spells of home tuition and state secondary schools. Although he was obviously quite intelligent with above average grades, school held little appeal to the teenage Cronin. He was a regular truant and ran away from home frequently, on which occasions he would live rough in Edinburgh. He was sent to one school for children with emotional problems where he managed to keep out of any serious trouble for two years. On one occasion he did, however, order several frozen turkeys on school note paper which he said he intended as a present for the chef.

Cronin began committing crimes within months of leaving school at the age of 15. His first criminal convictions were recorded in November 1987 when he admitted fraud and theft. Four months later, he faced several charges of fraud, using false cheques, theft and breaches of bail. At the same time he pled guilty at the sheriff's court to exposing himself and indecently assaulting a young girl he had met at St Theresa's Friary in south-east Edinburgh. He was sentenced to three months in a young offenders institution and sent to Glenochil Young Offenders Institution, near Stirling.

When he was released, Cronin's family did their best
to get him back on the straight and narrow. He was sent
to live in Ireland, where he still had relatives. Cronin,
however, was never out of trouble. On one occasion he
stole and altered his father's US Army ID and tried to
join the IRA in Belfast. He was sent home by the police.
Back in Ireland again he was jailed for 18 months for
fraud and forgery in 1989. He was released the same
year, but was quickly back inside for setting fire to a
farm building. Cronin had met a woman in County
Meath who was in a row with a male neighbour over
disputed land. Cronin torched his woman friend's barn
to try to frame the man. When he was released in late
1989 he went back to Navan and hurled rocks at the
woman's windows, blaming her for his arrest. Cronin,
then aged 18, was jailed again and given 16 months for
malicious damage. His actions drove the woman to a
nervous breakdown.

When he was again released from jail in Ireland, he
went back to Scotland. He was six-foot tall with a stocky
frame but his baby-face made him look years younger.
His looks, however, were deceptive as they put people
off their guard. By this time he had developed an interest
in the Church and politics. During his teens he would
inveigle his way into election campaigns in Scotland. On
one occasion he was warned off about his over-
enthusiastic canvassing style. Cronin combined his two
interests when he committed a crime that shocked
Britain in 1992. This time Cronin left no lingering doubt
about his capacity for sexual violence. A Conservative
Party worker known as Judy X had invited into her
home a plausible young priest calling himself Father
Sean Mulligan. He had phoned earlier and told her he
wanted to make a donation. They drank tea and talked.
Then without warning Cronin, posing as the politically

sympathetic priest, suddenly attacked. He repeatedly hit the mother-of-four across the head with a poker, with such force it was bent to a right angle. When he finally subdued his victim he forced her to commit indecent acts that left her near death. Cronin didn't try to disguise his face during the attack and thanks to his oddball behaviour in the past, police had little trouble in tracking down Judy X's attacker.

The case created a furore in the UK. Judy X bravely spoke about her ordeal at the Scottish Conservative Party conference. Her speech was carried by all the media. She was invited to speak at the British Conservative Party where she shared the platform with Prime Minister John Major. Her decision to speak out ensured that Cronin would never slip back into anonymity. Cronin didn't help his case either when he later wrote a letter from jail threatening Judy X.

Cronin was jailed for life for the shocking attack. That sentence was later reduced to six years by three appeal court judges who decided there wasn't enough proof that Cronin would re-offend. The judges were spectacularly wrong.

Cronin's family did their best to help their troubled son when he was again released from jail in 1996. Heavily-bearded and now weighing 20 stone, he was spirited away from Shotts Prison. He flew with his father back to Ireland where the family hoped they could keep him out of trouble. The very next day he turned up in Dáil Eireann dressed as a priest and tried to set up meetings with two female TDs. Suspicions were aroused and Cronin was arrested. Gardaí, however, had no choice but to release him because no crime had been committed.

Just one day later, Cronin then turned up at the home of Canon Sean Rooney in the quiet parish of

Mohill, County Leitrim. He told the Canon he was dying and wanted to leave IR£500,000 to the local community. The trusting priest took him in, wined and dined him. Cronin even stood drinks at a local party, where guests were taken in by his tall tales. When left alone in Canon Rooney's home, Cronin pocketed IR£1,180 which he found in a bedroom. He blew the money on a nine-day drinking binge in Dublin where the Gardaí caught up with him. Less than a month after his release from jail in Scotland, Cronin was given a 12 month sentence at Navan District Court for the theft.

Cronin went back to his parents' home in Tranent after his release in the summer of 1997. Immediately he was back at his old tricks, making nuisance phone calls to five local Tory party workers. He hit the headlines again when he admitted the offences but walked free from the court. Locally, in East Lothian there was a lot of anxiety about Cronin's presence and the failure of the authorities to keep tabs on him. Around the same time he began posing as a businessman and a doctor to get one-on-one meetings with professional women in Edinburgh. First he posed as a Dublin man at the city's up-market George Hotel. He persuaded a female sales executive to show him around hotel rooms on the pretext that he was interested in hiring a suite for the year. He left without doing anything out of the ordinary. Then he pretended to be a member of a top business family to con a woman into talking to him. He produced a fake business card to convince the market researcher to give him her name and address. It stated he was, "Charles F Jenner, CBA, BA (Hons), JP, Conservative Group Leader, City of Edinburgh Council". Cronin didn't realise that he was being watched by police while he sat staring at the woman for ten minutes in the city's Princes Street before going up to talk to her. He offered her and her colleagues a tour around the world-famous Jenners store to get her name and address. Cronin then went to a solicitor's office in Queen Street, Edinburgh and conned his way into meeting a female solicitor pretending to be a Dr James McDade, again from Dublin. He spent 30 minutes in one-to-one talks with her about a bogus story involving his non-existent mistress's love child. Again, Cronin didn't do anything, apart from pretending to be someone he wasn't. He was later arrested by police on a bus to Glasgow and charged with impersonation. Although Cronin had not actually tried to steal anything or attack the women the police weren't willing to wait to find out what he had in mind.

At the subsequent trial, the prosecuting lawyer said that although the offences were minor frauds, there appeared to be a sexual motive behind them all. His defence claimed that Cronin's offences just "wasted the time" of the victims. After an initial legal wrangle, Cronin admitted conning the three women. He was told by Sheriff James Farrell his offences were "bizarre". He was jailed for three years but served just 20 months before being released from Peterhead Jail in March 1999.

The next time Cronin turned up on the radar he did it in style. He arrived in Waterford City in November, 2001 where for a number of days he stayed in a hostel for the homeless. After a few days of roughing it, echoing the life of his early teens, he upgraded to a better establishment. Cronin booked into a guesthouse wearing a good suit, overcoat and carrying decent looking luggage. He was quick to tell the manager that he was a financial consultant on business in Ireland. He threw in unasked-for details about being married with two kids and how he sometimes missed his family when travelling on business. Apart from being free and easy with his personal information, he didn't seem in any way unusual. In a nearby pub he enjoyed plenty of pints, where again he told the locals he was a financial consultant. He gave money advice to anyone who would listen.

Over the next few days, Cronin tried to swindle bank staff at a branch of the TSB, but they didn't buy his story. He decided to take a different approach to getting cash. He checked out of the guesthouse, using a credit card to pay the bill, which included €400 in phone calls. Then he went to Mass after which he got a taxi to take him to the bank. While the driver waited outside, he entered the building armed with a starter pistol. He warned terrified staff he would "spray them" if they didn't co-operate. With a haul of €3,000 Cronin then got back into his taxi and asked to be driven to Dublin. Two hours later in Naas, County Kildare, just 30 miles from Dublin, the taxi was stopped and Cronin was arrested. He later told police he had planned to use the money to set up an operation to buy and sell imitation firearms. This time he was jailed for two years.

The day after he was released from jail and flown back to Manchester in October 2003, Cronin went straight back into crime. Bizarrely, he again embarked on a series of frauds in which he was always likely to get caught. A number of women fell victim to his lies and charm. He used company cheques to buy flowers and jewellery. He posed as an assistant to a French multi-millionaire and tried to lure a florist into a sinister midnight meeting.

Through 2004 to 2006 Cronin was in and out of prison in both Ireland and the UK as he continued the pattern of taking on and discarding personas. He passed himself off as the Mayor of Edinburgh while buying clothes, a former Mayor of Birmingham while donating bogus cheques to charity, a Scottish priest in Ireland and an Irish priest in Scotland. In August 2007 a man posing as a priest who matched Cronin's distinctive six-foot, 20-stone appearance, stole a cheque book from a guest house. His cover as a priest came unstuck in a local pub when he matched customer's dirty jokes with increasingly blue one-liners. Assuming that Cronin is the only 20-stone con-man who impersonates priests, he got away with it on this occasion. For the next three months he was in the British midlands where he stole goods using fake cheques. Then he turned up in Malmo, Sweden where he booked into the Savoy. Needless to say, he left without paying, before turning up in the country's best restaurant, the Operakallaren in Stockholm. He ordered scallops, steak and ice cream, a food bill which amounted to about €150. However he also ordered wine with each course and topped it off with a bottle of port. The most expensive wine was €4,500 from which he drank just a single glass. The total bill came to over €15,000. He simply told the stunned waiter: "I have no money. I can't pay for it. Call the police."

After four months in a Swedish jail he flew back to Gatwick, London, where police were waiting for him. He got another two and half years for the various frauds he had committed in his three year spree.

Cronin's 20-year criminal career has meandered from cruelty and sadism to what amounts to pathetic attention-seeking stunts. The fact remains that he is an inveterate liar and sexual predator which makes him a serious danger to women. He is also a skilled con-artist who persuades people to give him cash, or to cash cheques that are stolen or he knows have no value. Cronin is always capable of being perfectly charming. He is the type of criminal that exposes the inadequacies of our society's humane criminal justice system. He is bad enough to be in jail, but not mad enough to be locked up indefinitely in a secure psychiatric unit. Under a Californian style 'three-strikes' law, however, Cronin would be serving life without any prospect of parole. Even before his worst crime, in which he attacked Judy X, there had been enough red flags to warn the authorities he was capable of very serious violent offences. John Baird, a senior consultant psychiatrist who assessed Cronin for the Scottish High Court in 1992, believes his extensive psychiatric records showed: "a sustained pattern of outrageous and uncontrolled behaviour which is of enormous nuisance value and must have been the cause of considerable distress to those who he came into contact with." Other psychiatric reports about Cronin suggest he suffers from an incurable personality disorder. It is a safe bet that when Cronin next gets out of jail he'll turn up somewhere pretending to be someone else to get food and lodgings.

John Cronin, Ralph Cucciniello and Terry Kirby are all serial fraudsters. They come from different backgrounds but they share the same lack of fear of being caught. Police investigations, jail sentences and the ire of their victims, hold no terror for them. They also know how to inveigle their way into their victims' lives and how to quickly exploit opportunities for financial gain. They also play a game, at least in their heads, where they are just too clever and too smart for the rest of society. It's obvious they can't fool everyone all of the time, but there's always one person who'll fall for their story.

For them, that's enough.

TWO

No-good Nomads

For some reason the shopkeeper or waiter makes a mistake. Instead of the change from a €20 note he hands over the change for a €50. There's no way the error will be detected until the till receipts are done at the close of business. It is a simple thing to pocket the extra €30 and to pretend not to have noticed. It is a private test of honesty. If the retailer is a friend or the shop a regular stop, then it becomes easier to do the right thing and point out the error. After all, the honest customer will appear in a good light and it could even result in better service in the future. If the shop or restaurant is in a foreign country, however, or one that won't be visited again, it can become very easy to suppress any troubling little scruples about taking the money. The usual social constraints are considerably weaker if the person handing back too much change doesn't know the customer. It all comes down to the internal battle between right and wrong. Being anonymous can erase the usual rules of behaviour about stealing, lying and cheating.

The price of carrying out crude frauds is a life on the road dodging the consequences. It does, however, have the effect of blurring the edges around a con-artist's life. Most people tend to veer towards being polite and to give charming strangers the benefit of the doubt. A made-up persona or background can be difficult to check out without being brutally sceptical. Con-men and liars can find rich prey in cities where people are less likely to know their neighbours. It takes a lot more

personal skills to get into a tight community or family.
The corollary, however, is that once a person has
gained the trust of one member of the circle, the rest are
quite likely to follow without too many questions
being asked. The village of Loughglinn, located
between Roscommon and Frenchpark, is well off the
beaten track. A pleasant tranquil setting, it is the type
of location that has yet to recover from decades of
emigration despite the booming Irish economy of the
1990s and 2000s. With just one shop, a filling station
and a pub it is hardly the sort of place where a serial
fraudster would be expected to find rich pickings.
There's no problem finding a parking spot on the
single wide main street of Loughglinn which is
dominated by the church serving the surrounding
countryside. When Graham Peet and his partner
Tracey Heather turned up in the Roscommon village in
2007 he looked the part of a happy family man.
Developer Tommy Hanley remembered when 39-year-
old Peet arrived at his new housing development,
driving a Jaguar, with his young family in tow. If
anyone would sniff out a fraudster then it would be
Hanley. With his handlebar moustache and builder's
boots he cuts an unconventional figure. His mobile
phone rings constantly as he talks. Hanley is an
experienced builder and a canny property developer
who has worked all over Europe and Ireland. Peet was
keen to buy one the superbly finished houses at Hanley
Avenue, describing the area as "absolute heaven".

"He said he'd come down a week later to buy the
house and when he did, he asked was there any way he
could move in straight away because Dublin was such
a slum," said Tommy. There was never any doubt in
Hanley's mind about Peet, who was in such a hurry to
set up home in the sleepy Roscommon village. "I

thought he seemed a clean cut man. He was just the sort of good clientele I wanted in my estate."

Burly and balding, Peet told people that he was a former professional footballer in the north of England but now was a building contractor. Once they had moved into the first of Hanley's houses, Peet and his partner kept love-bombing Hanley. They told him what a great place it was they had moved to and Tracey would welcome the builder with a kiss on the cheek as if to thank him for their new life in a rural idyll. "Every day they'd thank me, shake my hand, say 'this is heaven'. He even bought me a bottle a wine and a bottle of whiskey another day," said Hanley.

Hanley was far from being the only person who was impressed by the personable dad-of-two who was so keen to adopt Loughglinn as his family's new home. Welshman Tom Baker was delighted when Peet promised to give him a quote for building an extension to his house at nearby Fairymount. Baker, a former long distance lorry driver, had moved to Roscommon just a few years previously. For years he had built up his savings nest-egg, working his shifts at night and then doing extra overtime at the weekends. For years he had been travelling to Ireland on holidays and when he wanted to get out of city life in Barry town near Cardiff, he decided to make a permanent move to enjoy quieter life in the west of Ireland. Graham Peet and Tom Baker met for the first time at the local health office where the pair began talking. Peet presented himself as a builder and offered to quote for the job to build Baker's extension at the house he'd bought four years ago. He told Baker that he'd have to start straight away because he was booked to do an extension for a garda sergeant in the nearby town of Castlerea. It was a convincing and plausible story.

"He sounded very genuine and offered to come up straight away to look at the site," recalled Tom. A contract was drawn up and he paid the Englishman €15,000 up front. Peet started work on Tom Baker's house on 4 July. From the beginning there were delays. It was a very wet summer and even the best of builders struggled to complete projects. Peet barely did any work. When deliveries of materials such as stone or concrete were being made, Peet was nowhere to be seen. On one occasion Baker paid €170 for a consignment of stone. Another time a young labourer employed by Peet was left without his week's wages. Baker's compassionate nature couldn't allow the young man to walk away empty-handed and he gave him his €640. By mid-August, Peet said he needed another €5,000 to continue the work which Baker handed over. Tom Baker still believed that the affable English builder would get the work done. Progress, however, was also hampered by Peet's apparent health problems. "There was a lot of rain and then he was in and out of hospital. It dragged on and on," said Baker.

Like Hanley, he then found himself at the receiving end of a charm offensive by Peet and his Irish wife. "After a couple of weeks he invited us down for a meal to his house. It was all very nice and very convincing." Peet used the occasion to tell Tom that he wanted him to be the godfather of his two young daughters. Peet had also started complaining to Baker about Tommy Hanley referring to him as "that bastard" claiming that the builder had put up the price of his house.

Peet's warm relationship with Hanley had indeed cooled over the wet summer of 2007. Just two or three weeks after moving into the house at Hanley Avenue, Peet told the builder he had a problem getting the mortgage. He had an outstanding loan and needed to pay off the €3,500 to get the mortgage approval to finalise the deal. "I gave him the money to pay it off to let him get the mortgage. I needed the money from the house sale to keep the business going. My solicitor was liaising with his solicitor. He'd tell me things were going well," Hanley said. Slowly but surely the details of Peet's life stopped adding up. That became even more apparent when Peet asked for a job as a carpenter with Hanley's firm. He turned up on the job equipped with discount-store tools and the foreman, Hanley's brother, knew straight away that whatever Peet could do, carpentry was not one of his skills. "He didn't know the difference between a hammer and saw. I let him go after two days," said Hanley.

A short time later Peet asked Hanley if he could put some business his way and gave him some newly printed business cards, T&G Construction. Hanley took the cards but sensibly never passed one on. Unbeknownst to Hanley it was around this time that Peet had smooth-talked Tom Baker into paying €15,000 up front for the house extension job. Things went from bad worse when Hanley's solicitor discovered that Peet had missed appointments with his own lawyer over the agreement to buy the house at Hanley Avenue. After five months time was running out for Peet's welcome in the village of Loughglinn. Just as Hanley knew nothing of Tom Baker's dealings with Peet, neither did Baker realise Peet had now been living in Hanley's newly-built house for six months without paying any rent. When he started bad-mouthing Hanley, Peet told Baker that he wasn't going to buy the house in Loughglinn. Instead, he told Baker, he would buy another house that was on the market. "He told me he had put a deposit on a cottage just over the road. I thought there's no way if he is moving in here that he is going to do a runner. He was doing all these things so you would have confidence in him," said Tom.

By the end of the summer Peet was still squirming and wriggling over the lack of progress on the extension. He told Tom Baker he was in hospital. At one point Tom even drove Peet to hospital in Roscommon. Peet told him that even if he didn't get out of hospital he had workers lined up to work on Monday morning. No one turned up. When the exasperated Baker confronted him at his house in Hanley Avenue, Peet went on the counter-offensive. "What are you doing shouting in front of my children," he told Baker. Then he told Baker that he had been diagnosed with suspected stomach cancer. But even then Peet continued to try and milk more cash. He sent pleading texts suggesting that he was in big trouble with some sinister figures and that his life was in danger. He asked for another €3,500 to keep the project going.

Tom Baker wasn't buying Peet's tall tales anymore and had a structural engineer examine the little work that had been carried out. The engineer said the jerry-built walls had to be demolished.

"We haven't seen him since," lamented Tom. "I worked nights five days a week and if I did overtime it would be at the weekends. To think I worked 12 hour shifts to give it to that bastard," he said. Peet had fleeced him for "a good portion" of his life savings and left him with a half built shell that was so unsound it had to be knocked down.

By now the penny had well and truly dropped with both Tom Baker and Tommy Hanley. They quickly discovered at least 16 people in the area had been conned for cash and goods. Peet had persuaded local suppliers to deliver furniture and electrical goods. Some of the furniture and electrical items were recovered when Peet did an overnight runner with his family.

Over the subsequent weeks there was a steady trickle of people turning up at the house looking for money, including builder suppliers, shop keepers, publicans and even a financial institution. It was an expensive lesson in trust for both Tom Baker and Tommy Hanley. There was some comfort, however small, in knowing they were not the only people who had been taken in by Peet. "It was a shock to the nation that I got caught out," said Hanley.

In the aftermath, Hanley was angry that it proved very difficult to persuade officials to get involved in the case. Gardaí kept telling Peet's victim that it was a civil matter. "Every official I went to, I was told that it was a civil matter. Why should a lay person have to do a private investigation? He cost me at least €9,500 which I'm never going to get back," he said.

In September 2007 Peet's escapades were exposed in the *Sunday World*. He and his young family took off again from a house in Lanesboro, County Longford where they had briefly lived after their abrupt departure from Loughglinn.

Peet's ability to talk people around has to be experienced to be believed. Like so many people who are taken in by a con-man, Baker tortured himself with sleepless nights and thoughts of how he had let himself be suckered. It came down to the fateful meeting in the health board office where he had gone to find a medical form. "The annoying part is that I didn't even need to go there," he said. It later emerged that the smooth-talking con-man also left people high and dry in his native Northampton. The list of victims included relatives of an ex-wife who he suddenly deserted one Christmas back in 2002. Peet and his then wife had travelled back to England to spend Christmas with her family. At the time he had been living in Dublin where he claimed he worked as a night-club bouncer. He departed from his in-laws after claiming that a fellow doorman in Dublin had been shot, never to be seen again. "He just went out the door on Boxing Day and hasn't been seen since. He had everybody fooled," said one of the relatives.

Con-artists don't need to fool everybody. They just need to fool one person at a time and for long enough to get what they need. In Ireland, Peet used his English background to concoct stories about his life that made him seem believable. He knew he couldn't get away with lying forever, but he also knew how to cloud the issue long enough to get what he needed. He is far from being alone as a con-artist whose labyrinth of lies and falsehoods can blur the truth to such an extent that the real person almost disappears. An air of mystery can be a vital tool for a con-artist. It can be used to explain the unexpected and to ward off searching questions.

Mystery certainly surrounded the young teenager found on the tarmac of a US airport. An Arca Airlines DC 8 had just landed at Miami International Airport, after a three-hour flight from Colombia, on June 4, 1993. Carrying a cargo of flowers, it took off from Bogota and flew 1,000 miles across the Caribbean at 35,000 feet. Ground staff were going through the disembarkation procedures when a skinny kid suddenly tumbled from the wheel well. Miraculously he was still alive. Airline workers were reported as saying they found him curled up in a ball, covered in frost. He made a quick recovery in a local hospital. The local media were gripped by the story of a young teenage immigrant who had survived such a fool-hardy escapade in freezing, high-altitude temperatures with no oxygen. Few stowaways in the undercarriage of aircrafts have survived such a trip. Luckily for him, this DC8 had pressurised wheel-wells. It emerged that 13-year-old Guillermo Rosales was an orphan whose parents had been tragically killed in a bus crash. He had been seen at Bogota Airport eating from rubbish bins to survive. The family of a local police officer, originally from Colombia, took him in while immigration authorities decided what to do with the plucky youngster. The Colombian consulate in Miami, however, had started looking into the incident and discovered that the 13-year-old was actually 16 years old and his name wasn't Guillermo. The teenager told a Colombian radio station that he had lied about his age because he feared deportation. But he still stuck to the story of his improbable journey in the aircraft's wheel-well. He admitted that his mother and step-father were also alive and living in Cali, Colombia. No one realised it at the time but the world was witnessing the beginning of a criminal career by a con-artist known as Juan Carlos Guzman-Betancourt.

Five years later Guzman re-emerged in the UK. Gone was the skinny teenager and in his place was a suave, impeccably dressed and confident young man. At ease in all the top hotels, designer boutiques and jewellery stores, Guzman could speak several languages. He was plausible and erudite in every one of them. At the Meridien Hotel in London he assumed the name of a guest and persuaded staff he had lost his key. Obligingly, hotel staff came to the rescue of their hapless 'guest' and let him back in. Guzman calmly plundered the room of its cash and valuables. He established a slick *modus operandi*. He would find a hotel guest's name, possibly from a register of guests at a swimming pool, gym or leisure centre. Then, simply posing as a clumsy Dad, blaming the kids for locking

him out of his room, he would persuade staff to allow
him to supposedly re-enter. They even handed him a
duplicate key.

Guzman's range and ability is simply stunning. In
1999, he was caught at Heathrow Airport trying to buy
expensive electronic goods with a credit card taken in a
hotel burglary in Tokyo. He was arrested under the
name Cesar Ortigos Vera. He appeared in court where
he denied the theft but admitted the deception. He was
let off with a fine. Two years later, in May 2001, he was
again back in London. This time he struck at the
Dorchester Hotel, Park Lane in London. An English
couple returned to their hotel room to find STG£35,000
worth of jewellery and a small amount of cash missing.
He went on to raid another three hotels. Using a stolen
Amex card he then booked a STG£400 chauffeur-driven
Bentley to Heathrow. He paid STG£250 for a flight to
Paris and blew another STG£8,000 in the departure
lounge at Terminal 4, while waiting for his plane. In
Paris he also did the rounds of the top couturier
boutiques. His spree appeared to come to an end a few
weeks later. He was arrested in the French capital when
he was caught in possession of four hotel keys. 'David
Soriano Martinez' was released on bail, however, and
again Guzman disappeared. A thief, using his *modus
operandi* was later reported to be operating in various
places including Moscow, St Petersburg, Thailand and
Mexico. He re-surfaced again in Las Vegas in the United
States. Cash and jewellery worth €235,000 were taken
from a British couple's room at the Four Seasons Hotel.
The con-man was identified as the prime suspect and
the Federal Bureau of Investigation issued a warrant for
Guzman.

During 2004 the Hotel Crimes Unit from Scotland
Yard set up Operation Magister to target criminals

raiding the city's best hotels. They couldn't be sure but Juan Carlos Guzman-Betancourt was top of the list of suspects for a series of thefts from Grosvenor House, The Royal Garden and the Dorchester hotels. A Bahrain businessman, Khalid Al-Sharif, had been on a pre-Christmas shopping spree in October 2004 and bought bags of designer goods. He left them in his room at the Mandarin Oriental Hotel in London's Knightsbridge. Although the items were only left in his room for a short time it was long enough for Guzman to pounce. He took all the designer bags, along with Al-Sharif's STG£2,000 Valentino leather jacket and a Franck Muller watch valued at STG£8,000, a total haul worth STG£40,000. The Scotland Yard officers had managed to track down one of his false identities but just when they thought the net was tightening Guzman seemed to disappear again. Police were convinced that he had left the UK to continue his thefts in another country. Two months later, however, on December 20, one of their detectives spotted Guzman by pure chance in a London supermarket. When he was arrested he was wearing Al-Sharif's stolen leather coat and watch. More evidence and stolen goods were found in a house where Guzman had been living in St John's Wood in north-east London. This time he claimed to be Gonzalo Zapater Vives. Through Interpol, and with the help of French police, the UK police were able to establish his true identity.

Later, in court, Detective Sergeant Andy Swindells from Scotland Yard gave a succinct picture of how Guzman operated:

"This man is a professional and prolific hotel burglar who uses a distinctive *modus operandi*. He uses the proceeds of his crimes for his own ends, even to the length of wearing stolen clothing and jewellery. He is a highly accomplished liar. He is plausible, believable and very professional – he commits these offences for a living, and is therefore incredibly well versed in identity theft, identity assumption, hotels and foreign travel. He is always immaculately presented and is very charming. He speaks several languages fluently. This man works internationally and it is doubtless that Interpol inquiries may shed light on the commission of other offences."

"Having acquired a guest's name and room number from, for example, a health club registration book, or a bar tab, he then assumes the guest's identity, acquires a key for the guest's room stating he has lost his. He then attends the room, and steals from within. On occasions, he will telephone reception from the room and claim to have forgotten the code for the room's safe. A member of staff then attends and, thinking him to be the genuine guest, opens the safe."

At six-foot, the 29-year-old fraudster still cut a dash at Southwark Crown Court, dressed in a black designer suit. With his smooth Latin looks, wavy black hair and dazzling smile Guzman looked every inch the ultimate charmer. Described as the son of a Colombian diplomat, Guzman admitted the thefts. 16 other offences were taken into account including possession of two forged passports. He was sentenced to three and a half years in jail in March 2005. Years of effort by police seemed to have finally brought the international con-artist's spree to a halt. Guzman, however, had different ideas. With no history of violence he was sent to Standford Hill, an open prison on the Isle of Sheppey in Kent. Just eight weeks into his sentence he persuaded staff to allow him to make a visit to a dentist on his own. They agreed and in May 2005 he walked out and disappeared.

Ten days later, in Dublin's up-market Merrion Hotel an American claimed he had managed to lock himself out of the Kirk Suite. First he asked a cleaner to admit him into the room. When she refused, he contacted reception staff who provided him with a duplicate key. Once inside he asked the cleaner to leave the room. Then he made a complaint that the kids had been messing with the safe code and hotel security staff were called in to unlock it for him.

Guzman was back in business.

In the short space of time since he had walked out of prison in the south of England, Guzman had travelled to Ireland and set himself up, yet again demonstrating his considerable resourcefulness. At the Merrion Hotel, Guzman stole $3,000, a ruby ring and put his new found credit card, in the name of Ms Robin Westbrook, to good use. Despite there being a woman's name on the credit card, Guzman was still able to indulge in some retail therapy. He splashed out €2,000 on CDs, DVDs and designer clothes. Then he walked into the city's top jewellers, Weirs and Sons, where he coolly spent €16,000 on a white-gold Rolex Daytona. He added a nine-carat gold chain and an 18-caret wedding ring to his shopping basket. The theft wasn't discovered by the family from Beverly Hills, California, until the next day.

But his luck was about to run out. Unfortunately for Guzman his easy escape from custody had caused a furore in the UK. With the incredible story and his good looks being irresistible to newsprint he featured in *The Times* and *The Guardian* newspapers. His notoriety brought him to the attention of the Gardaí. Once alerted to the possibility that Guzman, now thought to be a Venezualan national, was in Ireland he became a possible suspect. The theft at the Merrion exactly matched the con-man's *modus operandi*. It came down to the work of an individual officer, following up a hunch, to track down Guzman this time. Detective Garda Brian McGlynn had an idea that the Venezualan was likely to be staying in the north inner-city, close to Connolly railway station which links Dublin to Belfast. It was likely Guzman had travelled from the UK by boat and ferry to avoid the tighter security at airports. McGlynn was right. Some assiduous detective work found Guzman booked into a hostel as a Spaniard. He was even wearing the Rolex watch purchased with the stolen credit card when he was arrested. He also had the jewellery and two passports in his possession. One of them, an American passport, was in the name of a Hugh Hudson, but the photograph had been skilfully altered to carry Guzman's picture.

As usual Guzman did his best to confuse the police. He told the Gardaí that he was a Spaniard named Alejandro Cuenca from Cadiz. He was held on immigration charges for a week until French police were able to confirm, through Interpol, that he was indeed the infamous Juan Carlos Guzman-Betancourt, international man of mystery. The London Metropolitan Police also provided a match for the fingerprints sent from Dublin. Law enforcement agencies in the United States also expressed an interest in the man being held at Dublin's Cloverhill Prison.

Initially Guzman denied the deception and fraud charges but when his case came up for trial in November 2005 he admitted the charges. He remained steadfast, however, that his real name was Alejandro Cuenca. As the evidence at the trial was read out it was like a re-run of every other hotel raid by Guzman. Hotel CCTV recorded him using an internal phone to call the reception staff, making notes during the conversation. The helpful staff bought his story hook, line and sinker and Guzman was off on another shopping spree.

At the sentence hearing in March 2006 Judge Katherine Delahunt backdated Guzman's two year sentence to June 2005 to when he was first arrested in Ireland. She said he was "clearly a man who likes the finer things in life but might not be prepared to pay for them in the normal way". The Judge didn't buy into the media hype surrounding the man variously dubbed 'The Jewel Jackal' and 'The Jet Set Thief'. There were also comparisons with real-life con-man Frank Abagnale as depicted by Leonardo di Caprio in *Catch Me if You Can*, as well as the fictional jewel thief *Raffles*. Commenting on his continuous failure to elude law enforcement, Judge Delahunt said it was clear that Guzman was not a criminal mastermind.

With extradition queries from the UK, France and the United States, it was clear that Guzman would be on his way to another jail when he had finished serving his time in Ireland. He had already been tried *in absentia* in France for his raids on the couturier boutiques and sentenced to three years in jail. It was no surprise that he stuck to his claims of being Alejandro Cuenca as his legal team sought to fight off the three extradition orders. In July 2006 he won the first battle, when the High Court agreed to defer a British bid to have him extradited.

Five months later, however, it came down to Mr Justice Michael Peart to decide on whether the man in jail was Cuenca or Guzman. This time it was the French authorities who had got to the head of the queue with a European Arrest Warrant. Guzman provided an affidavit to the court detailing the harsh childhood of Cuenca. In the sworn affidavit 'Cuenca' said that his father had died in a car accident when he was three months old, that his mother had died in 1982 of tuberculosis and pneumonia. He said that he and his brother grew up in an orphanage in Seville, and then his brother was sent to a foster family. He later "escaped" from the orphanage at the age of ten, lived on the streets, had no education and never attended school. 'Cuenca' said that neither he nor his brother had birth certificates as their births were never registered. He explained that, according to gypsy tradition they were born in a house, not a hospital. He grew up in a number of different places, travelled around Spain and later Europe and other countries. When he tried to get ID from the Spanish authorities he was told that without a birth certificate this was not possible.

As the hearing progressed, his legal team argued over possible technical errors in the extradition documents, but the fingerprints were a match for the man the French police wanted. This was a coincidence, according to Guzman, who was clearly grasping at straws.

Mr Justice Peart didn't believe the story of an incredible coincidence. "I am satisfied that the person before the Court is the person who is sought under the European Arrest Warrant, and I am also satisfied by the expert fingerprint evidence referred to," he stated in his judgement on December 20, 2006. "The person before the Court is quite clearly a person who travels freely and easily between jurisdictions and within jurisdictions under a number of flags of convenience. He has no difficulty assuming a variety of names as required, and it is safe to presume as a matter of probability, given the nature of the offences for which he has been convicted already, that he is capable of changing his identity, availing of forged passports and other forms of identification in order to disguise his identity and travel around Europe. It is not surprising in these circumstances that he feels it possible to put up the sort of smoke-screen attempted in this case in order to try and cast doubt on his identity as the person whose surrender is sought by the French authorities."

Guzman was sent back to jail in France shortly after the High Court hearing when he was released from Irish prison. Presumably the next time a charming thief makes off with cash, credit cards and jewellery from an up-market hotel, the police will be calling France to find out when Guzman was released. He'll also have to dodge the outstanding warrants for his arrest from the US and the UK.

Of course being an international man of mystery doesn't have to depend on designer suits, Rolex watches and chauffeur-driven cars. Enigmatic con-artists come in all shapes and sizes. From 1999 until 2003 a little group of drifters crawled across America in a camper van and station wagon. They were an eccentric trio of friends. The middle-aged Irish couple and their male friend doted on their pet dogs. One of the animals was so old it was blind and was pushed around in a baby carrier. The three supposed travellers kept very much to themselves. Slowly they moved their way north up California in the United States, living quietly for a few weeks at a time, at different trailer parks. The woman would often spend long hours at an internet connection working on a computer. If anyone bothered to ask, the men explained they worked at refurbishing motel rooms.

In June 2002, they were staying at the Trailer Haven park on a bare asphalt parking lot close to the gate. They had recently been through Texas, Arizona and most of California. They lived a frugal and highly-mobile life, driving a well-equipped motor home and black station wagon with a trailer. Anthony Davenport, in his early sixties, was about ten years senior to his wife Linda Broderick. Their friend John Hay, a Scot, seemed to have been taken under their wing. He would sleep on the floor of their trailer. There was nothing to suggest in their scruffy, slightly dishevelled appearance that they had at least $1 million tucked away in banks accounts all over the US, as well as in Scotland and Ireland.

The long road trip through 24 US states had proved to be a lucrative affair. Although the two men regularly purchased bathroom and light fittings at Home Depot stores, their enterprise had nothing to do with kitting out old motel rooms. In fact Home Depot, the second biggest retail chain in the US, was their business.

For well over a year and a half, and possibly for as long as three years, the little group were making $2,000 a day from the retailer, in a very simple scam. First they copied the bar-code sticker from one cheap item. Then they stuck the fake bar code on a more expensive product. That item would be bought for the lower price, the fake sticker stripped off and the item returned for cash at the higher price. They stuck mostly to taps and light shades which fitted in with their cover as builders working on old motel rooms. They worked hard. In fact they worked very hard, hitting up as many as six Home Depot outlets in any given day. Hay would go in first with copied bar codes. He would, for instance, stick a bar code for $39 on a lighting fitting worth $169, and other fake stickers on items he would purchase. Then Davenport would return to the store with the same goods, minus the fake bar codes and seek a cash refund. If a member of staff asked for a receipt, he would pull out a folder and slowly start leafing his way through papers until the staff member lost interest. The checkout systems being used at the retail chain did not flag up items for which there was no record of a purchase.

This, of course, made it much easier for the fraudsters. In a culture of 'the customer is always right', low-paid retail staff didn't try too hard to get a receipt or look too closely at the ID being offered. If someone did persist, Davenport simply walked away. Each visit to a store would yield from $1,000 to $1,500. Whenever he was asked for identification he would produce an English or an Irish passport. Broderick handled the group's money, organising the cash and their various bank accounts. They had a well-organised and efficient system and they worked hard at making it pay.

It was a matter of good or bad fortune, depending on whose perspective you take, when Home Depot ended the policy of giving cash refunds in late 2001. Instead they offered gift cards for returned goods. Now the trio had to sell off gift cards at a discount price to convert their gains into cash. They sold the cards through newspaper ads and to people they met on their travels, quite often at a generous 30 per cent discount. One Texan who was building a house became a very good customer, buying $100,000 worth of gift cards for $70,000. When this man walked into his local Home Depot store and tried to pay for a new kitchen with $20,000 worth of gift cards from five different states, it raised a few eyebrows. The gift cards were soon traced back to Anthony Davenport and John Hay. Loss-making investigators analysing the information realised the pair had been pulling a bar-code switch but at that stage did not realise how much had been stolen from Home Depot. If the Texan home builder had been more circumspect, the scam could have continued on indefinitely. Slowly the pattern of frauds was linked together, showing how the strange little group had been winding their way all over the United States. They had worked their way through Home Depot outlets from

Georgia across to California and from as far north as
Ohio down to the Gulf states. Although computerised
records only went back as far as April 2001, a record of
an arrest of Anthony Broderick at a Home Depot store
in 1999 suggests that the fraud had been operating for a
lot longer.

The store detectives only knew that the group were
somewhere in California. The Federal Bureau of
Investigation showed little interest in getting involved
in the case. Surveillance photographs taken by in-store
cameras of the suspects were sent around to Californian
outlets in the hope that the pair would turn up. Fortune
intervened again when the store detective who caught
Davenport in 1999 recognised him from the pictures.
On the file an address at Trailer Haven trailer park was
listed. Unbelievably store detectives quickly discovered
that Davenport and the others were back in the same
place. When the two men went to the local Home Depot
store for a seemingly legitimate purchase they were
handcuffed by the retailer's security staff and placed
under citizen's arrest. The local police were now
involved.

A few hours later, police detectives went to Trailer
Haven where they found Linda Broderick packed up
and ready to go. Not realising that Home Depot had
unravelled their scam, Davenport did not object to their
vehicles being searched. What the police found
suddenly caught the interest of the law enforcement
community and the FBI. Stored on CDs were the details
of over a dozen bank accounts in which hundreds of
thousands of dollars had been deposited. On the day of
the arrests Linda Broderick had sent a money draft
worth $300,000 to a Bank of Ireland account in Scotland
which was subsequently frozen by the authorities. The
police also found bundles of pre-printed bar-codes, a

hand-held scanner, a lap-top computer and hundreds of Home Depot receipts. In a briefcase there were driving licences from different states, in each person's name as well as others with false names for Davenport and Broderick. Analysis of the computer hard drive showed the couple had downloaded documents for multiple Irish passport applications, while Hay appeared to always use his own name. For a brief period, investigators wondered if the operation was in fact a fund-raising expedition for Irish paramilitaries, although that was quickly ruled out. Despite their quirky lifestyle and frugal spending, it was clear they were running a professional operation.

As the scope of their fraud became apparent the US federal authorities took a greater interest in the case. It was transferred from local state authority, on the basis that the sales data from Home Depot stores was transferred to the company's Georgia headquarters every evening, making it a wire fraud and hence a federal offence. The three fraudsters didn't challenge the decision by the US Attorney's Office. Initially it was thought they had taken $400,000 from Home Depot, a figure that was soon revised upwards to $600,000. Considering Davenport's 1999 arrest it is quite possible the group took the retail giant for more than $1 million dollars, in less than four years. The FBI seized assets worth $821,000 belonging to the group, including the $300,000 money transfer Broderick attempted on the day of their arrests.

The group argued that some of the money was as a result of property deals done in the UK. Half a million dollars had been sitting in a bank account untouched for five years and had nothing to with the Home Depot scam. Lawyers for the three con-artists did their best to portray them as harmless oddballs who perpetrated a victimless crime to fund their retirement back in Ireland or Scotland. They all had a rootless early life and were accustomed to moving from place to place. Davenport grew up without parents and as an adult worked on civil engineering projects all over the world, earning a good salary. He took unpopular postings to Africa and the Middle East. In a court report it was stated that Davenport had worked abroad for 16 years and accumulated assets worth $3.9 million. His early criminal career, however, wasn't mentioned in the court report. He picked up his first criminal conviction at the age of 16 for breaking into an office. By 1986 he had 11 convictions and had spent five stretches behind bars for forgery, theft and assault. Broderick was raised by foster parents and as an adult worked as a hairdresser. She also made money by selling craft jewellery at fairs and accompanied Davenport on his trips around the globe. The couple seemed to know Hay from before they began their Home Depot scam. He had been deported from the US in 2000, but met up with them again when he had been allowed to re-enter the country within a year. The court reports seemed to raise more questions than were answered. Investigators were baffled why anyone with millions of dollars worth of assets would be bothered working a gruelling and labour-intensive scam, living the life of a nomad on the road.

A key to being a good con-artist is to win the sympathy of others. The police, FBI and the Home Depot investigators experienced just how charming and pleasant Davenport, Broderick and Hay could be. They were always polite and well-mannered. They all admitted the offences with which they were charged and were able to cut a plea-bargain deal. The agreement was that they would re-pay some of the cash to Home

Depot in return for shorter sentences. But their eccentricity didn't stop there. Davenport delayed signing his agreement in a bid to hold onto some assets to pay the couple who were minding their dogs. It meant that he had to spend an extra two months in Santa Rita jail until the deal was done. But it was typical of the trio's generosity – they always left money with anyone they stayed with.

At the US District Court in August 2004 Hay and Davenport were sentenced to 30 months in jail. Typically they accepted a deal that gave them more jail time but meant a shorter sentence for Linda Broderick. By that time she had already served her 15 month sentence. They paid $400,000 in restitution to Home Depot and their 26 months already served was taken into account. It meant that Broderick was released immediately and was deported back to Ireland. The two men had just a few months left to do.

Behind bars Davenport showed his stubborn streak even when it meant personal suffering. He had switched from being held at Camp Parks and its relatively easy regime to a tougher life at Santa Rita so that he would be allowed to write to Linda every day. He had also clashed with prison bosses there over his medical care. He suffered from a lung condition known as sarcoidosis which requires taking medication. Davenport felt he wasn't getting the right standard of care and he had put himself through a series of hunger strikes, one lasting 32 days, to make his point. On a number of occasions he had ended up on life support in the Highland Hospital at Oakland where he came close to death. He was also attacked by another inmate and was stabbed eight times. Despite his injuries, he never gave up the name of his assailant or explained the motive for the attack. Davenport is clearly an unusual personality who on the one hand was involved in a con-job and on the other stood up for his principles even to the point of risking his life.

When their sentences were served, Davenport and Hay were also deported from the United States.

Back in Ireland Davenport and Broderick lived for a short time in a run-down flat in Rathmines, Dublin, despite the fact that he still had the considerable assets identified by the US courts. Hay got work in the city as a security guard. For a while one of his postings was at Blackhall Place, where the country's solicitors train. He was also on the staff at the National Gallery, hired to protect the priceless paintings and artwork. When the trio's escapades in the United States were revealed in the *Sunday World* newspaper they moved on again. This time they travelled to Hay's native Scotland, where presumably they are finally enjoying a hard-earned retirement.

The Home Depot scammers almost pulled off the perfect con. It was such a low-profile scam it could have gone unnoticed if the retail chain had not changed its refund system and changed to gift cards. It is very possible the investigators never fully uncovered the full extent of the scam. The trio lived quiet, if eccentric, lives. They did nothing that attracted the attention of the police. Their nomadic lifestyle also added an extra layer for the investigators to work through, before they could catch their targets. It took determined security staff from the retailer to crack the case. Only then did the conventional forces of law and order get involved. Although it was perfectly possible to have executed the fraud without being caught, Davenport, Hay and Broderick failed to do so. Perhaps being on the road gave them a false sense of security. Like Guzman-Betancourt and Peet, their rootless lifestyle was a key factor in the fraud. Moving from store to store, never turning up in the same place twice and moving on if there was any hint of suspicion. Guzman's crime spree was at the opposite end of the spectrum in that he blazed a spectacular trail of con-artistry. His panache and flamboyance served to overwhelm the hotel staff who unwittingly helped to execute his scams. As a result the Venezualan has been compared to every type of con-artist from *Raffles* to Frank Abagnale. Peet on the other hand was mired in the mundane and the domestic. He stole cash from people who had genuinely allowed themselves to befriend him and believe all his two-faced lies. But, like the others, he relied on his anonymity to prevent his victims from learning about his predilection for cheating people out of their money. The private test of honesty in which most people would tell a waiter he made a mistake doesn't exist for such con-artists. They go out of their way to use and abuse the social etiquette which relies on people to show at least a basic level of ethical behaviour. Anonymity and role-playing makes it difficult for their victims to check out their stories without acting beyond the limits of the social norm. Some people are better at dealing with potential con-artists than others, but neither status, education nor money are any protection if a skilled operator manages to hit the right buttons.

THREE

The Skimmers

If the customer at the cash machine took longer than usual, no one noticed. His face, obscured by a peaked baseball cap drawn down over his eyes, was invisible. He appeared intent on completing his transaction. It is a routine action, carried out worldwide, by millions of people, every day of the week. The card goes into the automatic teller machine (ATM) and money comes out. The two men in the queue behind the young male bank customer looked relaxed. They were in no hurry and patiently waited their turn to use the machine. Eventually the man in the cap walked away, stuffing his wallet into his back pocket. The next customer stood at the machine and withdrew some cash. His friend then took his turn and the pair left together. Already there were two more customers waiting to use the ATM. This particular one was installed at a busy location on the south side of Dublin city. Nearby there is a convenience store and a pub. The traffic is heavy, but drivers still pull up at the kerb to get cash and to drop into the shop. Thousands of people are funnelled through this part of the city and a lot of money is dispensed through the machine.

The bank that operates the ATM started getting phone calls from irate and worried customers the following afternoon. A week later there were still calls coming through. Several hundred euros had been taken from all the customers' accounts in unexplained transactions, just before and after midnight. Weary bank officials knew straight away that the card skimmers had struck again.

Officers from the Garda Bureau of Fraud Investigation took a close look at security camera footage from the bank machine which all the affected customers had used. After trawling through hours of images the man in the baseball cap caught their attention. He hadn't been there to withdraw cash in the conventional sense. Instead, in a series of well-rehearsed moves, he quickly pulled some equipment from his jacket. He fitted a small device over the machine's card slot and placed a replica over the keyboard customers use to insert their secret personal identification number (PIN). A micro camera, concealed in a fake ATM frontage, filmed the customers' fingers as they pressed each number. For good measure, the fake keyboard also recorded the PINs onto a microchip. The device on the card slot then read and recorded the customer's details contained on the black magnetic strip. The two men who used the machine afterwards were part of the fraud. They had checked the equipment was securely fitted and was working properly. The trap had been set for unsuspecting customers who were about to unwittingly hand over all the information the criminals needed to empty their bank accounts. When the cash cards went into the slot they were stripped of their information. The transaction went ahead as normal and the skimmers' targets walked away, unaware their hard-earned money was about to be pilfered.

That evening the criminals sat in a parked car nearby, watching the machine and their carefully-crafted equipment on the ATM. Dozens of bank customers had turned up to withdraw cash. All the recorded details from the keyboard, the card reader and the camera were transmitted and downloaded onto a laptop computer. At a busy location, like the one they'd selected, hundreds of cards could be copied in a few hours. Later the fraudsters had returned to quietly remove the fake front, the rest of the gear and slipped away to their base.

The next stage of the operation was to use the stolen information to create replica cards. Each of the customers' card details were digitally transferred onto new cards, with magnetic strips. Supermarket loyalty cards, acquired for free, or phone cards are often used. With the right equipment and computer software, it is a surprisingly simple task to create the clones. Everything the professional skimmer needs can be easily acquired over the internet. Card readers supplied to retailers and restaurants can be bought second-hand and converted for use by the fraudsters.

Once the details are copied the newly-cloned cards are used to empty customer accounts. Then, to get around the daily cash limits imposed on card withdrawals from ATM by the banks, the cloned cards would each be used once before midnight. When the clock had struck twelve, the cards would be used for a second time. It takes most people 24 hours to realise someone has been dipping into their account, during which time the thieves can make four trips to the money trough. Often the stolen information is emailed to another country where the clones are manufactured and used. In one case, a card skimmed in Dublin was used in Spain to steal money just 20 minutes later. Each clone yields an average of €1,200. If a customer or bank doesn't notice the fraudulent withdrawals, then the fraudsters keep going until the well runs dry. The first time most customers will know about the theft is when the dreaded message 'insufficient funds to complete transaction' appears on the screen of an ATM.

Over the last decade ATM fraud has evolved into a highly-organised and tightly controlled industry. Much of it is overseen by elements of the notoriously violent and powerful Eastern European criminal mafias. Other gangs are controlled by people who are funding extreme Islamists with links to terrorists. Every step of the operation is meticulously encoded and recorded. The fraudsters know they have to account to their bosses for every cent that is stolen. At any time an 'auditor', the gang member who monitors everything, particularly how much money is taken, can arrive to check up on their progress. ATM skimming, for the most part, is the preserve of the criminal elite of the global underworld.

In 2005, fraudsters were very busy. They simply walked up to cash machines all over Ireland and pocketed €4 million in stolen cash. Card skimming frauds had reached an uncomfortable pinnacle. It was an epidemic. Over the years the scam had been improved and refined every time new security measures were introduced by the financial institutions. Slick and professional skimming operators could arrive in Ireland and leave three days later, with hundreds of thousands of euro, before the banks were even aware they had been robbed. What had, until the mid-1990s, been regarded as an urban myth, had become an everyday crime.

Ireland was far from being the only country targeted by highly-organised and well-equipped fraudsters. In the first nine months of 2004, an estimated €49 million was stolen in 17 European Union states in ATM scams. The London-based European ATM Security Team (EAST) released a report in January 2005 outlining how the organisation had been told of 2,377 card skimming operations at ATMs. The cash machine scam had clearly come of age. It was to change the way banks and their customers do business forever.

* * * *

The ATM was invented in 1939 and a mechanised cash dispenser came into use in London in 1967. Automatic teller machines did not start to appear on Irish streets, however, until the mid-1980s. There are now almost 3,000 in service all over the country in banks, on streets, in pubs, clubs and shops. Throughout 2005, Irish bank customers withdrew €24.1 billion from cash machines in 177 million transactions. It is the most common and efficient way for ordinary bank customers all over the world to withdraw cash from their accounts. There are an estimated one million ATMs in use worldwide. Some machines contain hundreds of thousands of euro, although financial institutions prefer not to comment on just how much is put into an average ATM. With so much money sitting tantalisingly close, it was only a matter of time before criminal minds began working out how to grab a slice of the cake.

The first ATM scams involved using a looped piece of plastic or a strip of video tape that was placed into the card slot. It was secured in such a way that just enough of the strip would be left protruding to allow it to be pulled back out again. An unsuspecting customer would then place their card into the slot, but nothing would happen. The fraudster, pretending to be a helpful fellow customer, would suggest re-trying the PIN number, while watching over the victim's shoulder in a practice known as 'shoulder surfing.' Eventually the customer would give up and walk away. The fraudsters would then retrieve the loop and the captured card from the machine and use it to withdraw cash. The scam became known as the Lebanese Loop after the country from where it is purported to have originated.

When it first started happening in Ireland customers had a difficult job convincing banks that they hadn't withdrawn the money themselves. In the early days, the fraudsters' job was also made easier because customer's account numbers were still printed on receipts which were usually discarded. There was no evidence of fraud or tampering with the machine. In the past, banks had insisted that all losses were the customer's fault and it was only as more and more customers complained that it became apparent that the so-called phantom withdrawals were more than an urban myth in the making. Denis Whalley, a Merseyside lawyer, represented over 400 bank customers in the UK who lost a total of STG£1 million as a result of 'phantom withdrawals'. By the early 1990s banks were being forced to admit by the likes of Whalley and consumer rights groups that the ATM system was not foolproof and that they couldn't force customers to take the hit for these 'phantom withdrawals'. The onus shifted and it was now on banks to prove that the customer has been negligent or fraudulent before refusing to compensate victims.

ATM fraud forced the banking industry to make sweeping changes. The limit on how much cash can be withdrawn in a single transaction was lowered to €300 from as much as €800. When cameras were installed at ATM sites, the footage provided proof that the defrauded customers were telling the truth. With the changes in banking culture the simple Lebanese Loop became more and more difficult to use. Newer machines were also designed to make the scam more difficult. Now most machines carry a message warning customers not to use it if anything appears unusual.

In the early 1990s, however, the ATM system was still extremely vulnerable to fraud and the early ATM skimmers were maverick independents. As it was, successfully using a loop and then 'shoulder surfing' a victim, took a certain level of skill and nerve that the average criminal would be unlikely to possess. The puzzle of how to access large amounts of money sitting in a machine has attracted some eccentric, highly intelligent minds, albeit with a criminal skew. To them it was a technically simple task to steal the information off a cash card. For some people who had a basic understanding of how the cash-card system works, the temptation proved too much. Jailbird Mindy Fairchild, serving time for stealing credit cards, put his hours to good use while in prison. He studied electronics and when he got out in 1996 developed his own system to skim ATM cards. He devised a camera hidden behind a false panel and a transmitter to allow him to watch customers key in their PINs. He then used a simple Lebanese Loop to retain the customer's card which he retrieved and used to empty funds from the account. Fairchild, who had changed his name from Mahinder Singh Rapul, hit bank machines in London and the Home Counties. He was caught after a tip-off to police. At his trial in Northampton Crown Court in 1997 it was estimated that he managed to steal STG£100,000. He was sentenced to five years in jail. Fairchild's equipment was nowhere near as sophisticated as later models used by Romanian and London gangs, but in the early days he was at the cutting edge of ATM skimming technology.

At the same time, in 1996, a security computer consultant in the UK also decided to use his talents to rip off ATM customers. Andrew Stone used a high-definition camera, bought for STG£8,000, from a considerable distance to record all the embossed details on a card, as well as the customer keying in their PIN. Using the information, he was able to make clones from supermarket club cards. Before he was caught, Stone stole STG£136,000, none of which was recovered. He was jailed for five and a half years. Two years previously he had been jailed for ten months for plotting to steal from ATMs in another skimming plot that had never got off the ground. Stone and Fairchild's scams were very simple. One used a long-range camera and the other a hidden camera to watch a customer input their PIN. That was all they needed to use the stolen card or a cloned card to empty a customer's account.

For the next decade ATM cards remained pretty much the same. Skimming, however, continued to develop. It became more organised and techniques were refined to make it more efficient and profitable. Security got tougher in the UK where the police and banks had by now recognised ATM fraud as a serious problem.

It had taken several years before ATM skimming hit Ireland. Since their arrival in 1996, however, there had been a steady rise in the amount of cash being stolen by skimmers. It rose by 38 per cent each year until 2002. In 2001, Gardaí issued a warning about a Lebanese Loop scam after two men were arrested in Tallaght. They were the tip of the iceberg.

In January 2003, there was a rare case of a skimmer using a Lebanese Loop being caught red-handed in Dublin's George's Street. Virgil Varga, a 20-year-old Romanian immigrant living in the city, was seen acting suspiciously by a uniformed Garda on foot patrol. As the Garda approached Varga and another man, they ran away, one of them dropping an object on the ground. Varga was collared on the nearby Stephen's Street. The discarded object turned out to be a Lebanese Loop fashioned from a doubled-up builder's measuring tape attached to a clear piece of plastic. Varga got a three month jail sentence for his efforts. But he was nothing but a bumbling amateur compared to the more sophisticated fraudsters that were already operating in Ireland. The Lebanese Loop was by now an old-fashioned method for stealing from ATMs.

Such was the level of ATM fraud in 2004 that the Garda Bureau of Fraud Investigation (GBFI) set up a special operation to tackle the criminals who appeared to be pillaging bank accounts at will all over Ireland. While some traditionalists like Virgil Varga were still knocking around, the real players had moved up a gear to stay ahead of the banks' counter-measures to stop the Lebanese Loop.

Once the GBFI were given the green light to tackle the problem, they quickly identified five separate gangs of criminals, all from Eastern Europe, who were running a slick and efficient criminal operation. They were milking millions from the accounts of unsuspecting bank customers in every part of the country. The investigators' first break came when they examined camera footage from a busy ATM in south Dublin which had been targeted by a professional skimming operation. They were able to glean enough information to tie it to another suspicious incident on the north side of the city. The net closed in on one gang as the GBFI tracked every possible intelligence lead in the operation to stop the card skimmers. Two members of the gang had previously been spotted by officers in July 2005 after reports of suspicious activity at a cash machine at Whitehall, Bray. A car, in which Sorin Condranche (25) and Rzvan Schiopu (26) were travelling, was later stopped several miles away, on the north side of the city. Gardaí found cards with magnetic strips, sticky tape and other bits of equipment in the car. They were released by the Gardaí after being questioned. Then, on September 10, two customers at a Bank of Ireland ATM in Deansgrange, south Dublin, became suspicious about the machine. When they began fiddling with the ATM, a silver tube with a tiny camera fell off. Two men approached the machine and ran off with the equipment. The fraudsters' failure to properly set the trap was to be their undoing.

The men were identified after a trawl through CCTV footage showed Condranche and Schiopu obviously setting up their skimming equipment. The GBFI officers, led by Detective Superintendent Eugene Gallagher, were able to trace the Romanians to their apartment at La Vallee in Bray where they were arrested on September 29, 2005. Also arrested with the two men was Daniela Ciocan, a 26-year-old woman who had been living in Ireland for the previous four years and a Russian woman, Tatsianan Povlyshko. When the apartment was searched by Gardaí they discovered two false fronts for an ATM machine, 100 home-made cards with magnetic strips and a number of skimmer units which are used to read a bank card's details. Sheets of coded letters and numbers contained lists of the customers' secret PIN numbers which the gang later matched up with the card's details. The cheeky gangsters had a sticker on their false ATM fronts warning customers of bank fraud. The equipment used by the gang meant they could download and copy the details from hundreds of bank cards every hour. The fake ATM keyboards and the covers to put over the card slot were machine-crafted to the highest standard. The fakes couldn't have been better made if the bank had ordered them from their own manufacturer. Properly fitted onto an ATM, even the most alert customer would be hard pressed to spot anything suspicious. It turned out to be one of the biggest cases of card-skimmers being caught red-handed in Europe.

The trio of Romanians were brought to trial in

October 2006. The Russian woman, Povlyshko, had already been deported for immigration offences. At Wicklow Circuit Court Judge Pat McCartan described the criminal operation as a sophisticated fraud detected by good police work. He said ATMs are a key financial support for bank customers and their accounts were abused by the gangsters. The judge described it as "a mean and nasty" scam that was capable of delivering substantial sums of money. In court the three fraudsters still looked shocked that they had been caught in what should have been a sure fire way to make easy money. They did their best to highlight how they had previously led blameless lives, came from good homes and were deeply embarrassed by their foray into the underworld of crime. Schiopu claimed he was a medical student. They hadn't told anyone back home about their run-in with the Irish authorities. They looked no different than any of the thousands of young Eastern Europeans who arrived in Ireland looking for work and an opportunity to improve their standard of living. The two men, however, had arrived in Ireland as illegal immigrants earlier in 2005. They had never intended to do an honest day's work. Their only purpose in coming to Ireland was to steal cash from ATMs. Ciocan had been in Ireland since 2002, working various jobs without ever getting in trouble with the law. The soft-spoken woman, who had residency status, had allowed them to use her apartment as a base for the skimming operation and had taken her share of the proceeds. Before he passed sentence, Judge McCartan said he was taking into account the trio's youth, education and the fact they had no previous convictions. However, he said a prison sentence had to be imposed to mark the serious nature of the crime and to deter other criminals from getting involved. They each got four years.

Even while behind bars Ciocan still managed to get in trouble over a bit of moonlighting from her prison cell. Eager to relieve the boredom and to earn a few quid, she was one of a group of prisoners who agreed to start work on a sex chat-line from behind bars. It emerged in May 2007 that the prisoners had developed a nice cottage industry posing as 'horny housewives' for punters who wanted to listen to someone talk dirty. Being in jail was not an obstacle to the women who were paid for keeping punters on the expensive premium lines, with smutty chit-chat. Ciocan promised the recruiter she'd keep the callers on the line all night. Sourcing mobile phones in jail wouldn't be a problem. Ciocan even sent a mobile phone photograph of herself posing in a mini-dress. Unfortunately, the recruiter was a *Sunday World* reporter, Niamh O'Connor, working on a story highlighting the easy access prisoners had to mobile phones. As a result Ciocan lost her jail privileges for a few days.

Condranche, Schiopu and Ciocan weren't the only skimmers caught operating in Ireland. A group of British career criminals, who set up a skimming and cloning operation in Cork City, were caught by a mixture of bad luck and rank amateurism. They weren't even among the gangs being targeted at the time by the GBFI. The Londoners, all of Pakistani origin, were old hands at various scams and criminal enterprises and had served time in British prisons. The men, Mohammed Majid (38), Ali Raza (48) and Mohammed Khaleed (25), arrived in Cork Airport from Gatwick on June 2, 2005, for the Bank Holiday weekend. To all intents and purposes they looked like a group of pals taking a short break, staying at the house of a compatriot in Wilton, Cork City. The real plan, however, was to clone cards and use them throughout southern Ireland. All the card details had already been

skimmed from people who had used their cash cards at
an ATM in Nottingham. The plan was to be back home
in England before the banks opened and before the
ripped off customers would even know their accounts
had been robbed. The decision to travel to Ireland was
to make it more difficult for any follow-up investigation
into the fraud from the UK. They had a good night's
sleep at the Wilton house. The following day they
started the process of making fake cash cards. It was a
fool-proof plan – easy street.

All day on Saturday, people from Nottingham were
apparently withdrawing cash around Cork City and
Killarney. It was estimated €25,000 was stolen from
bank accounts as the fraudsters worked hard to collect
as much cash as possible before heading home to
London. Everything was going perfectly to plan.

Things began to unravel at 8pm the following night,
however, when their host was pulled in by the Gardaí
as he drove his jeep close to his Wilton house. Two
Detective Gardaí, John McDonagh and Damien
Moloney, stopped the black four-wheel-drive with a
man and woman inside near the Sarsfield roundabout
in Wilton. A search of the car revealed a small amount
of cannabis and the man was arrested. He was taken to
Togher Garda Station, where he gave Gardaí
permission to search his home at Elmvale Avenue.
When they arrived at the address the officers could see,
through a living room window, the group of British
career criminals as they worked on creating more
cloned cards. The youngest, Khaleed, was using a
laptop computer, while Majid was busy writing on
paper. Raza and a fourth man were taking it easy in
armchairs while the other pair worked away.

As the arrested man arrived back at his house, he
used his own key to open the front door. In a belated

warning, he called "Police" as he walked into the sitting room. If the fraudsters had tried to act more suspiciously, they couldn't have done any better. The fourth man, who did not stand trial with the others, stood up immediately and threw away a gold cigarette box, drawing it to the attention of the Gardaí. Khaleed and Majid stopped in their tracks. The State prosecutor, John Edwards SC, was somewhat understated when he later said in court: "Because of the way they reacted the Gardaí thought there was unlawful activity going on." The gold box contained two fake cards and on the floor there were bundles of Tesco club cards and other cards with a standard magnetic strip for storing information. It was obvious to the two detectives that they had interrupted a major card skimming operation in full flow. The equipment they discovered had the potential to make 450 cash or credit cards and 87 already cloned cards were found in the house. The men were later charged with 16 different offences. Two of the charges were for possession of a card reader with criminal intent and the other 14 related to possession of cards and magnetic strips for use in a theft. During the trial the jury was shown a demonstration of how the men skimmed cards and then made clones to empty a customer's account.

Evidence was also given how Garda technicians found that the hard drive of the seized laptop computer contained deleted files of customers' card details which they had been able to recover. An external hard drive contained emails full of skimmed information. Installed on the computer was a programme called "Robo-swipe" which allowed the user to access card information. Raza, Khaleed and Majid pleaded not guilty to the charges under the Theft and Fraud Offences Act, but the jury at Cork Criminal Court had no doubts and returned a unanimous verdict on all counts. The court heard that the two sentenced men had extensive previous convictions for fraud and theft, including prison sentences for credit card scams in Britain. Ali Raza, who was on bail, disappeared on the third day of the trial and is thought to be hiding in Britain. He will be sentenced when he is apprehended and transferred back to Ireland. Mohammed Khaleed and Mohammed Majid were sentenced to five years in jail for the scam.

Throughout 2005 there were 110 skimming incidents in Ireland in which €2 million was stolen from customers' accounts. When the Romanian trio and the Londoners were arrested that year, a number of other suspects fled the country. The incidents of card skimming plummeted by 65 per cent. The three young Romanians fit into a pattern that suggests this type of card skimming operation is centrally organised by well-resourced criminal gangs who send out teams all over the world. Many of those who carry out the fraud are university graduates with technical qualifications, but living illegally at the time in a European Union state. Card skimming looks like easy money, but there are more sinister figures ultimately controlling what is a well-organised scam. It is suspected that much of the fake equipment is supplied by Russian criminal gangs. They in turn persuade illegal immigrants to take part in the scam. But once on board the skimmers find themselves under serious pressure to meet the demands for cash from the underworld heavyweights while still finding a way to make their own profits. They have to balance their fear of the sinister and dangerous figures from the Russian mafia, with the need to avoid being caught and jailed.

Fraud specialist Una Dillon, who works for the Irish Payments Services Organisation, which represents ten financial institutions including the five main clearing banks, has charted the rise of the skimmers, who are controlled by professional gangsters: "They are highly organised. The head honchos of these gangs literally cherry-pick off the street. They'll put people through four years of technical college. They'll be well trained on what to do. They are obviously studying bank processing systems. They know what they are doing. We haven't seen any Irish gangs doing any ATM skimming and it's because these Eastern European gangs are so well-organised. I've certainly seen information where there are links with Russian and Bulgarian mafia. Obviously Irish gangs are not interested in taking part in the fraud. We believe these people go around in groups of two or three but there's always someone we call the auditor in the group, someone who is checking up on everything that is actually obtained and how much is taken. They literally come into the country for a couple of weeks and leave again. Some cases we've seen, they have been in and out in one day and they are very much working for another source. The people we see are usually very well dressed. They look perfectly normal citizens, but they are not taking the money for themselves; it's usually for another source. In fact again the terrorist activity that we have seen around the globe, a lot of the European groups have proven that a lot of the revenue taken in from card fraud would go to fund more serious crimes like terrorism. Anyone we've seen they are highly organised and highly trained. They know what they are doing."

Any card with a magnetic strip can be easily copied and used to steal. It is very unlikely, however, that a fraudster is going to want to skim a supermarket club card to steal shopping points or to get into a lottery for a sun holiday. Credit cards are a different thing. The

potential rewards are far higher than what can be
gleaned from ATM skimming. It is a type of fraud that
has been around longer than ATM fraud and is
extremely easy to carry out, even with no equipment. In
December 2006, it looked as if this author was going to
have a great party on New Year's Eve. After all he
apparently phoned an off-licence to order a bottle of
Cristal champagne, two bottles of Rose champagne and
three bottles of Dom Perignon. The staff at the store
took down all the card details and asked for the security
code on the back, close to where it is signed. All was in
order and the so-called card holder's son was sent on
his way to collect the €950 worth of booze. The only
problem was that the caller had stolen the credit card
details or had been given them by someone who had
been in physical contact with the card. When the
fraudster tried to carry out the same scam in a different
branch of the same retail chain, a staff member noticed
the previous transaction. The Gardaí were alerted and
were waiting when the fraudster came to get the
champagne. It was a clear cut case and the cash was
refunded.

In 2006, €14.5 million was stolen from credit cards
issued by Ireland's five main clearing banks. That
figure amounts to what was lost by the banks. It doesn't
include losses suffered by card-holders or retailers.
Credit card theft far outstrips the theft of cash using
ATM cards, which have much lower cash limits. In this
day and age it is not uncommon for credit cards to have
a limit as high as €100,000. It is a tantalising honey-pot
for any determined fraudster. A report published by
Visa in 2005 found one in five Irish people have been
the victims of credit card fraud. Some are very basic
scams, like the champagne fraudster, but others were as
a result of far more sophisticated frauds in which credit

cards were electronically skimmed, cloned and fraudulently used. The biggest threat to financial institutions and customers, however, is posed by highly organised international crime gangs who are now increasingly targeting Ireland and its vibrant economy. The difference, however, between skimming an ATM card and a credit card is that the skimmer has to face their victim when quietly stealing the data from a credit card. A fraudster working in a bar or a motorway service stop has to carry a small data reader through which credit cards are quickly swiped. No bigger than a cigarette box they are easily concealed in the palm of a hand and can store the data from thousands of cards. A skimmer in a restaurant runs the risk of being caught in the act or else becoming the focus of suspicion as ripped-off customers and their banks spot a pattern. It also takes more organisational ability, using lots of different individuals in different locations to skim information, others to clone cards and to buy goods over the phone, which are then sold for cash.

In one case in November 2000, it became clear that a well-organised credit card skimming operation was up and running in Dublin. Irish cards that had been skimmed in Dublin were used to buy expensive goods in countries from the United States to Britain and China. In less than a week, one card that had been skimmed was used to purchase electrical goods worth €300,000 in Taiwan. It takes between two and three weeks before most legitimate credit card holders realise they have been billed for purchases they didn't make. In 2001 it was a systematic and well-organised global fraud operation. Nothing like it had ever been seen before in Ireland. Immigrant staff working in four city restaurants quickly became the suspects in the unprecedented skimming operation.

Between November 2000 and May 2001 the GBFI painstakingly built up intelligence on the gang which apparently had no links to Irish organised crime. The breakthrough for the fraud busters came on May 5, 2001 after the detectives learned that two new skimming devices were to arrive at the Federal Express bureau at Dublin Airport. The consignment was addressed to a Mr Abdul Kareem of Liberian Limited. The trap was set, as the fraud squad kept surveillance on the office for four days. Finally a man arrived to collect the suspect package.

The Gardaí made their move and arrested the North African man. The package was searched and the expected skimming machines were found, along with three counterfeit cards in the name of M. Santos Mendez, an envelope containing five gift vouchers and a piece of paper containing three credit card account numbers. It was more than enough for the Gardaí to search Liberian Limited premises and the man's home. The officers knew they were onto a professional outfit before the arrest, but the true extent of the gang's activity and global connections came as a surprise. The nondescript Liberian Limited office was the head-quarters. The search of the office at the Century Business Park (where the Liberian company was based at the time) yielded a laptop, a piece of hardware to read and write credit card data and a small, locked briefcase. The reader-writer was examined by an expert, who found it contained a program whereby data could be downloaded and uploaded to credit cards. Some genuine cards were literally ironed to remove their details and fake magnetic strips attached. Various gift vouchers for well-known retail stores including Debenhams, A-Wear, Next and Brown Thomas worth €5,080 were recovered at the Business

Park and at the man's home. They had been bought using the faked credit cards. The briefcase contained 416 blank, counterfeit and altered cards for which the arrested man accepted responsibility. Each card could have been used to defraud cash or goods up to €15,000, realising a potential haul of €6.2 million.

The arrested man was identified as really being Egyptian accountant Mohammed Saleem. The olive-skinned moustachioed North African looked the part of a cosmopolitan, charming, wheeler-dealer who could make his way anywhere in the world. The urbane playboy was a regular in casinos and gambling clubs where he played for high-stakes. Married with one child, the 34-year-old resided legally in Ireland with his wife in Ballymun, north-west Dublin. He had set up the company Liberian Limited in a small office that had become a hive of illegal activity. It had been a while since Saleem had made an honest living. He was an experienced fraudster with connections to organised criminals in Britain and Europe. He had served time in jail in both the UK and Holland before he arrived in Ireland, presumably to avoid the attentions of the various authorities who knew him well. The Egyptian's 'workers' were spread out across the city, quietly toiling away in garages and restaurants, stealing credit card information whenever the opportunity arose. The key to the fraud were the small skimming devices that were used by waiters and shop workers to swipe an unsuspecting customer's card.

Saleem later pleaded guilty to 17 sample counts, out of 44, involving cards issued by American Express, Visa and Mastercard. Two charges were from his arrest, when he was caught in possession of the data readers with intent to commit larceny on May 9, 2001. Seven of the counts related to altered or counterfeit American

Express, Visa and Mastercard credit cards recovered by
Gardaí at the airport and at the Liberian office in
Century Business Park. Saleem admitted to six counts
of handling stolen shop vouchers recovered from his
flat and to two counts of possession of a laptop
computer with intent to damage property, namely the
data strips on credit cards. It also emerged that Saleem
had nine previous convictions in England for the same
type of offence, including handling stolen credit cards,
fraud, forgery and obtaining property by deception. In
the past he was known to have used 18 different aliases.
It was clear that credit card fraud, not accountancy, was
Saleem's true profession.

At his trial in February 2002, by way of mitigation,
Saleem's defence lawyer said the North African had a
serious cocaine and gambling problem which brought
great shame on him because of the culture he came
from. The lawyer also pointed out that Saleem had
pleaded guilty from the start and co-operated with
Gardaí. But the trial judge, Desmond Hogan, described
the offences as very serious and said it was obvious that
Saleem had been involved in such activity for quite
some time. "It is clear that at the time of his arrest he
was gearing up and tooling himself for more and I just
can't ignore the fact that he is not unfamiliar with such
activity," he said.

The final year of the five-year sentence was
suspended because of the mitigating evidence and
back-dated to the time of Saleem's arrest. The urbane
playboy left the Four Courts in Dublin handcuffed to
prison officers, with a blanket covering his head.

Saleem was far from being the last credit card
skimmer to operate in Dublin or Ireland. In early 2008
another Romanian gangster ran a scam that
investigators believed was possibly making as much as

€200,000 a month. It combined the old-fashioned criminal skill of pick-pocketing, with the high-tech abilities of the card-cloners. The 30-year-old gangster who has no serious convictions in Ireland is regarded a criminal heavyweight. He is a prime suspect behind people-trafficking, prostitution and protection rackets against the Romanian community in Ireland. Well-spoken, with a perfect command of English, he is the Irish boss of a criminal network, headquartered in Brussels, which spans Europe. Instead of using expensive card readers and mini-cameras to skim cards, he used a gang of pick-pockets to simply steal them from tourists.

In one month, he organised for 110 petty criminals, many of them still in their teens, to travel from Spain to Ireland. There was a sudden surge of pick-pocket thefts in Dublin city centre, particularly at the tourist haunts surrounding Trinity College. In the three months following Christmas, hundreds of incidents were reported to the nearest Garda Station. This compared starkly with the usual rate of one or two a day. The young thieves, all Romanians, were prolific. Teams of undercover Gardaí were arresting them at the rate of eight a day, as they were caught in the act. One 16-year-old was caught two days in a row. Another, arrested just hours after landing in Dublin, was able to produce the business card of a local solicitor. Working in twos and threes, they would walk behind their targets in areas where pedestrians were crowded together. Using a scarf to cover their hand they would make the 'dip' and immediately pass off whatever they stole to their colleague.

The pickpockets were allowed to keep any cash they pilfered, but credit cards and mobile phones had to be handed over. Within hours of being stolen in Dublin, cloned versions of the cards were being used in cities such as Madrid and Oslo. The criminals used the cards to buy high-value goods which could easily be converted to cash. The pick-pocketing petered out by May as a result of constant Garda pressure. The criminal gangs presumably switched to another European city to continue their racket. Until credit cards are switched entirely to PIN-only, the way remains open for the Romanian gangsters to continue the scam.

It is not in the interest of banks and retailers to advertise how vulnerable credit cards and ATM cards are to fraud. The likes of Saleem and the Romanian skimmers have the potential to undermine confidence in the way card transactions are carried out. For that reason incidents of card fraud are played down and many frauds go unreported. The losses are simply being absorbed by financial institutions. Slowly, improved security measures have been introduced. Credit cards with customers' photographs have been suggested as a possibility, but tests on face-recognition by retail staff suggests that it would be far from a foolproof system. Using integrated circuits printed onto a micro-chip instead of the magnetic card will make it harder for the fraudsters, but not impossible. Likewise the use of PIN-only cards will not be a fool-proof safeguard against the skimmers. By March 2007, it was claimed that card skimming was on the verge of extinction as financial institutions introduced cards with micro-chips that could not be copied. However, many banks continue to use machines that still read both magnetic strips and the chips, leaving a gap in the market for skimmers to continue their trade. The tighter the security measures get, the more ingenious the methods devised by fraudsters to find a way to skim someone else's money.

FOUR

Insurance Fairy Tales

No doubt it seemed like a good idea at the time –
whiplash injuries are always worth at least €10,000.
There's the psychological trauma of being in a road
smash, not to mention headaches and the compensation
for the two weeks out of work to recover. A back injury
from even the smallest crash can have an impact on a
person's conjugal abilities, damaging relationships,
self-confidence and leading, perhaps, to depression. If
the insurance claim is done right, a bogus car crash can
be a tidy little earner for everyone involved. All it takes
is a bit of nerve and some basic acting skills.

By the end of the 1990s, if the insurers are to be
believed, bogus claims had become a cottage industry
in Ireland. Only in the United States – Ireland's spiritual
colony – are the citizens more compo-hungry than the
Irish. There is a compelling argument that the level of
fraud in Ireland forced up the price of insurance for
individuals and for businesses, such as hotels and
restaurants that deal with the litigious Irish population
on a daily basis. The then Irish Minister for Justice
Michael McDowell stated: "The growth of lawsuits in
Ireland has been deeply corrosive from an economic
point of view." Car insurance in particular was
prohibitively high. It was commonplace for people in
their 20s to be driving cars still registered in one of their
parents' names. By the early 2000s the insurance claims
culture had hit a peak. In 2003, for instance, personal
injury claims accounted for 60 per cent of all High
Court cases. The Army deafness cases, in which

thousands of ex-soldiers successfully sued the government for hearing loss, became the nadir of a cynical compo-culture society. The fact that the overwhelming majority of the cases brought by ex-soldiers were legitimate claims was glossed over, as the potential cost for the tax-payers steadily grew. An exasperated public had little sympathy when an Army bandsman, who sued for hearing loss, lost his case and had the legal costs awarded against him.

Local authorities lived in fear of public liability claims. In fact it became an excuse for not providing services. For years public parks lacked children's playgrounds with the explanation that insurance costs were far too high. If Ireland had become the world centre for bogus personal injuries claims, then Dublin city was most definitely the epicentre. Local authorities in the city continuously fought a battle against claims. People managed to frequently trip over paving stones, sometimes on more than one occasion, but always resulting in personal injuries claims. Work on laying pipes or other underground services was almost guaranteed to attract accident-prone pedestrians. Construction firms were also under attack and they began to take more radical measures to defend themselves from fraudsters. Private investigators were hired to check claimants' stories and to provide evidence that injuries were being exaggerated. In one case, where a man claiming a serious back injury had said he was unable to work, investigators provided a video tape of him carrying a TV up a flight of stairs.

A Dublin-based hairdresser felt her slip at work deserved compensation. In 2002, Amy Brunton was working at a hair salon in Clondalkin when she slipped on wet hair and moisture which had been allowed to build up on the floor. Although she didn't fall Amy twisted her back and neck which made it difficult for her to carry out even simple tasks. She sued her employer for €38,000 damages. One of the factors adding to the damages was the fact that her injuries affected her ability to play with her daughter. She had problems carrying out normal domestic duties such as vacuuming floors, gardening, housework, hanging out the washing or driving for long periods. Ms Brunton had claimed that she was someone whose whole life "during every waking moment" had been changed by the accident.

Her claims, however, failed to stand up to any scrutiny. Although she had told her doctor that she had gone home after twisting her neck and back she had been seen buying paint in a DIY store. A private detective was hired to check out the truth of her claims about her injuries and their debilitating effect. When the case came to court a video showed Ms Brunton playing with her daughter, trying to keep a paper aeroplane airborne. The tape was filmed exactly a year after she had slipped at work. She was clearly visible swinging her arms and shoulders and bending her neck and back. Judge Elizabeth Dunne described her claim as "grossly exaggerated" and ordered her to pay her former employer's legal costs.

Amy Brunton's case came at a time when the ever increasing costs of insurance created a public and political mood for change. The backlash allowed the government at the time to introduce new laws and methods for dealing with personal injuries. Business leaders, who were looking at soaring public liability insurance premiums, also began working on ways to reduce their exposure to dodgy claims. The third prong of attack came from the insurance industry itself, who had been guilty of making it too easy for bogus

claimants to succeed. Too many fake claims for
compensation were left unchallenged, as the firms
preferred to pay out rather than risk money fighting a
lengthy legal battle. Like the government and their
customers, the industry went about finding ways to
neuter Ireland's compo-culture.

By 2007, the insurance industry stated that the level
of fraudulent claims had dropped significantly. It still
costs, they estimate, €100 million a year. The key
change has been the change in public attitude towards
insurance fraudsters. The industry successfully made
people aware of the connection between high insurance
premiums and the level of fraud. The message went out
to the general public: 'fraudsters are costing you
money'. A telephone hotline set up to report bogus
claims proved to be an effective tool. It allowed the
insurance firms to use the paying public as their first
line of defence against fraudsters. The 'hotline' attracts
20 reports a week. Top of the list are exaggerated car
and motor-related claims, followed by public liability
claims against retailers and then employers' liability. It
is a crude and cheap, but very effective, method of
combating insurance fraud.

Winnie McDonagh is the perfect example of the
army of bogus litigants the insurance industry claimed
were bankrupting the system. She was determined to
get her share of the compensation pie when a car she
was travelling in was rear-ended in Finglas, north
Dublin on May 21, 2000. Winnie, her brother-in-law,
Martin Keenan, David Keenan and Julia Collins who
were all in the car, certainly caused a scene when their
car was hit. As the emergency services arrived, the four
were still in the vehicle, which was bought just the day
before for €40. The accident victims staged a good
drama. No less than three ambulances were called to

Ralph Cucciniello
© *Courtesy of Olwyn Triggs*

Terry Kirby
© *Andrew Downes*

Anthony Davenport, Linda
Broderick and John Hay.
*(Courtesy of Alameda County
Sheriff's Office)*

John Cronin
© *PJ Browne*

Joseph Smith
© *Padraig O'Reilly*

Juan Carlos Guzman-Betancourt, arrested in Dublin.
© *Cathal Naughton/PA*

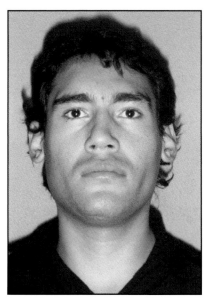

Guzman-Betancourt's mugshot released by the Metropolitan Police.

Graham Peet
and partner
Tracey Heather
*(Courtesy of
Tom Baker)*

Graham Peet
(Courtesy of Tom Baker)

Tom Baker and the half-built extension
© *Michael McCormack/Sunday World*

A card skimming device
© *Brian McEvoy/Sunday World*

Mohammed Majid
© *Provision*

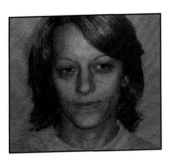

Daniela Ciocan
© *Sunday World*

Mohammed Saleem, *(right)*
leaving court.
© *Collins Photo Agency*

Rzvan Schiopu
© *Sunday World*

Sorin Condranche
© *Sunday World*

Michael Byrne, *(centre)*.
© Collins Photo Agency

Al Manning
© Collins Photo Agency

Brendan Murphy
© *Collins Photo Agency*

Dr Emad Massoud
© *Collins Photo Agency*

Gehan Massoud
© *Collins Photo Agency*

Noel Fitzpatrick on right, being escorted by a prison officer.
© *Collins Photo Agency*

Fugitive solicitor Michael Lynn.
© *Collins Photo Agency*

the scene, along with two fire engines, their crews and a Garda car. On paper, it certainly sounded like a major incident. Closer inspection revealed that while there was a lot of screaming and hysterics, there wasn't any blood. No one really got hurt.

It was always going to be a tricky case. When Winnie's claim for personal damages came through the High Court an independent eye witness to the collision, Joseph Smart, gave evidence. He saw the whole thing at Finglas village roundabout that night. He said he didn't consider the impact between the two cars a collision. Mr Smart thought it was so insignificant that nobody could have been injured.

Presiding Judge Vivian Lavan wasn't impressed, to say the least, with the evidence given by Winnie McDonagh. Evidence given by the other three people who had been in the car with her that night to support their claim for damages were just as bad. Ms McDonagh, it transpired, had drank six pints of lager between 6pm and midnight. The judge said that she and the other occupants were so drunk that their account of the accident could not be regarded as reliable or credible. Ms McDonagh had given "various accounts of events at various stages" and Judge Lavan had grave reservations about her version of events. The only evidence the judge was inclined to believe from any of the car's occupants was from David Keenan. His account was simply that he was so drunk he could not remember anything. This was "the only credible evidence I got from the Keenan family," said the nonplussed judge.

Apart from the conflicting and hazy witness accounts, the driver of the other car which hit Winnie and her relatives had also disappeared. He was said to be a 'John Ward' from Coolock but he could not be traced. In the end the law suit went ahead just citing the Motor Insurance Bureau of Ireland. One of the country's biggest insurers, Hibernian, ran the case for the Motor Insurance Bureau of Ireland (MIBI) during the four days at the High Court. The MIBI is the bureau which takes up the defence of cases where uninsured vehicles are responsible for accidents. The insurance investigators from Hibernian Insurance were not happy with Winnie's versions of events. It hadn't taken them long to conclude that the claim for damages was bogus. The MIBI disputed that there was any accident and filed a defence that the claims were fraudulent. They also argued that that the injuries suffered by Winnie and others in the car were coincidentally similar. The defence pointed out that neither Winnie nor the other occupants of the car made a complaint to Gardaí at the time.

Winnie's attempt to defraud an insurance company proved to be a laughably amateur escapade. The injured people staged "a holy show" according to the judge. Judge Vivian Lavan said according to the evidence the occupants of the car were "wailing and screaming" but that their behaviour was "bizarre in the extreme". The dramatics at the scene of the accident served only to arouse suspicions about the nature of the car crash and the evidence of eye-witnesses added to the hilarity of the case. But Judge Lavan wasn't laughing when he dismissed the case and awarded costs of the four day High Court case against her.

The lure of a compensation pay out can bring out the worst in people. In October 2001, an Irish-American tourist was enjoying a coach tour around Ireland. The driver decided to stop the coach at Carrickbrack Road to allow the passengers to enjoy the views of Howth. But barrelling towards them at high-speed, possibly as fast as 80 mph, was a young Dublin man showing off to his friends in his car. He ploughed into one of the tourists, 52-year-old Judith Martin. Her horrified daughter Jeanette saw the impact which killed her mother instantly. A year later the young man appeared in court where he pleaded guilty to dangerous driving and he was jailed for a year. Wracked with guilt, the driver said he had given up his career as a mechanic and would never drive a car again. An emotional Jeanette addressed the court and told the young driver: "It's taken me a year to get here and I don't know what to say to you. You just made a really bad mistake. I witnessed it and I can't tell you what I see every night before I go to sleep."

It fell to grief-stricken Jeanette to be the executor of her mother's estate. In that role she took a civil court case to sue the young driver for damages as a result of the trauma suffered by her and members of her family. The claim was brought on behalf of herself, her sister Gina, their two aunts and grandmother. On the face of it, the case appeared to be another routine High Court claim for damages. In court, however, the young driver's lawyer explained that the grandmother was in fact, deceased. Jeanette Martin, a Californian-based saleswoman, was accused of making a fraudulent claim. It was struck out.

Mr Justice Johnson who heard the case said in his 43 years as a judge and barrister he had never seen such a blatant and deliberate fraud. He described it as "cold-blooded" and "calculated." He directed that the papers be sent to the Director of Public Prosecution, although no charges were ever brought against Ms Martin.

Insurance fraud has not been limited to greedy individuals with a flair for telling lies. It has also been a staple for organised criminals all over the world.

Professional gangs can bring a variety of criminal skills to the mix that allows them to create more lucrative scenarios. They provide the muscle and the knowledge to bribe or cajole individuals into taking part in their scams. Police officers, investigators working for insurance companies and crash repair firms can all be sucked into a scam with enough cash or threats. Weak-willed individuals inveigled into taking a role in a fraud find themselves with no easy way out once the ball starts rolling. People of a criminal nature even derive a strong sense of self-esteem from fooling the official world of professionals into writing cheques for accidents, injuries, damages and losses that never happened. Compared to the ham-fisted attempt by Winnie McDonagh to scam an insurance company, the real insurance scammers leave no stone unturned when it comes to executing an operation to fleece insurers.

In the mid-1990s, one Irish-based outfit staged at least 100 fake car accidents. The gang created a whole history of crashes, shunts and head-ons, which simply never happened. A former cop, members of a feared paramilitary gang and a pillar of the community, were among those who colluded in a systematic campaign to make substantial and fraudulent claims for personal injuries and damage to cars, trucks and trailers. Insurance firms ended up paying out millions in compensation for the bogus claims.

At the centre of this web of deceit was a successful businessman and car dealer, Michael Byrne. He put together the various strands needed to make it all work. Based in Longford in the Irish midlands Byrne, then aged 39, appeared to the world to be a well-to-do car dealer, making a good living. In the early 1990s, he was seen as an ambitious young shaker and mover in the region. He was known for being ready and willing to do deals and keen to make money. There were, however, two sides to Byrne. One persona was that of the legitimate businessman but the other was a con-man. It was this side who recognised that the quickest way to make money was to file claims for damage to vehicles instead of claiming for personal injuries. Once he realised this he moved quickly to activate the con – paper work was forged, official stamps faked and one corrupt cop was bought off. It became Ireland's biggest and most organised operation to milk the compo-cash cow. This was no 'hit and hope' racket. Every possible angle was covered, including fake invoices for the cost of hiring replacement vehicles, which added to the eventual claim against the insurers. Byrne also ran a crash repairs company that provided useful documents and invoices to back up the costly recovery and repair of vehicles damaged in accidents which never even happened.

The operation was run on an impressive scale from 1994 until 1996. It was designed to maximise the payouts from the insurance companies so the conspirators made expensive trucks and machinery their preferred targets. Why have two cars collide when it could be arranged to stage an accident involving a truck towing a IR£50,000 crane on the back of a low-loader? Once the insurance firm had sent out a claims investigator to confirm the damage to the vehicles a cheque would be on the way. There would be no waiting around for medical appointments and doctors' reports and the need to fake a limp or a sore back and neck.

While some people were willing participants, others were gullible, greedy or just simply too scared to say no. In April 1994 a businessman from Newtownforbes was driving an articulated Iveco truck, hauling a

caterpillar digger on a low-loader. Al Manning, a 46-
year-old businessman, was well-known and liked in the
area and regarded as a real pillar of society. Words such
as 'integrity' and 'honesty' would be used to describe
the father-of-four. He ran a number of businesses
including firms involved in civil engineering, plant
hire, construction and quarrying. On the road at
Annaduff near Carrick-on-Shannon something
unfortunate happened. The result was that Manning's
truck collided with a Ford Sierra owned by a young
man, Gerard Smyth from Strokestown in County
Roscommon. It smashed into the Ford saloon which,
subsequent documents claimed, was later removed
from the accident scene by Byrne's crash repairs firm.
On the forms sent into the insurance company Smyth
explained that his car skidded and hit the truck driven
by Manning. Claims assessors later inspected the
damaged vehicles and a cheque for IR£35,000 was paid
to Smyth with another for IR£56,500 going to Manning
for the repair of his truck, low-loader, digger and the
cost of hiring replacement vehicles.

Nearly two years later, in January 1996, a brand new
Scania truck was travelling along a country road, again
at Annaduff, near Carrick-on-Shannon. According to
the subsequent accident reports, the driver, James
Murphy from Castlebellingham, County Louth, was at
the wheel. It was claimed that his truck, which was
hauling another truck on a low-loader, along with a
Hyster forklift, collided with a green Rover. Jeremiah
O'Donovan, a taxi-driver from Birr, County Offaly was
driving the Rover. He claimed he had been on his way
from Birr to see friends in Sligo when he lost control of
his new car. All the vehicles ended up down an
embankment. The evidence of the collision was soon
cleared away and the damaged vehicles were stored to

await the arrival of the insurance companies' crash investigators. The claims assessors saw the badly damaged Scania trucks and the mangled Rover. It was a miracle that no one had been killed. It seemed to be a straight-forward claim.

The insurance company Guardian/PMPA forked out a total of IR£151,000 to cover the claims for damage and injuries. The first claim to be settled was that made by O'Donovan, the driver of the Rover. He said he had been injured, but wasn't hospitalised. He had told the company that he wasn't sure if the accident was his fault because he thought the road was slippy. O'Donovan claimed that a Garda at the scene had told him he was to blame for the accident. Such mundane details are part and parcel of typical reports sent to insurance companies by customers making claims. The details are assessed and form the basis for the decision to make a payout. The insurance company settled O'Donovan's claim with a cheque for IR£18,500 in 1996 to cover the cost of the car and compensation for his injuries. The trucker, James Murphy, got IR£15,000 for injuries he claimed to have suffered. The company which owned the trucks, Portfleet Limited, were compensated to the tune of IR£101,000 for the loss of their vehicles. The rest of the IR£151,000 pay out went to the lawyers who carried out their duties while dealing with the claims in good faith. It was an expensive accident. In hindsight the collision was remarkably similar to the accident involving Al Manning two years earlier.

18 months later the same Scania truck, which had been written off by the claims assessors after the 1996 accident, was stopped at a Garda checkpoint in Rooskey, County Roscommon. The driver of the truck was a brother-in-law of Portfleet Limited Director

Michael McDonald. A check revealed that the truck shouldn't exist, let alone be on the road. By then the conspirators were already under investigation after insurance companies had expressed their concerns about different accidents. The investigation that was to follow unveiled a sophisticated and well-organised conspiracy.

The serious level of threat posed by those people involved in the racket was not lost on the investigating Gardaí. When the officers began working on the fraud scams, the team was based in a special room at Carrick-on-Shannon Garda Station. It was secured with a steel door, had iron bars on the windows and special alarms were installed. The Garda Superintendent Aidan Glacken, who led the investigation, described the precautions as most unusual. He said the only other Garda operation in which similar measures were taken was the probe into the murder of journalist Veronica Guerin. The gang behind that murder were a violent drugs gang, awash with money and with international connections. Officers felt that the insurance gang were the same kind of people, capable of anything to protect their lucrative business venture.

During the intense investigation, the true details of the almost identical Annaduff accidents were pieced together. Although the fraud was well-organised, it couldn't stand up to scrutiny, as every document and statement was double-checked. The scam also needed the threat of violence to hold it all together. It relied on the menace posed by dangerous paramilitaries to ensure innocent parties and greedy co-conspirators kept their mouths shut. As the Garda probe broadened out to include a whole series of accidents over the two-year period, a common thread emerged – Michael Byrne, the Longford car dealer.

Byrne's corrupt hands had touched the lives of all the people who were sucked into his world of deceit in which paramilitary thugs skulked in the shadows. It emerged that Smyth, the young man whose Ford Sierra was smashed in a collision with the Iveco truck driven by Al Manning, lived in fear of Michael Byrne and his associates. Smyth was a young labourer that the car dealer held sway over through such intimidation. He was approached by Byrne just days before the accident and told how to fake the car crash. Manning was also afraid of Byrne. Despite appearances and the high-regard in which he was held, Manning was a businessman in trouble. A long running legal dispute with Meath County Council had almost left him broke and he had to re-mortgage his home to keep the family business afloat.

On the day of the 'accident' Smyth drove in convoy with Byrne to the fake crash scene at Annaduff. His Ford Sierra was placed on the road and the two men withdrew to a safe distance. Manning then drove his truck into the car. A member of the Gardaí who later attended the scene, had previously worked as a qualified mechanic before joining the force. He noticed that while the car had suffered considerable damage, there was little done to the truck. The truck was perfectly capable of leaving the scene under its own power. It didn't need any recovery vehicle. He was surprised to later learn that the 'accident' had resulted in all the vehicles being written off.

Byrne was also to emerge as the figure behind another staged accident at the Lucan exit of the M50 in Dublin in December 1994. There had been a three-car shunt. Tallaght man Alan Nolan, who claimed to have been caught in the pile up, was also part of the fraud. When he was arrested in October 1996, Nolan admitted to Gardaí that the accident had been staged and confessed to his role. He refused, however, to give any information on the scam. He told the Gardaí that he had become "mixed up with the wrong people".

The investigation into the myriad car crashes and the labyrinthine evidence they created was a painstaking process. It took nine years from the time of the accident before Manning's trial came to court in 2003, at the Dublin Circuit Criminal Court. Manning was charged with fraud. The Garda who had attended the scene of the 'accident' said that the photographs of a damaged truck which were produced were not the same vehicle he had seen that day in 1994. The pictures had been taken by the claims assessor, who was shown an Iveco truck which had been in an accident. The officer said that the truck in the picture was so badly damaged it could not have left the scene of the accident under its own steam. The officer also didn't have a note of any oil on the road surface which Smyth had later claimed caused the accident.

As the trial continued it became clear that, using his contacts in the motor trade, Byrne was able to source vehicles which had been in genuine smashes to set up bogus claims. He had put the registration plate from Manning's truck onto the identical but damaged truck. It was this 'ringer' which was shown to the insurance assessor. Cars and trucks which had been written off in accidents all over Ireland and the UK were bought to be used in the scam. The 'identities' of the wrecks would be changed for the insurance assessors. It was a simple scam, repeated several times, and supported by fake invoices.

When initially confronted with the unequivocal evidence against him, Manning said that he was genuinely terrified of his co-conspirators. He told one detective that he was the "victim of circumstances" and said to them: "Look lads you are dealing with heavy stuff here."

When asked about Byrne's involvement he told the detectives: "Look lads, I can't tell you about this. I can't say anything. I have a wife, a family and a business."

Smyth was also frightened of Byrne. The young man had been so intimidated by associates of the car dealer that they had convinced him he had sold land he owned to a relation of Byrne's when in fact he hadn't. Smyth had handed over the €35,000 cheque he received from the insurance company to Byrne. It was then lodged into the bank account of a County Louth man. A few days later a corresponding sum of cash was withdrawn from that account and paid into a bank account belonging to the same relative of Byrne's who Smyth, in his terrified state, believed now owned his land. Smyth later took possession of his land back from Byrne's brother, Joseph, who had occupied it.

During the trial it emerged that the insurance claims made in Smyth's name were not even written in his handwriting. He was prosecuted for his role in the fake accident, but it was dealt at District Court level as a summary offence.

There was no such leniency on offer for Manning, even though his insurance cheque was also passed over to Byrne. Following an 18-day trial at the Dublin Circuit Criminal Court, Manning was found guilty of fraud. With no previous convictions, his defence team brought in a series of character witnesses to testify to Manning's standing in the community. His wife of 35 years, Elizabeth, described him as "a fantastic husband, a wonderful father of our four children and a true friend". She was one of 11 witnesses who took the stand on Manning's behalf. The parish priest described him

as a hard-working man, held in high esteem and said
that he would "trust him fully". Top businessmen from
Longford, a former Garda, council officials and a
Department of Agriculture inspector all expressed their
shock that Manning had become involved in such a
fraudulent scheme.

Judge Joseph Matthews said he had no choice but to
hand down a custodial sentence for what was "a
calculated and significantly well-planned crime."
Manning was jailed for two years for his part in the
fraud.

Just how dangerous Byrne and his associates could
be, became apparent during the trial in December 2003
for the second accident at Annaduff in 1996. It emerged
that the Rover 640 Jeremiah O'Donovan was driving
had been bought from a Wexford car dealer in
O'Donovan's name. Byrne had specifically acquired it
because it matched a green Rover, written-off as
wreckage, which he had also bought. This was the
green Rover later shown to the insurance assessors. It
was so badly damaged that it seemed a miracle that the
driver could have escaped without serious or even fatal
injuries. Byrne said it was the vehicle driven by
O'Donovan in the crash. In reality the Rover
O'Donovan was driving was never actually damaged.
It was even returned, without having been paid for, in
perfect condition to the Wexford dealer. When the
investigators tracked it down, after it was legitimately
sold on to another customer, it was found never to have
been in a crash of any description.

O'Donovan got a three-year suspended sentence. He
escaped jail because he paid back the money he had
received. With no previous criminal convictions,
O'Donovan was clearly a lightweight compared to
others involved in the conspiracy. By contrast, the

driver of the truck in the collision that never happened, James Murphy, was a man with a colourful past. In 1989 he had been jailed for six years on explosives charges for possessing nitro-benzine, a fertilizer favoured by the Provisional IRA's bomb-making units. For the fake crash, Murphy got three years after the trial judge described him as "the heart and soul" of the conspiracy. Byrne, of course, was the brains of the operation.

Another of those named in the charges over the Annaduff accident was Portafleet company director 38-year-old Michael McDonald from Riverstown, Dundalk, County Louth. A member of the Real IRA, his role in the fraud was to provide the supposedly damaged trucks, low-loader and forklift from his company Portafleet. He also provided fake invoices for the supposed use of replacement vehicles as a result of the crash. McDonald never came to trial in Dublin, having got into even more serious trouble abroad.

Ironically, McDonald, who in 1996 was busy creating fairy tales to defraud an insurance company, was himself to spectacularly fall hook, line and sinker for a sting operation. Just five years after Annaduff, in July 2001, McDonald and two other Real IRA men met a so-called Iraqi intelligence agent. The paramilitary organisation were desperate to find a State sponsor for their terrorist campaign. They wanted the same relationship as Libya had forged with the Provisionals in the 1980s, providing them with tons of explosives, ammunition and weapons. McDonald and two others, all from the same tight community in County Louth, had travelled to Slovakia to meet their contact. The man they thought was an Iraqi secret agent was in fact an M15 agent. The British secret service had set up an elaborate sting to snuff out any attempt by the Real IRA to re-arm itself. Undercover MI5 and police officers, taped and filmed conversations at an Arab restaurant in the Slovak spa resort of Piest'any. Afraid of being overheard, the men used a paper napkin to write down their wish list. They asked for 5,000 kilos of plastic explosives, 2,000 detonators, 200 rocket-propelled grenades and 500 handguns. As one of the Irishmen went to take it back, the MI5 officer pretended to blow his nose on the napkin and calmly put it in his pocket. The three men also asked for $1million in cash, wire-guided missiles, presumably to shoot down helicopters and sniper rifles capable of penetrating flak jackets. Once the MI5 team were advised by their lawyer that they had enough evidence the men were arrested. In May 2002, McDonald and his co-conspirators pleaded guilty to a number of charges under the UK's Terrorism Act. They each got 30 years in jail. The con-man had been well and truly conned by the spies and spooks on Her Majesty's secret service.

The involvement of McDonald in the insurance frauds in Annaduff lent credence to the statements by the junior conspirators that were in fear of the more senior members of the plot. McDonald, who had been on an international search for lethal armoury for a terrorist army, could easily have provided convincing threats of violence when needed.

It had been a long and difficult investigation for the detectives trying to unravel Byrne's scam. The Longford car dealer had spread his net far and wide, to draw in as many co-conspirators as possible. There were some further shocks in store for the investigation team based at Carrick-on-Shannon. They discovered that a former Garda, Desmond McGonigle, had thrown in his lot with the gang of dangerous fraudsters. The father-of-five, with a 31-year record of service with the Gardaí, was also charged with taking part in the fraud conspiracy. Driven by greed or fear, he had filed bogus reports with insurance assessors for the 1996 Annaduff accident. He had also made up details about another fake collision in February 1996 and claimed to have been in another non-existent crash in December 1995. He had retired from the force by the time he appeared in court.

At his trial for the Annaduff 'accident', evidence was given explaining that the crash would have taken hours to clear. It would have required lifting equipment and the road would have been closed during the clean-up. This didn't happen. A factory security man, Ib Thomosen, told the jury that his security hut was only about 20 yards away and if anything significant had happened there, before he finished duty, he would have reported it. There was no evidence of the crash apart from the paperwork sent to the insurance companies. It was obvious to the jury that the road accident never happened. McGonigle's role had been to submit an "entirely fictitious" Garda report on the accident. McGonigle, who had stood trial alongside Murphy and O'Donovan, was acquitted by the jury on the charges relating to the Annaduff accident.

McGonigle, however, was later convicted of taking part in a separate staged crash. He had falsely claimed that he was driving a Peugeot car when he crashed in December 1995. He made an insurance claim and received a cheque for €7,151 from the Guardian/PMPA firm. The car he was supposed to have been driving, however, had been previously written off by an assessor following an accident in March 1994. Both accidents were faked. In May 2005 McGonigle was sentenced to three years, although all but six months were suspended, after the father-of-five paid €9,000 as compensation to the insurance company. After serving six months behind bars he got another suspended sentence for the filing of a bogus report in February 1996.

Byrne had used paramilitaries, a corrupt garda and a hard-up company director, among others, to continue staging fake accidents. Investigating Gardaí were not surprised when they discovered that he had also drawn relatives into the morass. Jaqueline Kinlan, then a 36-year-old mother of two, was Michael Byrne's sister-in-law.

During her 11-day trial in May 2005, she denied the charge of pretending a genuine accident had happened on St Patrick's Day, 1994. She stood by her claim that she had skidded into the back of a car driven by farmer John Manning. The Peugeot she was driving was the same car McGonigle claimed he had been driving, in his collision, the following year. The Longford woman was found guilty but had two and half years of a three year sentence suspended after she handed over €12,000.

The man she supposedly rear-ended, farmer John Manning, was also brought before the courts. He had been paid IR£18,000 after claiming damages for personal injuries and to the Nissan car he claimed he was driving. Both the Nissan and Kinlan's Peugeot were supposed to have been repaired by Byrne's company, Longford Crash Repair. The firm assessed both cars and put the cost of repairs at IR£10,000 each. Investigators were able to prove that neither car showed any signs of ever having been in a serious accident. Manning who repaid the insurance company got a two year suspended sentence.

An insurance broker from Mullingar, County Westmeath was also involved. He made accident claims for clients through a solicitor. The only problem was that broker Peter Leahy didn't tell his clients about the claims he was making on their behalf. He was described as being a serious player in the conspiracy, who was close to Michael Byrne. Apart from Byrne, he had made the most false claims of any of the conspirators involved in the plot. Leahy received cheques worth a total of IR£92,415 over the two year period when the scam was in operation. He enjoyed a good lifestyle considering that he was just 25 at the time and had properties in both Ireland and Spain.

Leahy lied continuously when interviewed by Gardaí investigating the 90 suspect incidents. In one case a Longford solicitor innocently processed claims totalling IR£17,830 (€22,640) for Leahy, in the names of two people without their knowledge. Leahy pleaded guilty to three charges of fraud and false pretences. Two more charges were taken into consideration, arising out of incidents in 1995 and 1996. In these incidents more than IR£92,000 was defrauded from Guardian/PMPA and Cornhill Insurance. He changed his plea to guilty at the last minute. The Westmeath auctioneer and valuer was jailed for 30 months by Judge Yvonne Murphy at Dublin Circuit Criminal Court in December 2005.

The junior players all came to trial after Michael Byrne had first been convicted for master-minding the scam. The minor co-conspirators were mopped up by the prosecution once they had successfully got their main target, Michael Byrne. The probe had started in earnest in September 1996. Officers interviewed everybody involved in 90 suspect accidents and the subsequent insurance claims. Gardai took statements from 1,100 witnesses and trawled through 100 bank accounts. The Carrick-on-Shannon team had then spent months steadily building up evidence against the car dealer. Each accident and insurance claim was sifted through in fine detail. Every bribe, threat or piece of fake paperwork was logged and used to piece together the complex scam. By May 1998, there was enough evidence to arrest Michael Byrne.

Byrne was finally brought to trial in October 2002 on charges of conspiring to defraud the PMPA insurance company by falsely pretending that a genuine road accident had occurred in 1994 on the M50 near Lucan. Thanks to the detectives' focus on the paper trail of evidence, it was the M50 accident involving Tallaght man Alan Nolan, who had been too frightened to tell the Gardaí who was behind the plot, that the investigators could finally use to try to get a conviction against the Longford man. All three vehicles involved in the Lucan pile-up had been linked by investigators to Michael Byrne. The painstaking work in building up the evidence against Byrne was going to be paid off. He pleaded not guilty to the charge, but witness after witness was able to point the finger at the Longford man. It was dull and complicated stuff. The jury listened to hours of evidence of fake claims, ringed cars and bogus invoices during the ten-day trial. After five hours of deliberation they found him guilty.

A month later he pleaded guilty to additional charges of falsely obtaining money from the PMPA and from Cornhill Insurance for a further series of staged accidents and for falsely reporting that a car had been stolen. In November 2002, Judge Yvonne Murphy sentenced Byrne to a number of jail terms, parts of which were suspended. In total he would spend three years behind bars. The judge commended the Gardaí for what she called "exemplary work" in the case. She ordered that €5,000 of €50,000 which Byrne had lodged in court to repay some of the money he owed be paid to the Garda Benevolent Fund. It had been a long hard road for the investigation team, but their steady diligence had paid off with a conviction.

While the €50,000 scraped together may have gone some way towards avoiding a longer sentence, it wasn't enough to keep the Criminal Assets Bureau happy. The following January 2003, at Longford Circuit Court, CAB officers secured an order for €1.2 million against Byrne under the Proceeds of Crime Act. Byrne, the son of an ambulance driver who had built up a thriving business, had now lost it all thanks to his insatiable greed.

As 2003 progressed, things didn't improve for Byrne. He had to face an appeal by the Director of Public Prosecution service against the leniency of the three year jail sentence. Counsel for the DPP submitted that Byrne's offences had been carried out over a "not insignificant" period and that it was not a once-off incident. The appeal court judges said the offences were calculated, deliberate and sophisticated. The three-judge panel outlined how the offences involved careful preparation of a plan that created the circumstances where it would be believed a road traffic accident had taken place. Serious damage had been caused to particular vehicles and in some cases to individuals. Byrne was in the motor trade and had clearly used his own knowledge and expertise, they added. The panel took into account a number of mitigating factors put forward on Byrne's behalf, including that he had, in effect, "lost everything" – his business and his standing in the community. Until then he had a blameless record with no previous convictions. The appeal court, however, was satisfied that the sentences imposed in the circuit court were not only lenient but unduly lenient. The Court of Criminal Appeal increased Byrne's sentence from three to five years.

Even then Byrne's court room battles were not over. He filed a High Court claim that he was being singled out for special treatment at Castlerea Prison. He said it was because of an "unfounded belief" he was associated with the Real IRA. Byrne was given leave to seek an inquiry under Article 40 of the Constitution into the legality of his detention. In an affidavit Byrne outlined that he had been convicted of staging fake car accidents. On his transfer to Castlerea Prison from Mountjoy Prison, Byrne said he had expected that counselling he was receiving there would continue. A doctor at Castlerea had recommended counselling, but none was provided despite requests. Byrne also believed he was receiving different treatment to other prisoners in relation to his requests for temporary release. He explained that he had asked a family member to approach a TD to see if the Minister for Justice could inquire about him being allowed to visit his family for short periods of temporary release. He also wanted to know if the Minister could have him moved to Shelton Abbey, an open prison where his family could visit him. His brother told him that the TD had reported back that his requests would not be allowed. He said it was because there was a letter "on file" from the Gardaí suggesting that Byrne had an involvement with active Republicans, in particular the Real IRA.

The Governor of Castlerea Prison, Dan Scannell, rejected claims that Byrne was subjected to special treatment or that he was kept in his cell 23 hours a day. Scannell gave evidence that he did not hold any letter on file. Questioned about a claim that Byrne had spent Christmas Eve and Christmas Day in his underpants in a cold punishment cell, the prison governor said he had never placed anybody in isolation as a punishment. The jail chief rejected the suggestion that he was vindictive or unfair to Byrne. Despite all his efforts, Byrne lost his High Court bid to get moved to an open prison.

The outcome of the trials involving Michael Byrne and his various co-conspirators justified the insurance industry's assertion that Ireland was plagued by bogus claims for compensation but that they were moving against the fraudsters. Willie McGee, Fraud Investigation Manager for Axa Insurance, said after one of the trials: "This is part of another successful step in the fight by the insurance industry against fraud."

Insurance fraud is one of those animals that can be hard to track down. Insurance companies would love to have the paying public believe that all claims are bogus. The fact remains, however, that insurance companies in Ireland have made vast profits thanks to the high premiums they have been able to charge. In 2005 motor insurance companies made combined profits of €418 million, which dropped to €259 million in 2006. The entire insurance sector made €700 million in 2006. The industry spin is that bogus and exaggerated claims have forced up the price their customers have to pay for their policies and now the cost is falling because the amount of fraud has reduced. Like many of the stories that appear on insurance claim forms, the truth is not as simple. Some people believe that it is just as likely that increased competition among insurers, rather than detection of frauds, caused the price of premiums to gradually drop from 2000 until 2007.

Even so, tales of bogus personal injury claims are still myriad in Ireland's rumour mill. In the darkened corners of pubs there was even a certain Robin Hood kudos granted to those who were brave and clever enough to stiff a corporate body for a couple of grand. Of all the victims of fraud, corporate insurance companies elicit the least, if any, sympathy. In reality any type of insurance fraud is certainly not a victimless crime. As the insurance companies have pointed out, the true victims of professional fraud are their customers who have to pay higher premiums and charges. It is also clear from the strong arm tactics used by Michael Byrne and his Real IRA associates that there were victims in his fake car crash scams. The idea that insurance fraud is a victimless crime is perpetrated by people to assuage any guilt they may feel over committing the crime in the first place. After all, they might say, the insurance companies make vast profits from the steep premiums charged for insuring cars, properties and business – why not hit them for a few quid? No doubt the next Michael Byrne is already weaving a trail of paperwork to milk cash from the insurers, who continue to make almost obscene profit. We might never know if this person exists because the extent of insurance fraud can never be known. It is a simple truth that the best con-jobs are never detected. The cynical observer might even argue that the biggest con-artist in insurance is the industry itself. The lure of a large payout, however, lends a degree of certainty to the presumption that fraudsters won't stop trying to spin fairy tales to insurance companies any time soon.

FIVE

Pillars of Society

For many years the hard-working professional was held in high esteem by the great unwashed. Ordinary people and those in business deferred to experts such as solicitors, doctors, bank managers and accountants, for advice on the right course of action to take. With their suits and ties, they were the outside world's connection to the inside track. The relationship between a professional and their client is based on trust. It is like a partnership. As the professionals can't hide behind the protection of a limited company, in theory they share the same risk as their clients. A person in a position of trust, however, is well-placed to effect a fraud and then to bury their illegal deeds. Problems begin when professionals think too highly of themselves. Some professionals, to paraphrase Oscar Wilde, could not stop themselves being tempted by temptation. The theft stays hidden unless uncovered by some accident, an unexpected audit or the fraudster's own incompetence. Even then the dirty laundry is rarely aired in public by the professional body in charge of administering the slaps on the wrist. In Ireland, as in many other countries worldwide, the various professional bodies are allowed to regulate their own members' conduct. Until recently they have been closed shops. Few people outside the profession know or understand what was done on their behalf to rectify any misconduct. With this background, a professional career person is perfectly qualified to be a successful con-artist. Luckily the vast majority are honest.

Money and trust are uneasy bedfellows. Banks like to use the word 'trust', whether in a company name or financial product. A quick internet search with the words 'bank' and 'trust' provides a long list of examples. There was a time when banks based their business in strong looking stone buildings, with high windows and granite steps. It was all designed to reassure customers that their money would be safe. The physical solidity implied that there was no danger of collapse. Nowadays brokers and financial advisers use slightly different tactics to give clients the impression of solidity. Slick buildings of steel and glass convey the same impression. Old school connections, expensive suits, membership of the right golf clubs and of the most fashionable charity circles, also help to fill in the requirements. Their fellow professionals all use different techniques. Lawyers have centuries of jurisprudence behind them to lend them the necessary air of authority. They also have client accounts from which money can be moved to pay fees, deposits or do whatever the client asks. The usual notification rules regarding the deposit of cash amounts higher than €12,000 to safeguard against money-laundering, don't apply to bona fide solicitors. They are afforded this courtesy from their fellow professionals – the bankers. As Ireland's Celtic Tiger economy began to slow in 2007, that unquestioning faith in the country's legal practitioners took a serious blow.

Mayo-native Michael Lynn was a young man determined to be successful. As a young solicitor he boosted his income moonlighting as a wedding singer. He was well able to promote himself and took stands at wedding fairs to drum up business. When he set up his own practise he quickly jumped on the property bandwagon. He used minor celebrities and sporting figures to help push sales in overseas development projects by his company Kendar Global Properties. By 2007 solicitor Michael Lynn was a significant player among the recently wealthy Irish property speculators. The 39-year-old lawyer and developer owned properties in nine different countries. He acted as the solicitor to other property entrepreneurs and developers, fearlessly betting on rising property prices all over the world. Lynn and his wife Bríd Murphy moved from their up-market home in Sandymount to the magnificent Glenlion House on the Hill of Howth, overlooking Dublin Bay. Lynn was, without doubt, a true cub of the Celtic Tiger.

Then someone in his office blew the whistle.

Suddenly the Law Society was called in and there was a scramble by the banks to get to the High Court first, as each bank vied to lay claim to the available assets. It soon emerged that there were multiple mortgages on various properties. Ten banks fought to secure their interests in Lynn's properties. It became clear that the solicitor had been treated with an unusually high level of trust by the financial institutions providing Lynn and his clients with mortgages. His close connections in Ireland's financial institutions had even allowed Lynn to sign off on his own conveyancing files. This relationship had opened the door for an unlimited and unrivalled supply of credit. Lynn had simply taken out more than one mortgage on the same property. For instance, both the Ulster Bank and the Bank of Scotland had provided mortgages for the full amount of the Sandymount house.

In October 2007, with debts of €85 million, the High Court ordered his practice to be shut down. For six weeks he sat in court and listened as his legal

colleagues argued who had a claim to what. He showed
a remarkable capacity to absorb stress, chatting with
friends, colleagues and even photographers waiting for
him outside. Finally, on December 12 Lynn had been
due to allow himself to be cross-examined on his
dealings. He didn't turn up and effectively became a
fugitive. Files in one case were passed on to the Garda
fraud squad and a civil arrest warrant was issued by the
High Court. His houses in Sandymount and Howth
were sold off by the banks. Even his €3,000 wine
collection went under the auctioneer's hammer. Lynn
apparently continued with his property business in
Portugal and central Europe while the row he'd caused
in Ireland rumbled on. The Law Society finally got
around to striking him off the solicitors' rolls in May
2008 and fined him €2 million. It has yet to be paid.

The news of Lynn's financial troubles came as an
omen of doom for the Irish property market which had
already started to slide. Just days after the allegations
about Lynn came to light another solicitor was shut
down. Crumlin-based Thomas Byrne had debts of €50
million. The High Court froze his assets as
investigations were launched into various mortgages
he had taken out. As if to finally destroy any vestige of
respectability enjoyed by the legal profession, more
cases of professional misconduct emerged within
weeks of each other. Two partners at one firm were
caught operating a secret slush fund worth €32 million
to evade tax and another solicitor was accused of
stealing €1 million from clients' money.

It shouldn't have come as a surprise that
professional practitioners could be tempted by the
heavy flow of cash passing through their fingers.
There's no reason why there shouldn't be as many
thieving, lying, cheating professionals who are crooks

as there are criminals in any other walk of life. There had been plenty of warning signs in the past. The best known example was that of Dublin solicitor Elio Malocco. Always keen to turn a quick buck, he had business interests in various parts of Dublin. Married to a member of the De Valera family, to the outside world he was a stalwart member of the establishment. He acted for the De Valera's *Irish Press* newspaper group. With this blue-chip background it came as a bit of a shock when he was jailed for five years in 1993 for stealing money from his clients' accounts. As the Lynn scandal unfolded, it emerged that Malocco was back at work with a legal firm in the UK. He was employed as a consultant which ironically, Lynn had retained to represent his interests.

While there was public outrage over the behaviour of these solicitors there was little sympathy for the banks and financial institutions who had got caught out. Few regular customers would enjoy such preferential treatment when taking out bank loans or providing proof of collateral. The favoured position enjoyed by the likes of Lynn is confined to the legal profession. Anyone bringing in the right amount of business can expect the red carpet treatment.

Noel Fitzpatrick was an unremarkable insurance agent in his mid-30s. He was plodding along making a living. Selling insurance and pension schemes is the drudge work of the financial world. It's hard going and there's nothing glamorous in the chase for clients and commissions. Affable and sociable, there was nothing unusual about Fitzpatrick's modest lifestyle. He came from a solid middle-class upbringing. While he had some marital difficulties, he got back with his previously estranged wife in 1999. They had three children together. This time he was determined to make a better go of things. Being reunited with his wife coincided with an upturn in business for Noel Fitzpatrick and Associates. In June 2000, he bought a house in Cabinteely for €630,000. Things were looking good. The dawn of the new century was also the beginning of a new and exciting phase for Fitzpatrick.

By December 2001, he had managed to secure commission for bringing some high-end individuals into an executive group pension scheme. He went from strength to strength, using his connections in the insurance companies to negotiate pension deals for clients. His biggest coup came in March 2002 when he secured an up-front commission from Friends First. Thirty-six employees of a fictitious company, a software consultancy called Terrintech, had supposedly signed up to one of the company's group schemes. The deal was backed by letters of undertaking in which he agreed the money would be paid back if the contributions were not made. In just one month, between June and July 2002, Fitzpatrick earned commission worth an impressive €725,000. Based in offices in Stillorgan, south Dublin, Fitzpatrick wasn't shy about spending his new found wealth. He splashed the money on a new BMW X5, two Mercedes and a dazzling array of jewellery. He enjoyed an active social life and wasn't adverse to buying rounds of drinks for his friends and associates. Fitzpatrick's new status was underpinned by his €46,000 membership of the Druids Glen Golf Club in County Wicklow. By the end of July the insurance agent had earned total commissions worth €2.3 million. There was no doubt he was a serious player in Ireland's rapidly growing economy. He invested some of his new found wealth in two start-up companies. One was involved in pub design, the other in advertising.

The fast and spectacular rise of Noel Fitzpatrick came to a sudden halt in September 2002. Friends First called in the fraud squad when the contributions to the bonus scheme for the fictitious Terrintech employees employees were not made. They stood to lose €1.5 million. The financial firm won the race to the High Court and froze his assets. It soon became clear that other institutions had also been hit. New Ireland was exposed to the tune of €480,000 and Canada Life had lost €336,700. On top of that Fitzpatrick had taken out a €507,895 bridging loan from Anglo Irish Bank, using forged documents to show he owned three properties. That had been used to pay off a loan for IR£290,000 taken from Allied Irish Banks and the rest of the money had been spent to prop up the façade of success. He had been robbing Peter to pay Paul until the cash ran out.

It wasn't so much a case of someone living the dream as playing out a fantasy. Fitzpatrick did it all with money that didn't belong to him. Terrintech Ireland didn't even exist. He had set up an entirely bogus company, using forged documents about non-existent directors, to register it with the Companies Office. As the Gardaí and the banks closed in, Fitzpatrick took the only course of action open to a true con-man and he fled the country. In his absence the banks got to work on dividing up what was left of the spoils. The house in Cabinteely was sold off with the proceeds going to the mortgage company Irish Permanent and to set up his wife, again estranged, and children in a new home.

At first Fitzpatrick travelled to South Africa, then to Uganda. His scam had left him both professionally and financially ruined but he formed plans to settle down and go back into business. Ex-pats involved in fish-farming, agriculture and commodities can live lavish lifestyles in the central African country. To get started in

Uganda, however, Fitzpatrick needed some seed capital.

In 2003, he returned to Ireland. Any pretence that his financial antics from December 2000 until June 2002 were out of character were soon to be dispelled. During his six-week stay in Ireland in 2003, he set up a series of loans from Irish banks which he had no intention of paying back. To carry out the new fraud he stole his brother's identity. Fitzpatrick took a copy of his brother's wage slip, birth certificate and P60 from the family's home. With his unsuspecting brother's passport, Noel Fitzpatrick borrowed money from the Bank of Ireland, Ulster Bank, National Irish Bank and Permanent TSB over ten days in November 2003. The amounts came to a total of €84,000. He lodged €64,000 in a Bank of Ireland account which was to be used to pay out the initial repayments and kept €20,000 in cash for his expenses. He removed €38,000 from the Bank of Ireland account, in ten instalments, and returned to Africa with his €58,000 'profit'. The first his brother knew of the loans taken out in his name were when the banks made contact looking for their repayments.

On Fitzpatrick's next trip back to Ireland, on February 18, 2005, the Gardaí were waiting for him at Dublin Airport. He was arrested and questioned about the loans he had received when he was using his brother's identity. He admitted everything and was charged with 27 counts of obtaining money by false pretences. He was remanded in custody to Cloverhill Prison to wait for his court date.

In January 2006, after spending almost a year in jail, Noel Fitzpatrick went on trial for the pensions scam which he had operated in 2002. He appeared at Dublin District Court where he pleaded guilty to seven charges of falsely claiming he had customers applying to join pension schemes with the three insurance companies Friends First, Canada Life and New Ireland. He also admitted to taking out the €507,895 bridging loan from Allied Irish Banks under false pretences.

A month later he was brought back to court for sentencing. Judge Catherine Delahunt said Fitzpatrick had got away with the fraud because the financial institutions had failed to carry out adequate checks on him. She added that the scam: "Had a limited life span and that the house of cards collapsed in a relatively short space of time." During the court hearing it was calculated that Fitzpatrick had cleared €1.6 million from the bogus schemes. He spent €153,000 on cars, €54,000 on jewellery, clocked up €100,000 on his credit card as well as the €46,000 membership of Druid's Glen. He was sentenced to four years. By this stage the insurance companies and banks had retrieved what they could. The cars and jewellery were sold off. The investments made by Fitzpatrick into the start-up companies were given back. Friends First cut their losses to €300,000, while New Ireland had to write off about €100,000. Canada Life never gave any indication how much they lost to Fitzpatrick.

But the criminal justice system still hadn't finished with Noel Fitzpatrick. In February 2007 he was back in court for the loans he had taken out in his brother's name. He got an extra two years behind bars. The judge in the case said Fitzpatrick had "significantly abused the trust of his family".

Fitzpatrick had stolen money that he knew was going to be missed. There was no way his fraud wasn't going to come to light. Realising this he used some of the money to buy time, making the initial payments for the loans and pension schemes. In the meantime he enjoyed the luxuries the cash could buy and the status they gave him – before he had to flee the country. For some reason he thought no one would still be looking for him when he returned to Ireland just over a year later. It is not unusual for white collar criminals like Fitzpatrick to somehow persuade themselves they won't be caught or that they'll be able to pay the money back before it is missed. Fitzpatrick was able to hoodwink the banks despite being a small, one man operation. The potential for fraud by someone well-connected and working in a business regarded as blue-chip is far greater.

Located on Cork City's South Mall the firm of W&R Morrogh ticked all the right boxes when it came to exuding the professional kind of gravitas. Even the street, with its high Georgian buildings and wide thoroughfare, suggests an unshakeable record of professional integrity. For 114 years the merchant class of Ireland's second city had entrusted their savings to the firm, founded by local man Walter Morrogh in 1887. W&R Morrogh had an impressive pedigree. It had a seat on the Cork Stock Exchange when the city was one of a number of centres around the country with their own exchange. The stock exchange continued to trade until the late 1960s, when it was amalgamated with the Dublin market. Up until 2001, the firm also had seats on both the Dublin and London stock exchanges. It was the only stockbroker outside the capital and one of the few independent brokerages left in Ireland. It was as close as it possibly could be to aristocratic banking in Ireland. Old money, wrapped in a patrician Catholic sense of duty to its clients, meant that the firm's reputation was pure blue-chip. They had such a reputation for absolute probity that people didn't even ask for share certificates.

A grandson of the founder, Alec Morrogh, was the

senior partner in the firm. The junior partner was his cousin, Stephen Jeremiah Pearson. Between them they owned 60 per cent and 40 per cent of the firm respectively. At university Pearson had studied French and Theology. He then spent seven years in Glenstal Abbey where he had trained to become a Benedictine monk. In 1987 Pearson decided life in a religious order was not for him. He left the Benedictines to go into the family business. In 1992 he became financial controller. When his father, Peter, retired in 1997, Stephen inherited his father's share of the business and became an owner of the brokerage.

By 2001, Pearson was a married man with three children, from the ages of four to nine. He loved France and regularly went on holidays there with his family. Quiet and calm, Pearson wasn't flash or ostentatious with his wealth, driving a modest car and living quietly with his family at Stonleight, North Esk in Glanmire, Cork. Pearson appeared to be the perfect person to trust. He was a real Mr Reliable in a business where trust was everything. Many clients had nominee accounts which gave the stockbroker complete control over their assets. The arrangement saves time and allows transactions to be carried out quickly to maximise profits and minimise losses. In some cases a client would hand over their entire life-savings, entrusting their nest-egg to the company. Bereaved spouses who received life assurance pay-outs or disabled accident victims who got insurance compensation turned to W&R Morrogh to safeguard their financial future. The firm was rooted in the community and independent of financial corporations seeking to maximise earnings from commissions and fees. Pearson was a stalwart of a firm that had been in the hands of the same family for three generations.

All, however, was not as it seemed. In 1993, when he was seven years into his new career, Pearson had first shown his potential for some wayward judgement. He had taken some risky gambles on futures and options on the London Stock Exchange. The gamble didn't pay off. The disastrous transaction had come to light when he admitted it to his father Peter. The senior partner, Alec Morrogh, was assured that the money had been paid back. No lasting damage had been done and he decided to allow his junior partner and cousin, to stay on in the business. He had accepted the assurance from Pearson and his family that it would not happen again. Throughout the 1990s the firm had continued to quietly and smoothly operate as it had done for over a century. As Ireland enjoyed unprecedented financial growth, W&R Morrogh were in an unrivalled position. Then, on April 19, 2001, a trader working at the firm noticed an unusual journal entry. He took it to Alec Morrogh, who saw that IR£275,000 had been taken from a solicitor's account for a transaction that had never happened. The cash had then been lodged with a dealer in London with whom Pearson had been trading high-risk futures and options.

The senior partner was left shaken by the revelation. He confronted Pearson the next morning. After being told the secret debt amounted to IR£500,000, Morrogh sold off IR£800,000 of Pearson's shares to cover the losses. This time the regulators and the Central Bank got involved and preparations were made to investigate the true extent of the fraud. The Garda Bureau of Fraud Investigation was also called in. Alec Morrogh was initially hopeful that the firm would quickly recover from the blow. That confidence was short-lived.

That weekend Pearson went missing. His family

feared the worst. He had driven to Dublin and booked into Jury's Inn at Christchurch. Alone in his hotel room he attempted to end his life by slitting his wrists. He ended up in hospital where he underwent surgery to repair the self-inflicted damage. The Gardaí, the officials from the Stock Exchange and their long list of questions would have to wait.

By Tuesday, the senior partner, the grandson of the founder, was getting messages that as much as €3 million could be missing. On April 26, the firm was suspended from trading by the Irish Stock Exchange. The investigators had discovered a network of false accounts within the firm's own system. Pearson, as the financial controller, had set up the system to hide his mounting losses. Half of the company's €12 million assets didn't actually exist. Pearson had lost the money playing financial roulette in high-risk, and illegal, trades. Effectively the firm was insolvent.

Within a month, an application was before the High Court to wind up the firm. There was no chance that the stock-broking firm could trade its way out of trouble and it was put into receivership. The Central Bank's Head of Securities expressed his concern that the 1993 fraud had not been reported to them or to the Stock Exchange. The Receiver, Tom Grace, told the court that he had spoken with Pearson in St Patrick's Hospital, but that it would take some time to discover the full extent of the losses. After 114 years, W&R Morrogh was shut down.

The collapse of the company sent shockwaves through its 9,000 strong client list and the Irish financial world. Pearson had used clients' money to hide the losses he had racked up. Money given to him to buy shares was stolen. Shares were sold without the customers' knowledge and the cash was used to fund his reckless trading. Other clients were shown forged share certificates. It emerged that from 1995 until 2001 Pearson had been engaged in a precarious juggling act in which he had succeeded in hiding the massive hole he had made in the firm's finances.

The effects of Pearson's fraud would reverberate for years. One client, unlike Pearson, successfully committed suicide after learning that the life savings he invested with the firm had disappeared. Another client, whose account had been pilfered, developed Alzheimer's and there was no cash left to pay for medical expenses. Another was a man who had been in a car crash suffering serious spinal injuries. The insurance pay-out he lodged with W&R Morrogh would have been his only income for the rest of his life. Pearson even stole money from L'Arche charity by manipulating the accounts ahead of an Annual General Meeting.

As more information came to light it was clear that Pearson's scam was Ireland's biggest securities fraud. It was a real shock to the financial community as the details of Pearson's reckless scam slowly emerged. There were comparisons to Nick Leeson whose trading in Asia brought down Barings Bank. Leeson hid STG£827 million losses. In that case, however, Leeson was using his employer's money. Leeson's fraud can be partially blamed on the lack of controls within Barings. Pearson, on the other hand, was the man who was supposed to be exercising control over his firm's dealers. While Leeson lost a truly staggering sum of money, Pearson's fraud, while materially less, was more calculated and crueller. Unlike Leeson, Pearson knew his victims personally. One of them was his grand-aunt, Veronica Guy. He lost the €213,000, which the elderly woman had given him to purchase shares.

Pearson fully understood the depth of his deceit. This was to become apparent in the subsequent interviews he gave to investigating detectives. He knew the company he was destroying was his family's legacy.

Over the course of the next two years the former financial controller was interviewed 22 times by officers from the fraud squad. It quickly became apparent that the fraud had been carefully perpetrated. Although he co-operated, Pearson only confirmed illegal deals and fraudulent transactions when confronted with the documentary evidence. Otherwise his account of his dealings remained vague, lacking the details the officers needed. He had used the name Gerard Stevens to carry his high-risk trading in futures and options on the London Exchange. He had also opened accounts in his own firm's system using names like 'Bear Bull' in which he moved money about to disguise the losses.

At his trial in October 2005, Pearson pleaded guilty to 47 charges of fraud, amounting to €4.3 million. As a result of his guilty plea, much of the case dealt with Pearson as an individual. It focused on why, despite his life of moneyed-privilege, he was such a troubled soul. The prosecution case was read out in court and included some of the victims' statements. Pearson was not cross-examined about his motivation. Neither were any of his victims asked to give firsthand testimony of how his actions had affected their lives. Pearson's legal team put forward the factors which mitigated in favour of their client. It was stated that he had a personality disorder and craved the approval of his family and colleagues. Beneath his calm demeanour, Pearson was beset by anxiety and depression. Combined with an addiction to gambling, it all led to the catastrophic illegal trading. His lawyer said that since the firm's collapse Pearson had sought treatment for his addiction. There was no evidence that money had been channelled into a life of wild excess. It simply didn't happen. His only extravagance appeared to have been the IR£150,000 he put into an investment club to which he belonged with 20 other friends and colleagues. The IR£150,000 had been given to him by a widow to keep her comfortable in her declining years and to pay her daughter's way through college. Pearson's crimes meant that she had to return to work and her daughter was forced to drop out of her third level course. More victims' stories were read out in court from statements they had given to Gardaí.

In April 2005 Judge Desmond Hogan sentenced him to three years at the Dublin Circuit Criminal Court, but suspended the final year, saying he had regard for the effect prison would have on Pearson, his wife and his family. The sentence was greeted with outrage.

His former business partner, Alec Morrogh, told reporters that Pearson had "got away with absolute murder".

"I'm very disappointed, I thought that was a totally inadequate sentence for what he did, totally inadequate. There was a case in court some years ago when two ladies stole money from a credit union for which they were working. And I think the sentence was seven years, and I think it was less than IR£1 million. I think he got away with absolute murder. The presentation of the case was all about him. As he pleaded guilty, all the case was skewed towards mitigating his sentence and suggesting that he was a victim himself of his own addiction. In my opinion, what he did was extremely evil.

"Nobody is given an audience as to the damage that has been done to them because the victim impact regulations don't cover people who have lost money.

The judge said the profile of the people from whom he stole, they were mostly elderly, past the earning time of their lives and incredibly damaged by what he did."

The fraud committed by his cousin, former friend and business partner, was a blow to the heart of what Alec Morrogh believed his family company had stood for. It clearly had left him shaken and unable to forgive. "I don't want to speak about myself, it is just very raw and I have been lost for the last four years. I don't have a past, I consistently think about it, I don't really have a present and I don't have a future."

Alec Morrogh lost everything so that clients could be compensated. He paid €3 million to the Receiver to cover losses. Under the industry regulations, however, the maximum compensation was limited to €20,000 per person. That left bigger clients considerably out of pocket, especially one who had lost €1.4 million. The wrangle over who owned what ate up any of the remaining assets. It was a mire of legal wrangles and dispute over ownership, thanks to the complex web of deceit weaved by Pearson. Clients who knew what shares belonging to them were held in the firm's nominee accounts challenged the receivers' claim on the assets.

In the end the receivership and associated legal fees cost €5.6 million, more than the €4.6 million Pearson had stolen. In May 2006, Pearson's jail sentence was appealed. He was given an extra three years in jail after the Director of Public Prosecutions had challenged the undue leniency of his original two-year sentence. "The word must go out to the public that white collar crime of this nature will attract serious sentences," said Mr Justice Nicholas Kearns.

Pearson had been born into money and followed his father into the family company. It could be argued that because of his privileged background he felt entitled to a life of success and money, a flaw which drew him to committing the devastating fraud. This sense of entitlement, however, is not reserved to people from a privileged background. Being a self-made man doesn't provide immunity to temptation. Doctor Emad Massoud didn't have the benefit of an old-school network as he worked his way up the medical hierarchy. Skilled and clever, he had to drudge his way through a career in medicine. He studied hard and in 1981 got a joint degree in medicine and surgical medicine in his native city, Alexandria on Egypt's Mediterranean coast. It is a place that has a long tradition of medical study. Medical texts dating from 2000 BC attest to Egypt's incredible record and the city itself was a centre of ancient Greek medicine. After Alexandria University, Dr Massoud entered the gruelling world of the junior doctor. Instead of a modern hospital, with more senior colleagues to call on, the newly qualified doctor found himself based in a remote mountain village. With a hinterland of 150,000 people, he was the only doctor on call. He had to perform whatever medical tasks were necessary, such as Caesarean sections and amputations, with rudimentary equipment and poor lighting. It was a tough learning curve where the young Dr Massoud had no choice except to rely on his own abilities. Then, in 1985 the 29-year-old doctor met a woman, Gehan, who was nine years his junior. As he was a Muslim and she a Christian, they had to move to England where they secretly married. Such an inter-faith union could have caused serious problems for their respective families in Egypt where religious tensions bubble under the surface.

For the next 12 years Emad and Gehan, who qualified as a nurse, lived the nomadic lives of

immigrant medics picking up contracts in the
provincial hospitals. They landed jobs in which the
careerist native Irish and British doctors had no interest.
In a dozen years they worked in almost as many
hospitals. There was Chesterfield and Norwich in
England, then Mullingar, Letterkenny, Bantry,
Enniskillen and a stint in the Mater Hospital in Dublin.
By 1997 the couple had their second child and decided
it was time to settle down for a better quality of family
life. Dr Massoud had worked hard and was already a
wealthy man by normal standards. He bought a house
in Castleknock and went about setting up his own
private surgical practice in Dublin city. He worked from
the Wellman Clinic in Eccles Street, where he was the
Medical Director. The clinic specialises in male-related
medical procedures and treatments such as vasectomy,
hair-loss, erectile dysfunction and diagnosis of prostate,
bladder and testicular cancer. The company's website
refers to their medical director: "He has been in general
medical and surgical practice for the last 20 years with
a special interest in men's problems." The years of slog
had finally paid off for the Massoud family. The
Wellman Clinic was set up just as the Irish economy
boomed and the public health service got worse and
worse. He had property interests in Egypt and
Romania.

In 2000 the doctor was interviewed as part of an
article about men's health. "There are specific problems
which will bring a man to the doctor. If a man has a
broken ankle, he will look for help. But men are proud.
'I'm not bad enough to see a doctor,' seems to be the
attitude. It's the way we were reared; to be tough, so
that a man can feel ashamed at admitting there is
something wrong and may be scared that he will be
regarded as weak or foolish," he intoned. Clearly, he

was a man who could see a marketing opportunity when it arose, obviously having developed his business acumen along the way. "What needs to be done is that representatives of the medical profession need to be out there offering education and generally raising awareness. Media reports, public meetings, cholesterol testing in shopping centres, all have an impact. We took a stand at the Ideal Homes Exhibition last year. If men don't come to doctor's surgeries, we have to find a way of going to them. And if I could say one thing to men it would be take care of your health the way you take care of your car."

By 2001, the jowly, grey-haired doctor was the father of four children and they had dual Irish and Egyptian citizenship. The family had moved to an impressive property in County Meath. He had come a long way from the remote mountain village. He certainly could allow himself to be a little smug or self-satisfied. But that year an event happened which would irrevocably change the comfortable lifestyle the Massouds had worked so hard to achieve. Back in Egypt Gehan's mother was diagnosed with breast cancer. She contacted her daughter and son-in-law for their help. While surgeons in Egypt carried out an operation to remove the cancerous breast tissue, back in Ireland Dr Massoud discussed with his colleagues the best way to help his mother-in-law. He had samples sent over from Egypt for testing in Ireland and he sent for her pathology report. It was at some point after that, that Dr Massoud saw a golden opportunity. He realised that with one small scam his mother-in-law's illness could be used to further enrich himself.

He went about setting up a unique fraud. It was a con that only someone with his level of medical expertise could possibly have carried off. The couple must have realised that to risk such an undertaking would put their careers and business in jeopardy, as well as their personal liberty, but they decided to go ahead with it. Dr Massoud would later claim that one night in September 2001, as the couple prepared for a night out to celebrate Gehan's birthday, she discovered a lump in her breast. The skilled surgeon was distraught with worry and opted to operate immediately on his wife. He seemed unconcerned by Irish medical guidelines which forbid surgeons from operating on family members. "If a tiler can tile his own bathroom, why can't a surgeon operate on his own family," he would later say. During the operation Dr Massoud said he removed the tumour and a large amount of tissue from his wife's breast. The surgeon, who had specialised in men's health, did this with just local anaesthetic, no assistants and in his clinic.

As it turned out, Gehan had been insured for just such a calamitous medical problem, to the tune of €730,000. Mindful that he could be in trouble with the Medical Council for carrying out the procedure alone, Dr Massoud listed a colleague as the operating surgeon on the insurance claims. The claims went through and Massoud appeared to have successfully carried out his scam to hoodwink the insurance companies. Scottish Provident paid out €685,658 and Lifetime Assurance sent a cheque for €45,338 in settlements made in February 2002. A lot of the money was spent refurbishing the family's home in Brownstown, Ratoath, County Meath.

Nearly two years later, a whistleblower finally came forward to suggest that all may not have been as it seemed. The Gardaí began investigating and the insurance companies went to the High Court to start proceedings against Dr Massoud to get their money

back. On November 4, 2003, the couple were both
arrested at their home. They strenuously denied the
allegations that they had defrauded the insurance
companies by faking Gehan's breast cancer. The couple
were both remanded on bail.

The Massouds had a lot to protect and fought the
case every inch of the way. Their arrests were challenged
in the High Court, which ruled against them, paving the
way for the criminal trial in January 2008.

Six and a half years after the Massouds first cooked
up the scam, they appeared in court. In his suit and tie
and with an air of haughty importance Dr Massoud
went out to face down his accusers. Gehan appeared to
have less of her husband's self-assuredness. It can't
have been easy to listen to how they had set out to use
their hard-won position to deceive insurance
companies. A former colleague and close friend of the
Massouds, Dr Mohamed Elsayed Attia, gave evidence
against the couple, but denied being the whistleblower.
The anaesthetist had seen a jar of human tissue in the
Massoud family home after Gehan's mother's breast
cancer had first been discussed. He said that a man who
worked for the Massouds had brought the tissue to
Ireland in his suitcase. The doctor painted a different
picture of Emad Massoud than that of successful
surgeon and businessman. He said that Massoud had
grown pompous and arrogant and that there was even
a sinister, dark side to his personality. The pair had
clashed and fallen out over three Egyptian men who
had gone to Dr Attia for help. They had been working
for Massoud, who had paid for them to come to Ireland
to work on his house. He said that they had come to
him because Massoud had thrown them out in the
middle of the night, after abusing them. When Massoud
found out that Attia gave them food and shelter he said

he should have closed the door in the men's faces. Dr Attia claimed that Massoud had said if they had been left out in the cold they would have gone back to work for him. The two men had been close friends and Dr Attia said he would definitely have known if Gehan Massoud had breast cancer, just months after her mother had been diagnosed with the same illness. Attia denied claims that he had fabricated the story against the Massouds after the row and a disagreement over medical fees he had been charged by Massoud for a report.

Another friend, Dr Mohamed Hilal, whose name had been put down as the surgeon who operated on Gehan Massoud, denied carrying out the procedure or signing any medical or insurance documents. He too had been a close friend of the family and they had holidayed together in 2003. Massoud had lent the younger doctor money and had also paid his registration fees with the Irish Medical Council.

The most damning evidence against the Massouds came from the Irish medical experts. One forensic scientist, for the prosecution, had no doubt that the sample tissue provided did not come from Gehan Massoud. Another, working for the defence, said that the tissue sample was so degraded that any DNA results would be unreliable. Cancerous tumours can cause genetic damage to cells that will cause a mismatch. Neither expert could say if it was Gehan's tissue. Another consultant, who has carried out 150 lumpectomy operations, pointed out that Dr Massoud's claim to have removed 237 grammes of tissue, which would have amounted to half his wife's breast, just "didn't add up".

Dr Emad Massoud put on a good show when he took the stand in the Central Criminal Court on January

28, 2008. He broke down in tears as he recalled the
moment his wife discovered a lump in her breast.

"I'll never forget it. She was taking a shower because
we were going out to celebrate her birthday. As a
human being you don't think the worst is going to
happen to you." He said he decided not to follow the
usual medical protocols and opted to operate on his
wife in his clinic. "A doctor is a human being and
human beings can sometimes be happy and sometimes
sad, sometimes laugh and sometimes cry, sometimes
can be brave and sometimes can be a coward and I was
scared," he said.

He admitted that he had carried out the operation,
not Dr Mohamed Hilal whose name had been entered
on records as the surgeon. But otherwise he stuck to his
story branding Dr Attia "a clever illusionist".

"He just made up the story. The insurance company
welcomed the story, the insurance company, out of
greed, then went to the Gardaí who welcomed the story.
I was arrested on the basis of one statement from Dr
Mohamed Hilal. There was no Garda investigation
whatsoever to prove I had committed fraud," he said in
court.

He rejected the prosecution claim that he had used
his mother-in-law's tissue sample to create a bogus case
for his wife. He dismissed as coincidence the discovery
of a lump in his wife's breast the day after her mother
had had one removed.

It was a long trial, with expert witnesses for both the
prosecution and defence. It took 15 days, over two
months and the book of evidence was 900 pages long. A
jury of seven men and four women took just two hours
to deliver a guilty verdict.

Judge Patrick McCartan described the fraud as: "an
appalling tragedy entirely of their making." Both

medics had brought an end to their professional careers when there was no need to have done so. The judge pointed out that he was not impressed by the fact that the couple had both stopped working when the matter was investigated by the Gardaí and there appeared to be no prospect of paying the money back to the insurance companies. The Massouds had received legal aid for their defence. The judge also depicted the fraud as "a particularly evil and nasty offence" in which the surgeon had deliberately scarred his wife. The offence was at the higher end of the scale and had been committed "simply to satisfy the greed of two people well capable of supporting their family." He jailed Emad Massoud for four years. He suspended a three year sentence for Gehan Massoud because he didn't want to leave the children without both parents.

Dr Massoud had been arrogant enough to think he could perform a bogus surgical procedure on his wife to create the impression that a lumpectomy had been carried out. Then, he used a colleague's identity to defraud two insurance companies. Typical of so many fraudsters, and even professional con-artists, he thought he was cleverer than everyone else. In court he cried as he stuck to his story in the face of damning evidence. For a man who had worked hard to achieve a comfortable lifestyle the fraud attempt was of breath-taking stupidity. But it was one he almost got away with. Massoud's downfall was his haughty, conceited manner. He rubbed up a colleague the wrong way, once too often, with his high-handed arrogance. It was enough to bring down his scheme and end the career he had worked so hard to establish.

It can take a strong combination of factors for a professional person to turn their backs on their chosen career and to abuse the trust they have earned. Dr

Massoud found himself in a unique position to attempt a breast cancer fraud. Even if a corrupt doctor had wanted to defraud an insurance company, he still needed samples of cancerous human tissue and a willing accomplice. When he heard about his mother-in-law's illness, Massoud found himself with a set of circumstances that made him believe that he could successfully pull off a con and he tried to do just that. But there is an even bigger source of cash, than the money that's available to insurance firms. The vast pot of gold that is the public purse is one that has always tempted fraudsters. For the carousel VAT fraudsters it was like shooting fish in a barrel. The sheer amount of cash processed through the Revenue Commissioner is staggering. Yet rarely have tax officials been found with their fingers in the till and, unlike Massoud, they are in a position to commit fraud every time they go into work. They have access to hundreds of thousands of people's personal and financial details and valuable inside knowledge. But they have a reputation of probity that is second to none. The tax man, like justice, is blind when it comes to dealing with the citizens of the State. The tax system is a vital pillar of the community that must run smoothly and without any hints of wrong-doing. Corruption in such a sensitive government department would lead to chaos and anarchy. A country can barely exist without an honest and efficient body of civil servants. There have been cases of corruption among government officials but thankfully they are rare. The Revenue Commissioners, however, have to be on a constant alert for attempts to defraud the State – whether through tax evasion, false claims or smuggling.

One day in June, 1997, an assistant principal officer in the tax office noticed something unusual. Sam Gill was processing a VAT reclaim form, normally a routine task. This one, however, was more than a little unusual. A cheque for IR£3.4 million was about to be paid out to a company called Unirock Enterprises. In the file was a claim for VAT repayments to the company. Included were six documents, some of which were purportedly signed by six senior officials in the Department of Revenue, including a future chairman, Dermot Quigley, and the then chairman, Cathal Mac Domhnaill. The letter stated the IR£3.82 million payment was part of a scheme agreed between the Minister for Finance and the Revenue to allow the Criminal Assets Bureau to repay money to companies without undue publicity. The letter told revenue officials dealing with the case to act in secrecy. Gill decided to double-check the contents of the file and he spoke to Dermot Quigley by phone. Quigley hadn't heard of the secret scheme. The letters were forgeries and the cheque was stopped immediately. The intervention came just in the nick of time. 20 minutes later businessman Brendan O'Doherty walked into the Collector General's offices in Ennis, County Clare. He had come to pick up the expected rebate due to be paid to Unirock. Instead he was arrested and taken into custody. The Gardaí, including the Criminal Assets Bureau, launched a major investigation.

The detectives did not expect what happened next. The trail led all the way back to the Revenue Commissioners at Sarsfield House in Limerick. The next day one of Gill's superiors, Brendan Murphy was arrested. Murphy wasn't just an ordinary official. He was one of four principal officers based in Limerick City. His job was to manage the VAT reclaim system for the entire State. He had the equivalent position to a Garda Chief Superintendent. Originally from Trim, County Meath, he moved to work in Limerick as part of the government's plan to decentralise civil servants from Dublin. He lived in Parteen, County Clare with his wife and three children. He became an enthusiastic amateur aviator, learning to fly both a helicopter and a plane. At the time he was earning a generous salary of IR£47,000, after 18 years of service with Revenue. As a sideline he did a bit of construction work through his company Meckfield Limited.

When he was arrested by Gardaí on June 18, Murphy broke down. He gave a long statement to the Gardaí in which he claimed he had been threatened. He said that threats were made against his family and would be carried out if he didn't take part in the fraud. Murphy said the plot had it origins in a meeting with Brendan O'Doherty. They had met in Artane, north Dublin in January or February that year, when they discussed general tax issues. The pair knew each other from Trim, County Meath where they had grown up. They met a second time and again discussed taxation, with O'Doherty appearing to have become more familiar with the system. At a third meeting O'Doherty was joined by a number of associates. Murphy claimed that O'Doherty appeared to represent a criminal gang. They pushed him for details on how the VAT reclaim system worked. He believed that O'Doherty had passed on what he had learned to these other people who realised he could be used if he was 'got at'. One of the men asked him how his wife was and also if his daughter still enjoyed horse-riding. According to Murphy the man commented that horse-riding could be a dangerous sport, which the VAT man took as being a threat. During the conversation Murphy said he was told that if he opened his mouth he would end up under a coffin. At yet another meeting one of the mystery men, who was armed with a hand gun, said that they intended to make a false VAT claim. They wanted a copy of a fully certified claim which had gone through the system. Murphy said he refused to give it to them and never gave them a copy. More meetings followed. In Murphy's version of events the gangsters produced a VAT return form and a covering certificate on which an inspector had authorised payment. He told them that it was incorrectly completed and that no inspector would have done it that way. According to Murphy the gangsters were determined to make the scam work. He claimed that he was given no option except to co-operate. Murphy was told that if the fraud worked he would get half of the proceeds. If it didn't, his family would be harmed. Murphy said he was told: "All you have to do if something comes before you is to pass it or ignore it." He told detectives he thought the fraud was also an attempt to get back at the recently formed Criminal Assets Bureau. Shortly after this last meeting the cheque had been drawn up in the Revenue Commissioners. O'Doherty had been on his way to collect it when he was arrested.

Both Murphy and O'Doherty later pleaded guilty to conspiracy to defraud the State when they appeared in Ennis District Court. O'Doherty, then aged 47, went on trial first and was described as the "front man" of the operation. His job had been to collect the cheque and to lodge it to an Allied Irish Bank account in Dublin. From there, the money was to have been transferred to an unnamed account in Austria. He was due to get just €20,000 for his role in the operation. He was jailed for four years in February 1998. That August, as he was serving his sentence, he died from natural causes.

After O'Doherty's unfortunate death, Murphy then tried to change his earlier guilty plea to one of not guilty. He claimed in court that he had developed: "a frightening dependence on tranquiliser tablets." As a result, his lawyers argued, Murphy had been in a disabled mental state and was not fit to plead at the time. He had been bewildered and went along with advice he did not understand to plead guilty to the charges. Reports gave details of his medical history which included a battle with thyroid cancer in 1978 which re-occurred in 1997. He had also suffered from depression, voluntarily admitting himself to hospital in 1985. After that he gave up alcohol but was prescribed tranquilisers for anxiety and became dependent on them. A psychiatric report submitted for the defence described Murphy as a chronically restless individual. He took up martial arts, learned to fly helicopters and aeroplanes. It added that he was involved in five cases of litigation at the same time. He was constantly dogged by problems. It went on to claim that Murphy had been ostracised by his family as a result of the case and lived in his garage.

The trial judge, Kevin Haugh, who heard the application, said that there was no evidence of any permanent impairment of Murphy's ability to instruct his legal team. He spent 45 minutes delivering his judgement rejecting the application. He pointed to the fact that Murphy had been able to operate as normal in his demanding post within the Revenue Commissioners at the time. He added that through the 1990s Murphy had learned how to fly a plane and would have been subject to medical examinations for his licences. If addiction to tranquilisers had left him in such a severely disabled state, it would have been evident at a much earlier point in time. There were also letters to his solicitor in which he showed a good grasp of his legal position. He said they were sensible and incisive letters.

With O'Doherty dead, it is quite probable that the prosecution case against Murphy would have failed if he had been allowed to change his plea to one of not guilty but the judge's ruling ensured that the trial would go ahead with Murphy's guilty plea.

Murphy's criminal trial got underway in September 1999. Yet again Murphy's version of events, put forward in mitigation, was regarded as a complete cock and bull story. Judge Haugh said that Murphy had misused his power and had carried out a gross breach of privilege as a trusted employee in a major fraud. He described the conspiracy as "very clever and ingenious" and one which could only have been planned by someone with an in-depth knowledge of the system. He was satisfied that all the forged documents had originated from Murphy. The Criminal Assets Bureau had investigated Murphy's claims that the plot was organised by a sinister gang with paramilitary connections. They were found to be without basis. Murphy was sentenced to seven years, with the final three years being suspended. Amazingly, despite the jail sentence, it emerged that it was not an immediately fireable offence to attempt such a massive fraud. He stayed on the State payroll even while he was behind bars. His wife received hardship payments from the Department. He also kept his 18 years of pension rights. Obviously the careful procedural approach, used by Sam Gill in double-checking the facts for the Unirock rebate in the first place, is applied equally in the Revenue Commissioners when it comes to firing miscreants.

Brendan Murphy was the ultimate insider when it came to using the knowledge of a system's inner-workings to pull off a fraud. Similarly Dr Massoud, Michael Lynn, Stephen Pearson and Noel Fitzpatrick knew the mechanics of how transactions worked in their various areas of expertise. They used that knowledge to enrich themselves. When Ireland's Celtic Tiger boom was close to its peak there was no end in sight to the money that could be made. To have sat down at a dinner party with Dr Massoud, Stephen Pearson, Michael Lynn and Noel Fitzpatrick, would have probably have been an expensive affair. A guest would be privileged to have been in the company of a group so apparently switched on and clued into how the world works. They would have seemed like the real shakers and movers, forging ahead of the pack, making millions thanks to their brilliance. The bent tax man, Brendan Murphy, would have been another welcome guest at the dinner table. It would have been impossible to know then that all the expensive cars parked outside, the heavy wrist watches and fine wines on the table were just a façade. The con-artists used their professional credentials for dishonesty and their victims had simply trusted the system to work as it normally does. They knocked on the professional's door and stepped into an office where everything was based on trust. Behind those doors, and behind the façade of wealth, lurked the professionals' real characters – liars, cheaters, sharks and charlatans.

SIX

The 419ers

In a down-at-heel cyber café, there is a young man feverishly working the keyboard. Each day, every day he drills out hundreds of emails. The young man is not alone. Sometimes he is working from a flyblown suburb of Lagos, Nigeria, other times he is on a backstreet where immigrants congregate, in the cities of the wealthy West. The vast majority of the messages are sent automatically, using simple computer software, as new addresses are culled from the internet. When they elicit a response a human touch is eventually needed to begin luring in those people who have replied. There are thousands of others just like the young man, who are making a meagre living looking for stupid, rich Westerners to make contact. The kid in the café is at the starting point of the 419 scam.

The 419 scam originated in Nigeria and they take their name from the paragraph of the Nigerian Constitution that bans fraud. Estimates put the number of active 419ers at one million, an army of con-men using the Internet to reach around the globe. Anyone with an email address is familiar with the letter sent out by the fraudsters but there are many different versions of the initial scam letter. Some play on a person's religious beliefs by suggesting the writer is a wealthy person who is terminally ill. The proposition is that they want to distribute their wealth to needy causes without their relatives finding out. Other letters are supposedly from bank officials who want help to steal the cash of dead customers who have no known next of kin. Then there are rich children looking for a guardian to help start a new life in the West. More again are from nubile, sexy young women who desperately need help to smuggle their dead parents' millions into the West. Needless to say there are no vast sums of money. Most emails are greeted with the delete button. But surprisingly, a tiny minority, just under one per cent, actually get a reply. Those who are sucked into the web of deceit are then asked to pay cash up front to ensure the deal goes ahead. For that reason it is also known as the advance fee fraud.

Nowadays the 419 scam has been adopted and refined by other criminal gangs, but it remains primarily a fraud organised by Nigerian crime gangs. The scam is not unique to the West African country, but such has been the industriousness of their fraudsters, it is a reputation Nigeria will be saddled with for decades to come. In Nigeria there is, at an official level, some embarrassment at the activities of the prolific fraudsters. On the other hand there is a certain grudging pride among the public for anyone who cons a stupid rich Westerner out of their cash. To some people, the 419ers are seen as a modern day African version of Robin Hood. In the summer of 2005 Nigerian comic actor, Nkem Owoh, even had a hit with the song *I Go Chop Your Dollar*: "You be the mugu, I be the master, Oyinbo I go chop your dollar, I go take your money disappear, 419 is just a game, you are the loser, I am the winner." *Oyinbo* is slang for a white man and can be a derogatory term, depending on how it is used. *Mugu* means fool. For some the scam is a case of giving the former colonial powers and their rapacious corporations a taste of their own greedy medicine. For others it's another way of showing that sometimes white people are really stupid.

Nigerian fraudsters have been successfully chopping dollars for well over two decades. The kid in the café, who may even be a university student, is likely to earn $500 dollars a month, many times the national average income in Nigeria. When the keyboard kid gets a promising lead it is sold onto the fraudsters working at the next level. His bosses will earn considerably more from the tiny minority who reply to the email. The internet has increased the scope and catch of the industrious and resourceful 419ers who work tirelessly to separate fools from their money. The scam works from the best starting point of every good con: it exploits the victim's greed, the lure of easy money. The victims are also invited to help by bending or breaking the law. As a result, people who get caught out by the 419ers are not usually in any hurry to go to their local police to explain how they were conned. Victims, particularly in Japan, have been known to pay hush money to the scammers to stop them being exposed in their home countries. Who wants it known that they were trying to help a poor 19-year-old girl smuggle $20 million dollars out of Africa?

The letters have evolved over the years, each version adding a new twist or a different slant on the same old message. The 419ers were working scams even before email existed. One effective fraud during the 1980s, for instance, exploited the use of fax machines. Invoices for small amounts of cash were sent en-masse to companies all over the world. The necessary accountancy controls weren't always in place and the fraudsters very often received cheques that were sent out automatically in payment for their bogus bills. Usually the fake invoices would be cleverly named, using a fictitious company name that bore a close resemblance to a well-known supplier of office materials or other services.

One ambitious scam operation used Ireland as a base to set up wealthy business people from all over the world and had been going since 1993. Instead of using emails the fraudsters sent out old-fashioned 'snail-mail' letters. One German victim had travelled to Nigeria a number of times after being lured to the country with promises of an incredible business deal. He was fleeced of the equivalent of €500,000. In February 1999, the same group of con-artists travelled to Ireland where, using fake identities, they set up a genuine registered company called World Wide Clearing and Finance. The sole purpose of the firm was to rip-off more victims. During the month the company was up and running, the fraudsters were in contact with 50 foreign-based business people who had previously been contacted by accomplices in Nigeria. Some of the people contacted had already been scammed and were told they could recover their money through the Irish company. Others were enticed by a lucrative share of massive lump sums that had to be laundered through international bank accounts.

Thomas Smith, owner of the American Plumbing Company in Baton Rouge, Louisiana, was one of the people contacted by the fraudsters. A Nigerian professional had originally contacted him claiming to represent officials at the Works and Housing Ministry of Nigeria. They explained that a foreign-owned firm, involved in a large scale housing contract, had gone bust and that they had completed the work themselves. However, as government employees they couldn't receive the $32 million payment for the project. They needed the help of Smith's company. They promised him $4 million if he said his company had completed the project. As part of their plan to lure Smith into their trap, the con-artists also sent a fax, supposedly from their Ministry, acknowledging that he had paid income tax on profits made on Nigerian projects. He then received another fax, this time from the Nigerian Central Bank, confirming he would receive the cheque at the offices of World Wide Clearing and Finance (WWCF) in Dublin. The American businessman took the bait and travelled to Ireland to meet them that same month.

The day before he was due to collect the cheque, Smith had a look at the WWCF's Dublin office. Based in Baggot Street, in central Dublin, the offices gave the company a veneer of plausibility. The next day, he met his contacts as planned and they travelled together to a bank. The con-artists went through a charade of collecting a draft for $32 million, supposedly issued by the Bank of Ireland and drawn down on funds from Chase Manhattan. Smith appeared to be unaware that the con-artists were simply engaged in building up his confidence in their credentials as international financiers. Back at the Baggot Street office, an 'auditor' told Smith he'd have to pay $2 million to finalise the housing project before he could get his $4 million share from the draft. Smith smelled a rat and after making his excuses, left and contacted the Gardaí.

12 days later a German businessman arrived in Ireland. He too was due to collect a cheque for $56.5 million through WWCF. This time the Gardaí were waiting, thanks to Smith's tip-off. As members of the gang and their German victim travelled by taxi to the Bank of Ireland at College Green in Dublin city centre, they were arrested. The WWCF office was then raided by fraud officers and another potential 'client' was discovered, waiting for the 419ers. Five of the accused gang members were arrested. They included Nigerian refugee Christian Obumneme who tried to swallow the

fake bank draft for $56.5 million. He was desperate to dispose of the evidence. Three Gardaí pinned him to the pavement in an attempt to retrieve the fake draft. It was another half an hour before he spat out the blood-stained forgery in a nearby police station. One of the other fraudsters was Englishman Raymond Folkes. He was also found with a forged $15 million bank draft. In total three Nigerians and two English con-artists were arrested.

After a 23-day trial which ended in July 2000, Folkes and Obumneme were jailed for four years and a third man Thomas Anthony O'Brien was jailed for five. Two other Nigerians were acquitted during the trial due to lack of evidence and walked away free men.

The American businessman, Thomas Smith, gave evidence that he had treated his correspondence with the Nigerians as a hobby. He said he knew all along it was a scam, but decided to travel to Ireland anyway because he wanted to trace his ancestors. Smith's tip-off was crucial to catching the gang. It had been the Irish fraud squad's first taste of the 419ers in action and it was a rare success, anywhere in the world, to catch the con-men red-handed.

The first time police had any idea that 419 gangs were operating in Ireland was a year earlier in October 1998 when bags of black paper, the size of bank notes, were found in a raid at a property in County Meath. One of the successful scams favoured by the 419ers revolved around so-called "black money" and secret stashes of foreign currency that had to be smuggled out of Nigeria. The scammers show their victims a suitcase full of black notes which are then 'washed' to be revealed as genuine currency. The fraudsters simply wash black paper with water and then, using sleight of hand, switch a few samples of the paper for real $100 bills. By using dollars bills the fraudsters stepped into the jurisdiction of the United States Secret Service. Apart from watching over the President, the Secret Service is also charged with the task of protecting the currency from forgeries. As a result, the officers, popularised as sharp-suited individuals with sunglasses and microphones up their sleeves, have been all over the world in the fight against the never-ending wave of 419ers. Once the 419ers' "black money" victims had bought the story and agreed to take part, they would then be presented with a series of problems and hitches. Usually these would include a demand for cash bribes to get the consignment through customs or money to purchase more chemicals as they had all disastrously dried up or some other skilfully delivered cock and bull story. There would often be an element of menace added by the presence of big burly bogus bankers or fake corrupt officials, to make it all more urgent.

Members of the Secret Service, whose motto is 'Worthy of Trust and Confidence', are the antithesis of the scammers. They came to Ireland in 2001 after a sting operation was set up in Dublin designed to snare a 419er. A man known as both Blessing Ogbishe Erejuna and Michael Colomo was part of an operation that had persuaded a group of Americans to participate in the black money scam. A 25-strong syndicate believed they were going to get a quarter share of $25.5 million that had been coated with a black dye to allow it be smuggled out of Africa. By the time Erejuna or Colomo was called in to do his part, the American syndicate were already into the scheme for $900,000. A female member of the syndicate had been asked to travel to Ireland from Seattle with an additional $90,000 to buy the chemicals needed to clean the concealing dye. After

already handing over $900,000 the syndicate had
realised they had been stung and the fraud operation
was reported to the Secret Service.

Working with Garda fraud officers in Ireland, the
Secret Service allowed the meeting between the
syndicate member and the 419er to go ahead at the
Burlington Hotel in September 2001. The con-man was
arrested as the woman handed over the cash. In his
pocket was the mobile phone through which he had
been contacted by the American 'investors'. When his
apartment in a west Dublin suburb was searched,
Gardaí found two large plastic sacks filled with black
paper. Colomo was the real deal and he had been
caught red-handed. He had entered the country under
a false passport and had applied for asylum under the
name Blessing Erejuna. His application had been
turned down. A week after his arrest, the investigating
officers still didn't know the man's real identity so his
fingerprints were sent to Interpol. Before any serious
charges could be brought against him, despite Garda
objections, he was given €1,000 bail after a High Court
hearing. He fled the country, never to be seen again.

The operation that Colomo took part in was clearly
organised by a professional network that can operate
easily across international borders. They have fake
passports and identities to move around the globe. The
fraudsters can change names to avoid arrest and to
disappear. Another 419er who was caught as he
attempted to leave Wales, provided an insight into the
scale and scope of what a professional con-man can
achieve. In late 2003 Peter Okoeguale (33) was arrested
as he was about to board a ferry from Holyhead to
Ireland, where his wife and son were living. He also
had fake documents, one of which was headed
'Nigerian Police Force Contract Investigation Section'.

The document urged the recipient to forward the details to the unit of any contact by corrupt government officials. Okoeguale had been planning to trick victims of previous scams into handing over more cash by pretending to help them. The computer software the police discovered on his laptop underlined the level of sophistication with which the 419ers operate. The Nigerian had floppy disks which could scan websites for email addresses and for sending spam messages. North Wales Police said that discs found on Okoeguale also contained thousands of email addresses, telephone numbers of companies and individuals from Scotland, the USA, the Middle East and the Far East. Using the documents, the police traced 11 victims, including one in Scotland who lost up to STG£20,000, and a retired 72-year-old American businessman who lost $46,500.

Okoeguale later pleaded guilty at Caernarfon Crown Court to 'going equipped to cheat'. He claimed he was not a fraudster and that he had simply been asked to deliver the items to someone else who he refused to name. Judge John Rogers QC remarked: "This is international fraud. Only a period of imprisonment is appropriate." Okoeguale was jailed for 20 months.

Considering that Colomo and Okoeguale are just two members of a million-strong army of hard-working con-artists, the potential damage they can cause is truly immense. The advent of emails enabled the fraudster to streamline and expand their operations to previously unimaginable levels. Now, they are no longer constrained to commercial companies as they were with fax machines. They can reach right into the homes of gullible private citizens. Another version of the advance fee fraud has exploited the growth in buying and selling through internet trading websites. Everything and anything can be found for sale on the internet from puppies to yachts, to jewellery and jeeps. Ordinary people have become part-time wheelers and dealers. Goods are bought, sold and shipped all over the world. It is a quick and virtually free way of doing business. The cash for the deals is usually paid to a third party such as PayPal which holds the money until everyone is satisfied with the deal. It is known in legal terms as an escrow account. It is a common business practice when two complete strangers are dealing with one another and one the internet quickly adopted. The fraudsters, of course, have found ways of enticing people out of their security zone. For instance online auctions can be manipulated and the seller then contacts an under-bidder and offers to sell the item, asking for direct payment through a wire service transfer. In many such cases the so-called seller was using a bogus identity and the money is gone before anyone realises it. Another scam is to offer to buy an advertised item for over and above the asking price. The bogus buyer sends a money draft for more than the agreed amount. He asks the seller to cash the cheque and to wire transfer the surplus to a shipping agent who will organise the collection of the goods for sale. As most banks credit a draft cheque to an account before they are cleared, the victim will have transferred the surplus before learning that the cheque was a forgery. It has proved to be a very effective fraud for the 419ers who are prepared to stalk the internet's classified ads, searching for a victim.

Ken is a livewire business man. His energy allowed him to hop from deal to deal in Ireland's booming property market through the late 1990s and on. He followed the business to the new EU entrant states from the old Eastern bloc, getting into the market early and selling before the weekend speculators arrived. The fast-talking Irishman is well-versed in dealing with lawyers in various jurisdictions, smoothing over the paper work, organising fixers and moving funds across international borders. He is not the type anyone would expect to be hoodwinked by 419ers. In 2007, he put an old Izusu jeep up for sale on an Irish car website for €2,000: "To be honest I was using it for storage. It was in the way and would have paid someone to take it away. Someone rang, said they were from Tipperary and asked about the jeep. They didn't seem that interested. Then he sent an email offering to buy the jeep. We agreed the sale and the cheque came from Tipperary for €4,950."

In a further email 'John Henry' told Ken that he was involved in exporting second-hand vehicles to Africa and Canada and that the shipping would be handled by a London-based agent. From the cheque Ken was told to deduct €2,000 for the jeep and to keep €400 for the trouble of wiring €2,500 to London.

"I lodged the cheque and didn't think anything about it. I was in Poland when someone in the bank rang me to say 'I have bad news for you, the cheque is a dud.' I laughed," Ken admitted. "It could have been a lot worse. I had a yacht up for sale as well for €90,000. What bothered me is that no-one seems to give a fuck. I rang up the bank whose name was used on the cheque and they are not doing anything about it. It was all so easily done. My own bank paid me back €1,000 only because I'm such a good customer for them."

Ken is far from being the only victim. In an identical scam at around the same time, in early 2007, another Irish woman had been on the verge of cashing a forged bank draft sent in payment for her Volkswagen car. At the last minute she admits her husband became suspicious. Like Ken she was shocked by how easily the scam is being facilitated by banks who credit drafts to customer accounts before they are cashed. The banks were crediting bogus cheques to customer accounts, because such banker's drafts are meant to be honoured as cash. They seemed to fear disrupting the system more than protecting their customers who usually suffered the loss. The woman pulled out of the bogus deal and didn't lose any money, although for a while she feared the con-artists would send someone to her house demanding back their fake draft.

No matter how lucrative their other activities the 419ers are still prodigious when it comes to their output of spam emails in the search for new *mugus*. There is a constant flow of 419 mails to email addresses all over the world. One Monday morning there was a typical collection of 419 emails in this author's inbox. There was one from 19-year-old Martha Bamba and her $10 million of hot money. Another was from brother and sister Williams and Suzan Alfarouk, orphaned by war, trying to deal with their $18.5 million which was left by their deceased shipping-magnate dad. All three were looking for an adoptive parent to help handle their cash and further their studies. Terminally-ill Doris Moore had also made contact, with the help of God, from the Ivory Coast where she was languishing in her hospital bed. She desperately needed the help of a fellow committed Christian to send her late husband's cash to somewhere it could be used for God's work, preferably an orphanage. Doris, from Kuwait, explained that her late husband, Kevin, had worked for the Kuwaiti Embassy in the West African country. Before he died he had provided for their future security by depositing $2,800,000 in a security box. If you answered her heartfelt plea for help, a second email seeking the name and address of "the servant of God" who had replied, would be sent. She explained this was needed to bestow power of attorney over the box and its contents. Once the details were supplied, in reply would come a copy of a 'Certificate of Deposit' from the United Trust and Securities Company in Abidjan. It came complete with stamps and signatures, including one from the deceased Kevin Moore. Surrounded, as she was, by her late husband's greedy relatives, the good Christian Doris Moore asked her fellow Christian to partake in a few white lies to ensure the money would reach a place where it could benefit God's work. Firstly, there were the contents of the box which were officially listed as containing family valuables and medical equipment. The $2.8 million, the real contents, was a secret. Then there was the importance of making sure her grasping relatives didn't find out about her scheme. The sentiments expressed and the apparently covert nature of the communications helped to build up the burgeoning relationship and the shared trust. Indeed by Wednesday evening, three emails later, it had become a conspiratorial partnership. 'Doris' even supplied a picture of herself as a hospital patient, complete with a respirator. It was probably culled from an internet news source.

The train of correspondence then switched to the United Trust and Securities Company. Director of Operations, Dr Blaise Konan, promised to organise the tricky business of shipping the box from West Africa to Ireland. Dr Konan sent a businesslike email, complete with an attached scanned copy of 'A Letter of Authorisation' from the Ministry of Justice, signed by poor Doris. Also attached was the new 'Ownership Certificate'. It detailed Doris's new friend as the owner of the box held by the firm. On request Dr Konan also sent a scanned copy of his badly forged Ivory Coast passport. Everything seemed to be going smoothly. A trunk full of US dollars, until recently owned by a woman who was now on death's door, would soon be on its way to Ireland.

Then there was a hitch. The insurance policy had just run out. There was also the fee for the courier. "I HAVE ENQUIRED FROM THE INSURANCE COMPANY AND WAS MADE KNOW THAT THE INSURANCE INDOMITABLE BOND COST TWO THOUSAND SIX HUNDRED AND TWENTY FIVE EURO (2,625EURO). THE DIPLOMATIC COURIER SHIPMENT COST IS FOUR THOUSAND FIVE HUNDRED EURO (4,500EURO)," wrote Dr Konan.

From opening the initial email it had taken just four days to the first request for money. This is the point when the scam becomes real. The targets are asked to send cash by money transfer. Even as the emails went back and forth the con-artists constantly tried to make contact over the phone. Presumably the scammers wanted to lay it on thick and fast and even speed things up if possible, but their command of English was so poor all attempts at conversation failed.

By now 'Doris' was too sick to send emails herself. Instead, another co-conspirator, attractive, 22-year-old nurse Charlotte, took over the job. She responded enthusiastically to a picture request from the potential victim. She was pictured posing in a tight-fitting evening dressing with a slit cut high to the top her thigh. It was all getting hot and heavy with the scammers. Charlotte got involved in some virtual flirting while asking for updates on the transaction because she wanted to ease poor Doris' worries. Dr Konan helpfully suggested that the money should be made in two separate payments, in case the transfer company started asking questions. He sent scans of identity cards of the people who were to collect the money. It is possible the photographs were actually those of the scammers.

In reply, Dr Konan was given fake money transfer control numbers and a scan of a fake receipt. The forgery was admittedly a bit of an amateur job. When they went to claim their cash from a Western Union agent somewhere in The Ivory Coast they were turned away. Even so, there was no sense of the scammers showing any fear of being reported to the authorities. They continued to try and cajole their would-be victim into transferring money to Africa.

Dr Konan was immediately back on the email. He advised: "THIS TO COMFIRM TO YOU THE RECEIPT OF YOUR MAIL ALONG WITH THE INFORMATIONS REGARDS TO THE TRANSFER BUT ALSO TO INFORM YOU THAT OUR SECRETARY HAS GONE FOR THE MONEY AND WAS TOLD THAT IT HAS NOT BEEN TRANSFERED YET S THE INFORMATINS ARE INVALID. PLEASE RECONFIRM FROM THE AGENT AND LET ME KNOW AS WE ARE ARRANGING FOR THE SHIPMENT TO BE EFFECTIVE AS SOON AS THE MONEY IS RECEIVED."

The Director of Operations wasn't happy with the confusion. Eventually the penny must have dropped and he made vague threats of calling in the police. Ironically, he seemed upset that someone would send him a fake letter: "YOU MUST UNDERSTAND THAT YOU ARE DEALING WITH INTELLIGENT PEOPLE THAT HAS BEEN UNDER THIS COMPANY FOR MORE THAN SIX YEARS. MIND YOU, YOU HAVE NOT SEND ANY MONEY TO ANY WESTERN UNION AND NOTE THAT WITH THIS WESTERN UNION PAPER YOU USED IN FORGING A

TRANSFER, I MIGHT CREATE A VERY BIG
PROBLEM FOR YOU BY CALLING MY MEN IN USA
TO GET YOU ARRESTED THROUGH SCOT YARD
POLICE. ANYWAY, BE VERY VERY CAREFUL IN
WHAT EVER YOU ARE DOING THATS MY ADVICE
TO YOU AND DO NEVER USE A FIRM LIKE
WESTERN UNION TO CREATE PROBEM FOR
YOURSELF. LOOKING AT THE PAPER YOU SEND IT
LOOK LIKE WHERE A KID IS JOKING. OK HAVE A
GOOD DAY.   REGARDS, DR BLAISE KONAN.
DIRECTOR, UTSC, ABIDJAN CI."

Realising the would-be victim was online at the time,
with an instant messenger turned on, the scam artist
switched to sending live messages. The tone was now
aggressive and threatening. "You must be a stupid
person indeed. Do I look like an idiot like you who take
his precious time in searching for western union money
transfer paper sheet," he wrote. "Ok I promised you
that I am going to send these paper to the authority and
will let you know the out come. Watch and see the
scotland yard police." This was the communication
from Dr Konan, who clearly wasn't going to put his
hands up and admit being a con-artist.

The caper with Konan and Doris Moore was internet
horseplay. It is better known among the white knights
of the internet as scam-baiting and the real person
behind Konan and Doris had walked right into the trap.
There are people who take it half-seriously, working
hard to get the 419ers to send pictures of themselves in
stupid and ridiculous poses. It can be an entertaining
way of avoiding work in the office and morally justified
on the grounds that while the 419ers are wasting their
time a real victim is not being targeted. For the real
victims, however, 419 scams are not a joke. Just as
amateur scam-baiters have set up websites dedicated to

having fun at the scammer's expense, there are other people who treat it as a serious fraud. Ultrascan is a private investigation firm which has built up a vast database of the various 419 scammers. The Dutch company has collected details of where they operate from and the techniques they use. Frank Englesman, an investigator with the company, has 12 years experience probing the 419 scammers, many of whom are based in Holland. Scam-baiting aside, the 419ers can sometimes be extremely dangerous people. Victims who are persuaded to travel to Nigerian, Ghana or The Ivory Coast are gambling with their lives.

"There have been significant numbers of murders, maybe 20. We expect more kidnaps and that type of thing in Cote D'Ivoire. We see a lot of foreigners going there. The victim is not willing to pay or cannot afford to pay a single cent anymore. He is in a foreign country and these fraudsters have other connections, with other types of criminals," explained Frank.

Once a foreign victim turns up he or she could be the subject of an auction between crime gangs. Businessman James Lafferty from County Clare found out the hard way. The 48-year-old company director was well-known in his native county where he had been the Chairman of the County Clare Ladies Football board. He coached teams, including one which won the under-16 All-Ireland final. The grey-haired football fanatic was a popular figure who is well able to talk. His construction business was involved with various projects, including one at Dublin Airport. In 2007 business, however, had not being going well. He left home in Clare for a break in London. It was a bolt from the blue when he suddenly hit the international headlines as a kidnap victim rescued at gunpoint by police in the Ghanian capital of Acra. It later emerged that Lafferty had travelled to the

West African state in November after being sucked into a deal by a 419 operation. Initial reports suggested he had been scammed in a honey-trap and had lost 200,000. On his safe return home, Lafferty offered a more considered version of events in which he admitted: "I was in a bullin' mad lunatic of a fit, I didn't even tell my wife. It was lunacy." In an interview with the local *Clare Champion* newspaper he laughed at reports he had been lured to Africa by a woman. "Chasing women in Ghana for money would have been a bit of a joke. There were no women in Ghana. End of story," he said.

Lafferty was lucky to survive the escapade in which he was held at gunpoint in a hotel room by kidnappers, who demanded €500,000 for his release. A man called Stanley had persuaded the Clare man to make the trip. "The biggest joke of it all was they pulled out the gun, put two bullets into it and said 'we want $500,000'. I looked at them and I said 'of all the people in Ireland you picked, you picked the poorest man in Ireland'." Lafferty said that over the course of the next five days he negotiated the kidnappers down to a sum of $12,000. He persuaded one of the kidnappers to text the name and number of the hotel to the Gardaí in Ennis, telling them it was his wife, Ann. His local police made contact with their colleagues in Ghana where the police came to Lafferty's rescue.

"I was on the phone to Ann about the money coming through when the Ghanaian police opened up the door. Stanley was there lying on the bed with a 'James Lafferty and Associates' top on him," he said. Lafferty never revealed how much he lost, but denied it was anywhere near the €200,000 that had been reported in Irish newspapers.

James Lafferty came face-to-face with the 419ers and lived to tell the tale. But not everyone has to be in physical contact with them to feel intimidated by the gangsters. The scammers can add a significant level of menace to their messages if they need to keep a victim compliant. A Japanese woman, Yuko, who was targeted in a romance version of the 419 fraud ended up being terrified for her safety. Like Dr Blaise Konan, her tormentor denied being a con-artist when confronted with the obvious truth. When Yuko found that her local police had little enthusiasm to investigate she turned to Ultrascan, making contact with Englesman.

The Japanese woman's story had begun with a typical 'inheritance scam' story, often used by the 419ers. In her email to Englesman she explained: "I am a Japanese woman living in Tokyo. I was contacted by the person called Michael Sanders [sic] by msn.match.com. Our conversations by emails started in late January of 2006. He told me he is a banker of Barkley [sic] London. He was looking for a business partner and he wanted to be like a Mr. Trump, a millionaire. Well, he started his conversation how he is doing at Barkley [sic] bank. He told me that there is a huge inheritance (US$43.6million) in the Barkley [sic] bank untouched for several years." It took some persuasion but Saunders managed to get Yuko to agree to accept the money on their behalf. Once the deal was done, he promised, they could live together in happiness. After all he loved the woman he had met through the internet.

The next step was to ask Yuko to pay taxes that were due on the inheritance. An official looking letter was sent to her by a 'Mrs Catherine Packer' explaining the amount that had to be paid to HM Revenue. Although she was nervous about handing over the money, Saunders used his skills to persuade Yuko to go ahead with the transaction, even sending her a Saint

Valentine's Day gift. She continued her story: "So I paid that amount to through [sic] Western Union on February 03 and February 06. Mrs Catherine Packe contacted me again assuring me my name was duly registered. However to transfer the funds to Japan, she asked for STG£7,100 for transaction fee. So I paid again through the Western Union in February 12, and 13. On Feb 14, I received a present (Champaign bottle, flowers, teddy bear, candy) from Michael Saunders [sic] for Valentine's Day saying he loves me and appreciated what I did."

It was an expensive Valentine's Day gift for Yuko. Saunders continued to mercilessly exploit his victim's vulnerability. The scammers don't stop until they know their victim has been bled dry. The first request for money was soon followed by another. This time it was for STG£33,000. Again Saunders turned on the charm and pressure to ensure the victim coughed up her hard-earned savings: "I had an argument with Michael Sanders [sic], but you know he persuade me to keep saying he loves me, we are together.... whatever....   So I wired STG£33,000 through the bank. The beneficiary's name I wired to was 'AJR International & Financial Services', AIB Bank, Western Retail Park, Blanchards-town, Dublin 15, Ireland."

Sure enough there were yet more problems with the transaction. Saunders said that a deal also had to be struck with the Nigerian government. He said they had to be paid a cut of the funds. Then a Western Union transfer was somehow stolen: "I waited and waited for the transactions to be completed to transfer the funds to my bank account. Nothing. I called Michael Sanders [sic] about what happened to the transferring money to my account. He said that Ministry of Nigeria is busy and somebody of his relatives died recently and cannot sign the agreement now. So he asked me to wait and be patient."

As more requests were made for cash, Yuko eventually realised she had been conned. It is a horrifying moment when someone realises that a person they had trusted has in reality been a liar and a cheat from the very beginning. "Now I found myself, I am in trouble after paying more than UKP50,000..... which is fortune I saved this money working for 20 years. I contacted one of my friends here and he told me that it is a Nigeria 419 scam," she wrote.

Yuko had made her last payment in April 2006, but hadn't told 'Saunders' she knew he was a fraudster. He continued to post messages looking for cash, cajoling her and trying to manipulate her emotions. He said: "All I explained to you yesterday was going into your first ear and coming out of the other, you don't listen to me. A good wife should love and listen to her man, a good wife is by her man in good times and bad, besides this is not a bad time, its the fee to release the funds we are paying for which altogether is less than 2% of the funds. Yuko, you know you can't get this opportunity anywhere, never, this is a lucky chance for us, do you want to keep working for that company all your life? Or do you want to assist me finalize this one problem and make us a rich couple?"

The stress of keeping up contact with the scammers in the hope that the police would organise a sting operation was taking its toll on the Japanese victim. "Am I going to be killed by these scammers because I do not pay money? Or because I am ignoring them? Are they going to send someone to find me and threat to the death? I am getting scared now. Will you please give me some advice?," Yuko asked in an email to Englesman.

Although thousands of miles apart from the

scammers, Yuko was in just as much physical danger as Lafferty had been. Englesman later commented: "We try to coach the victim. Most of them want to commit suicide when they are Japanese. We have to keep them busy. If they have no opportunity to go over their story for the police, they will keep on worrying and get mental problems."

She ignored Saunders final mail. "Dear Yuko, How stupid can you be? What is wrong with you? What is Nigeria scammer? Are you ok? If someone is saying this to you then you are getting the wrong information my dear, this is the way you have ended our love we shared, our destiny Yuko, I have finally made it and I am only asking for you to allow me prove myself Yuko, I have the money to pay you. I am doing great now Yuko and it is because you made this thing work this is why I am able to get to this status. I still love you Yuko and not because you helped me. I am caucasian white not a Nigerian scammer. I am rich now Yuko and because you helped me start off this transaction, you made it happen and I want you back now my love and stop this nonsense. Withdraw your words now and I will love you and give you all I have, I am real Yuko. If you doubt it please fly to Maldives now and meet me where I am on holidaying."

The email provides an invaluable insight into the scammers' mindset – even when it is obvious the well of cash has run dry they never come clean to their victims. Unlike Lafferty, Yuko didn't accept the offer to travel abroad to meet the scammer. Englesman advised her to contact both the police and the Irish embassy to try and recover the STG£33,000 she had sent to the AIB account in Dublin, Ireland.

"In the end the police finally helped her. I gave her the name and the address of somebody in the guards in

Ireland. I gave her the email of somebody in the bank. From there it was supposed to be handled by someone in the bank. In these types of cases banks don't want any type of media exposure," said Englesman. "Once any cash is transferred to Nigeria it is gone forever. There have been money transfers and swift bank transfers recovered because there has been instant police action. If you're fast enough, like three to four days after the transfer, you can still block the money and get it back."

In Yuko's case the money trail had already gone cold. There was, however, a case in Holland where a woman working for the 419ers had received about €500,000 in her account. The police were able to freeze the money that was still there, according to Englesman.

Unfortunately Yuko lost her life savings and she is not alone. According to Englesman's estimates, the Japanese woman was one of thousands of people who lost a total of $3.8 billion to the 419ers in 2006. In the absence of any official statistics on the size and effect of the 419 scams, Dutch investigators have come up with the best guess. They suggest that the scammers have stolen $28 billion since the 1980s. "There are about 20,000 to 30,000 new users of the internet in the world. We should protect them also," he said.

The number of active scammers is conservatively thought to number at least 300,000 and could be as high as one million and growing every year. Of those, there are 18,000 based in Western Europe who work full-time at scams. Englesman explained how some of the estimates of the scale of 419 scams are being formulated: "They [the Nigerian authorities] sampled all the outgoing mail for a month from Lagos. They caught about €2 billion worth of fake cheques."

It is a problem that police forces and governments

have failed to get to grips with in any meaningful way. About 35 scammers could be singled out as 'Mr Bigs', according to Englesman, but even targeting these individuals alone would not reduce the level of fraud. "Let's say if you arrest one and convict him for 20 years. That wouldn't stop the organisation because it is an open source, anybody from 12 to 60 can go on," he said.

The 419ers are a community with their own set of rules, honour codes and hierarchy. Englesman described one multi-millionaire scammer who is a major figure and has expanded his network throughout the world. "He started off in 2003 with 800 people in his scam-ring in Europe and Nigeria. Now he has more than 3,500 scammers under his command in Asia, Europe, Africa. He is even investing in countries such as Malaysia and Thailand where it is dangerous for fraudsters to operate because of the harsh penalties and prison systems. He sends people there to grow his networks. It's not like he's a stupid guy. He has the skills of an accountant. We found records that he plans his book-keeping until 2011. He travels to Madrid, Dubai, London. He keeps doing scams himself with the million dollar victims. It's a matter of honour."

Even though this Mr Big has millions of dollars at his fingertips, there is no question of his walking away from fraud and joining the legitimate business world. "This same guy, every month, he stills scams a Chinese couple in New York. The husband was scammed for three to four years, lost all their money. The wife said 'now we know, forget about it' but he doesn't stop. These people when they are two years hooked they are completely brainwashed. Every two weeks she gives him $50 so he cannot lose anymore. This man, who is one of the top bosses in the world in the 419 scams, makes the effort to get the $50 sent to him wherever he is. You know how much is left when you wire $50? Something like $31. It's not about the amount of money it's also a matter of honour. It's also an honour if someone loses their house or is evicted, that type of thing."

It seems that just as the scam-baiters collect their trophies, so do the 419ers. The scammers go to great lengths to set up their victims. Fake 'tax offices' operate in Holland and the UK where foreign targets are brought to pay for certificates or pay tax bills to free the non-existent stash of money. These locations are carefully chosen. Usually they are close to the international airport. The scammers will rent meeting rooms in a building that houses some official office, giving the location an air of authenticity. The victim, who they are possibly trying to lure abroad, is met by well-dressed officials and taken to the location by limo. Everything is made to look as if it is above board.

Any meaningful effort to make the 419ers work harder for their money will take an unprecedented level of co-operation between various police forces, government agencies and financial institutions all over the world. Banks and money transfer companies such as Moneygram and Western Union do try and warn their customers when they have information about con-artists. But in reality the scammers can adapt too quickly for any security measures to be effective for long: "Most of the time when you try to send money, they ask you questions. They try to warn clients. The last victim I had in London, for instance, she went four times to send a total of STG£8,000. At the fifth time she went to the Western Union office she was told 'we cannot send money to this person in Holland anymore.' Western Union does have a database of people whose names are used a lot. Of course it's never up-to-date and Nigerian networks are too large. If one name doesn't work in five or ten minutes they have another name. This was quite an experience for this woman. She doesn't want to go near a Western Union office again," explained Englesman, with measured understatement.

The 419 scammers can change and adapt their tactics quicker than any official agency or corporate body can introduce counter-measures. Englesman, who probably knows more about 419 scams than anyone else, believes the situation needs urgent international action. The Dutch man argues for a non-governmental agency to be set up specifically to combat 419 fraud. "This type of crime network works too fast. The decision cycles of governments and large companies are too late to ever win over the Nigerian scammers. We know people fall for it so we should do something about it. As soon as police get a little bit structured in organising this problem the crime network adapt very fast and try to get local front runners."

At best, the 419 scams can provide some light entertainment for idle office workers willing to indulge in some scam-baiting. At worst, the cash being generated by the frauds is being channelled into international criminal networks. While the initial emails from the keyboard kid may seem amateurish, they are sent by organisations with capabilities that rival any of the dangerous crime syndicates involved in drugs, guns and smuggling. There have also been murders and suicides as a result of 419 frauds. People have been left financially ruined after falling under the spell of the scam-artists. Every day there are 20,000 to 30,000 new users logging onto the internet. At the moment the only thing standing between their cash and the 419ers is common sense.

SEVEN

The Cash Carousel

Carousel VAT fraud is the ultimate get rich quick scheme. It ticks all the boxes for someone with a business mind who doesn't actually want to work all that hard. It is the perfect quick fix for individuals who crave the international jet-set lifestyle. In the European Union fraudsters and criminals who have executed the VAT scam can count themselves among the super rich. They have been able to divert a fast-flowing pipeline of cash into their pockets with ridiculous ease.

VAT is a consumer tax. It is collected by VAT registered traders on their supplies of goods and services. They in turn then pass it on to the government. In the simplest form of the Carousel VAT fraud, a trader imports goods free of VAT, then sells them on to someone else, with the tax charged, and duly disappears without passing on the tax monies to Revenue. If ever there was a licence to print money then it has to be the Carousel VAT fraud. It has been made possible by the internet, email and the increased speed of international financial transactions that comes with it. It has also been made possible by the failure of the EU to harmonise VAT rates between the various member states. There are a huge variety of VAT rates between all the various countries which are applied to hundreds of thousands of different products. For instance in Ireland nappies have a 0% VAT rate, while most other goods incur a 21% rate. In the UK the standard rate is 17.5%, while in Denmark it is 25%. To ease trade between member states Brussels has insisted that all goods exported in international trades are exempt from VAT.

In the legitimate business world the necessity of dealing with tax officials and the prospect of the complicated task of making VAT-returns created a specialist niche for tax advisers. It has also created an opening for the specialist fraudster willing to take the time and make the effort to learn the system. Under the current system the import companies selling on the goods act as the tax collector. They are then supposed to pay back the VAT to their country's Exchequer. The fraudsters, who are in control of the import company, simply collect the VAT money from their customers and then disappear.

The Carousel scam is based on the fact that an EU company can reclaim the VAT paid on goods if they are sold to a company based in a different European Union member state. The EU's current system, which exempts exporting firms from paying the tax, was only intended to be a temporary measure, a transitional system. The plan was to move VAT payments to the so-called "origin system", in which VAT is paid in the country where the goods are first bought. This would mean that the same rates of VAT would have to apply to the same products in every EU member state. As a result there would be no zero rating for the goods when they are imported into the UK and no right to reclaim VAT from the Exchequer at the point of export. There would no longer be an opportunity for the Carousel VAT fraud.

Over the last decade the scam has developed various standard operating procedures. It involves setting up a minimum of three fake companies, at least two of which are based in a different EU state. Then consignments of high-value goods, such as micro-chips or mobile phones, are 'sold' between the three companies, one after the other. The company in the middle of the chain reclaims the VAT it supposedly paid on the transaction from revenue and then disappears. For instance Firm A based in Ireland exports STG£10 million worth of mobile phones to Firm B in the UK. Firm B then sells the consignment to Firm C. The sale from B to C is within the UK and therefore attracts a VAT rate of 17.5% so Firm C pays STG£11.75 million for the phones. Firm B is acting as the collector of the VAT for the UK Exchequer and is supposed to pass the STG£1.75 million onto the Inland Revenue. Firm C then sells the phones to Firm A which is outside the UK. This is an export transaction so it is exempt from VAT. Under the system Firm C is then entitled to reclaim from the UK government the £1.75 million VAT it supposedly paid to Firm B for the consignment of phones. When the scam works, as it usually does, Firm C gets the money from Inland Revenue before anybody realises that Firm B hasn't passed on the VAT. Firms B and C then disappear. Firms B and C are the so-called 'missing traders'. The companies are bought off the shelf and set up using bogus documents and false identities or dupes are used as directors. Firm A now has its consignment of phones back and starts the procedure again with two new companies Firms D and E. The trading has no commercial value. Its sole purpose is to defraud money from the taxman. In the more sophisticated version of the scam, the consignment can be passed through several companies, each one of which will disappear with the rebated VAT money.

The tax bill left behind by the fraudsters could run from a few thousand to several million euros. All the inspectors have to follow is a complex paper trail, full of cul-de-sacs. To follow the paper is to enter a bureaucratic maze laden with false leads that suck up investigative resources for a case which may never be solved. Even if the fraudsters are tracked down there is no certainty there will be enough proof to secure a criminal conviction. The first sign of the fraud is usually detected deep in the bloodless heart of a government tax department, when a previously anonymous company is suddenly involved in multi-million euro worth of international export trades. By that stage it is too late and the fraudsters have long gone. To all intents and purposes it is the perfect crime. It is best known as the Carousel VAT fraud, but more formally as Missing Trader intra-Community fraud (MTIC).

In early 2005, Carousel VAT fraud was costing the United Kingdom's Exchequer two pence in every pound of revenue – the criminals were taking two per cent of the country's income from tax. The scale of the 'industry' is truly staggering. According to figures from the UK's Exchequer, an estimated €75 billion in fraudulent transactions is moved around every year. It is equivalent to the cash spent on the Common Agricultural Policy by the entire European Union. The best bit is that the clever fraudsters can still get away with it, even if they get caught

In the last two decades the criminals have refined the operation to the point where 'virtual' carousels are set up using fake companies and fake invoices to pay for non-existent goods in transactions that never actually happen. The con-artists pocket the reclaimed VAT on transactions that sometimes only happen on paper. A new bogus company is set up and the chain of transactions start again. The goods travel around in a circle, hence the term carousel. Once a Carousel operation is up and running it becomes a simple job to suck the cash from government coffers. One consignment of mobile phones was found to have been re-crossing the Swiss-German border for five years, during which €165 million was reclaimed from the German government. The more sophisticated operations use an entire string of companies, all controlled by the same group or person. The VAT is reclaimed at every point along the Carousel. For instance a non-existent consignment of micro-chips, worth €1,000,000, with a VAT rate of 17.5%, nets €175,000 every time it is 'sold' on through each step of the chain. As customs and revenue officials began to put mobile phone and computer companies under greater scrutiny, the fraudsters are suspected of having turned to other high-value goods such as razors, ink and even pornography. Money is funnelled through untraceable accounts in tax havens all over the world to places such as Dubai, Singapore, Curacao and the more prosaic, but equally effective, Isle of Man. The authorities in such places care little about the source of a customer's money and investigators face long and difficult battles to seize ill-gotten gains. In any case the cash can be quickly transferred and moved on well before the authorities even get close.

In 2006, Her Majesty's Customs began to get traction on a group of VAT fraudsters in Britain. They realised that several individual fraudsters all used the same bank on the Caribbean island of Curacao. The First Curacao International Bank held 2,500 accounts used by British-based fraudsters, to fund each turn of the VAT Carousel. The money made on the fraud was then invested in off-shore banking centres. This single bank was responsible for channelling 40 per cent of the money estimated to have been stolen. The bank is reported to have warned its clients well in advance to move their cash before a penny was seized.

The scale of VAT fraud is so high in the UK that it has skewed the country's trade figures. In early 2006, according to export figures, it looked as if trade between Britain and the little desert kingdom of Dubai had really taken off. Dubai, with its population of just 900,000 had become the UK's tenth largest trading partner. In one month alone there was official trade between the two countries worth STG£325 million. But then it was realised the figures represented the complex carousel of siphoned-off tax-payers' cash that was being circulated between the two countries. Consignments of goods were simply being sent in a constant loop between the two countries. There were reports of Asian-run factories in Dubai changing the serial numbers on mobile phones, as the same batch went back and forth between the two countries.

Different individuals in various EU countries first began to work out how to execute the VAT Carousel fraud around the mid-1990s. In Ireland the beginnings of the fraud had its origins in a former tax official who went to work as a financial adviser in the private sector. His inside knowledge and expertise equipped other people with all they needed to start their own Carousel. The first known VAT fraud in Ireland involved a number of well-connected and capable business people.

Builder and businessman Daniel O'Connell set up a computer component business in April 1996, with his financial partner Bernadette Devine. O'Connell was brash and flash and well-known in his native Limerick. Devine had found success across the water in the UK, where she had originally worked as a nurse. A native of Keash, County Sligo, she became involved in politics and was elected a Tory councillor for Ealing, West London. When the pair went into business together, O'Connell had already bought five off-the-shelf companies. In 1996 he used them to buy high-value consignments of computer micro-chips in the UK. His plan was to then sell them in Ireland. Devine set up offices for the new company in Perivale, West London, under the banner Keash Systems International. Soon enough there were staggering sums of money flowing through the company coffers. By 1999, their various companies had handled STG£100 million worth of Intel Pentium Two processor chips. O'Connell, then a 47-year-old father of two, knew how to enjoy the fruits of his success. He decorated his mistress in diamonds from royal jewellers Asprey and Garrard and was planning a life of retirement in the sun. He toured the Bahamas looking for a suitable hideaway. Devine was equally adept at spending her share of the cash. She used it to fund the sort of lifestyle usually enjoyed by Premiership footballers and A-list movie stars. The 34-year-old bought six properties, as well as a luxury country club called Ballymote Castle in Sligo, and drove a Ferrari Testarossa.

On the surface, Devine and O'Connell looked like high-flyers, who had entered the international trade in computer micro-chips at the right time. In reality the entire operation was a scam. They had been faking the re-export of mirco-chips, claiming back the VAT from the bogus sale and then selling off the goods at a profit in legitimate transactions. The net had been slowly closing on Devine and O'Connell as, apparently acting on a tip-off, UK customs began to investigate the series of high-value trades associated with their companies. In December 1998, the fraud briefly stopped after an article in an Irish newspaper about the existence of VAT fraud in the import and export of micro-chips. The fraudsters must have feared that the authorities were about to act but nothing happened and they decided to

get back into action. The scam was just about to re-start
in March 1999, when Her Majesty's revenue men made
their move against the pair. They raided O'Connell's
hotel bedroom at Grosvenor House Hotel in London's
Park Lane. The revenue investigators found a surprised
O'Connell still in bed in the Crown Suite with his
mistress. More importantly they also found diaries
containing references to suppliers and purchasers. They
also discovered airline tickets used as proof of export.

The subsequent trial, which began in February 2000,
was a complex affair and lasted six long months. There
were huge volumes of paper evidence and hundreds of
witnesses called to testify to every detail of the intricate
fraud. The first witness was a director of a company
that specialised in selling off-the-shelf companies and
his testimony was heard over two days. He gave
evidence about the five limited companies which
O'Connell had set up to buy the computer chips from
London dealers as part of the scam. O'Connell used a
myriad of front companies to hide his dealings,
produced fake paperwork and deliberately bought
misleading airline tickets, while he was searching the
Bahamas for the ideal hideaway. Every bit of evidence
had to be supported by a prosecution witness.

The majority of the STG£100 million worth of Intel
Pentium Two processor chips was brought by a trusted
employee to a warehouse in southern England. The
ownership of the chips changed to another company
run by Bernadette Devine. O'Connell's firm 'kept' the
VAT on the transactions which amounted to millions of
pounds. The chips were then sold off separately.
O'Connell and his associates were accused of pocketing
STG£20 million from the fraud by reclaiming the VAT
from the transaction between companies which they
controlled.

In the witness box O'Connell claimed that a former government minister, Michael Keating, was the real mastermind behind the fraud. He maintained that his problems began when he borrowed IR£150,000 from Keating to bail out one of his building firms. When he tried to back out of the computer chip business, he said he was threatened by Keating: "He told me I would be in a wheelchair. He said 'We know where you live. We know where your wife and children are.'"

A UK customs investigator said in court that the only reason Keating was not in the dock was because the extradition treaty between Ireland the UK did not include fiscal crimes. He added that Keating would be arrested if he ever set foot in the UK.

The jury didn't believe O'Connell's story that he was forced into a life of crime and he was convicted. In August 2000, at Middlesex Guildhall Crown Court, he was jailed for eight years.

The trial judge, William Rose, told O'Connell: "The fraud in which you played a major part was on a totally massive scale and its result has been to set at a loss to Her Majesty's Customs and Excise and therefore the public purse of a sum in excess of STG£20 million. I have little doubt that had you not been apprehended as you were, the frauds would have continued using the number of companies that had been specially prepared for the purpose and that you would have continued playing your part of continuing to relieve the public purse of huge sums of money."

Michael Keating, a former Fine Gael minister, stuck to his vehement denials. He even went as far as saying that the statement by the customs' agent was an abuse of court privilege.

A few years later, Keating's denials looked paper thin when the truth about the sinister backgrounds of some of his 'business' associates began to emerge. In 2002, he was forced to settle a tax bill with Ireland's Criminal Assets Bureau, who had originally hit him with a demand for €1 million. He was confronted about his association with Peter Bolger, a convicted fraudster based in Dublin. The ex-Fine Gael man was also challenged about a meeting he'd had with George Mitchell, otherwise known as The Penguin, one of Ireland's biggest drug dealers. Bolger was Mitchell's money launderer and on one occasion, in 1997, Keating had been arrested in possession of money drafts made out to the drug dealer. The association with such highly-placed international criminals wiped away any shred of credibility Keating had left. It also lent a ring of truth to O'Connell's outlandish claims of intimidation at the hands of the ex-Government Minister.

O'Connell's partner-in-fraud, Bernadette Devine, then aged 34, was also brought separately to trial. She had used false paperwork to claim products were sent to Ireland, when in fact they were sent back to the London office via a company in Wales. At the peak of the scam, it was claimed in court, Devine was raking in STG£1 million a month of British taxpayer's money. Needless to say, Devine didn't go quietly. Halfway through the trial there were doubts over her mental stability. Two psychiatrists decided that she was psychotic, but another two said she was fine. Devine was found fit to plead and the case continued.

Again, a jury, which had sat through an incredibly complex trial, returned a verdict of guilty. Devine was sentenced to six years behind bars for tax evasion. Two years later, in 2003 Devine was the subject of a confiscation hearing. It came after a lengthy investigation into her assets. She was also ordered to pay almost STG£1.5 million in fines. The case had been the UK's largest Carousel VAT fraud and was heralded as a landmark result in combating the fraudsters.

Daniel O'Connell and Bernadette Devine's VAT Carousel scam came to its abrupt end just when another young millionaire with Limerick connections was getting into his stride. Dylan Louis Creaven was an ambitious Irish businessman determined to carve out a successful niche for himself in the ever burgeoning computer and technology industry. The young entrepreneur, however, emerged as the unlikely focus of the biggest VAT fraud ever detected by the British authorities, even beating the record set by O'Connell and Devine.

Creaven grew up in the village of Newmarket-on-Fergus, a few miles south of Ennis and home to famous Dromoland Castle in County Clare, on Ireland's west coast. He is one of two boys and three girls born to parents Louis and Harriet. His father, Louis, is well-known in the local community. He was Chairman of the Mid Western Hospitals Development Trust which has raised a lot of money for medical services in the region. Louis also runs a successful aviation instruments business based in Shannon with another family member. As a youngster Creaven went to primary school in Shannon and later to Saint Flannan's College for his secondary education. Tall and athletic, young Dylan Creavan was a cocky, but likeable character who played rugby in Ennis. It would have been a comfortable life for young Creaven in which he lacked for nothing – he would have been far better off than many of his contemporaries.

In July 1996, then aged just 22, he rented a unit at the Clare Enterprise Centre in the town of Ennis. The centre is typical of such facilities set up to support young indigenous entrepreneurs. The rent would not have amounted to more than €12,000 a year. Many of the units would have been rented by craft workers and were subsidised by the State-run Shannon Development Agency. Full of confidence and with a charming manner, Creaven set up the company Silicon Technologies Europe. The plan was to custom-manufacture computers for clients. The following year, amid a great deal of media hype, Ennis was selected as Ireland's first Information Age town. Millions of euro was invested in the town's telecommunications infrastructure to ensure that the information technology experiment worked. Creaven, it seemed, had set up business in the right place – at the right time.

To describe his success as meteoric would be an understatement. From the County Clare backwaters, Creaven, by 2001, had grown his little start-up cottage enterprise to a company with a turnover of a staggering €416 million. Silicon Technologies now had offices in Singapore and Boston. The company was surfing the global IT bubble in an industry that was going through incredibly swift changes. Investors were climbing over each other to throw money at techie whiz-kids. It was nothing unusual for young IT entrepreneurs to become, suddenly, filthy rich. Creaven seemed to fit neatly into that category. Despite his massive success, Creaven was far from being a household name. He was however, known among those who traded in computer products such as micro-chips. In October 2002 he told an Irish trade magazine, *Computer Reseller News*, all about the secrets of his amazing financial success, presumably with a straight face.

"Spotting an untapped position, good planning, trusting your own judgement, not being risk averse, low paper clip bills and a sense of humour," he said. He also mentioned how he could solve the Rubik's Cube puzzle in 40 seconds, something that the world of computer geeks might be impressed by, if the size of his bank accounts left them unmoved.

But if Creaven was not a household name in Ireland he was certainly creating a local reputation. Such was his opulent lifestyle he had acquired the nickname 'Hollywood' from those more used to the down to earth surroundings of County Clare. In the same interview, when asked which he thought was the better status symbol, a car or a yacht, he replied: "You can throw a better party on a yacht." He played the part of the brash young buccaneer of the runaway Celtic Tiger economy. For Creaven, money was all about enjoying the status it conferred. He built a large house on the outskirts of Ennis and filled it with high-tech gadgets. He drove a top-of-the-range Mercedes and as a rugby fan was a sponsor of Garryowen Rugby Club, one of Limerick city's famous clubs. He was also a regular customer at the bar and restaurant in the upmarket tourist haunt, Dromoland Castle. With a string of racehorses to his name, Dylan Creaven was every inch the successful face of the country's new generation of confident, daring and rich young entrepreneurs.

'Hollywood' had greater social ambitions than just being a patron of Garryowen RFC. He set up home in the implausibly upmarket Knightsbridge, London. The huge mansion block, just down the road from Harvey Nichols, with views across Hyde Park, is home to some of Britain's most fashionable addresses. In 2007 apartments there were selling for €2.25 million. It was a suitable place for 'Hollywood' to enjoy his fabulous wealth when enjoying the diversions London has to offer. He even had his place in the sun, another luxury villa in Marbella worth €2.1 million. Creaven was a businessman on top of the world, enjoying the sumptuous fruit of his incredible success. In the same trade magazine interview, when asked which of the world's greatest software and computer giants he most aspired to be, he replied: "I plan to leave my own mark." His ego had matched his wealth and possibly his capacity for self-deception.

What 'Hollywood' Creaven failed to grasp is that sudden and vast wealth very often attracts curiosity from the authorities. The massive transactions between his company and traders in the UK that suddenly went missing had become a cause for concern for UK customs. On a number of occasions he was interviewed on their behalf by Irish Customs and Excise officers about his links with 'missing traders' in the UK. In early 1998, Customs raided his business premises in connection with an inquiry into another company with whom he had been trading to the tune of STG£250,000 a week. A man called Mark Humber was later jailed for six years at Manchester Crown Court for VAT fraud in connection with that investigation.

The Criminal Assts Bureau, then headed by Felix McKenna, began to take an interest in Silicon Technologies and Dylan Creaven. Previously, the official view had been that because no crime was being committed in Ireland, there was no point in investigating Irish-based Carousel VAT scammers. McKenna changed the official outlook and sought to co-operate with UK agencies.

The joint investigation into Creaven's Carousel scam was christened Operation Chipstick as the newly-formed Assets Recovery Agency (ARA) in the UK got their teeth into what was to be their biggest case. It took until November 2002, just a month after his trade magazine interview and not long after ordering a

€200,000 Mercedes, before Creaven was arrested in London. It was a dramatic moment. A squad of armed police officers, kitted out in full tactical body armour and helmets were used to stop his Range Rover at gunpoint. He was spread-eagled on the ground and the mobile phone was taken from his hand. With CAB and the ARA, planned raids at premises in the UK and Ireland went ahead including Silicon Technologies at the Clare Enterprise Centre, along with Creaven's house and his accountant's office. 'Hollywood' Creaven had to swap the luxury of Dromoland Castle and Knightsbridge for the more austere surrounds of Wandsworth Prison. Charged with fraud, totalling STG£240 million, he spent a year on remand as investigators picked their way through the complex scheme of missing trader transactions in which registered companies disappeared with the UK Exchequer's VAT cheques for millions of pounds. It was a classic Carousel fraud, but was immense in its complexity and its execution. Creaven was eventually released on bail after agreeing to surrender his passport.

'Hollywood' had no intentions of going down without a fight. He denied the fraud charges. In 2003 he successfully challenged the November 2002 search warrants used by the Criminal Assets Bureau. He claimed in the High Court that the seizure of company documents was illegal because the letters sent from the UK were defective. He also maintained that the search warrants issued in Ireland were invalid because they had been issued in the wrong District Court. It didn't prevent the ARA from going ahead with their prosecution although it meant that they couldn't use any evidence gleaned from documents found in the searches by the CAB officers.

In April 2005 Creaven went on trial at Blackfriars
Crown Court. Although originally charged with fraud
totalling STG£240 million when it came to trial he was
facing 28 specific charges relating to STG£14 million
worth of fraud. The ARA alleged that over a period of
time, 99 per cent of the business conducted by Silicon
Technologies Europe involved fraudulent transactions.
Creaven played the innocent abroad who had suddenly
found himself out of his depth, led astray by more
canny people. It was a stark contrast to his previous role
of a brash playboy. The 32-year-old claimed, without
providing any useful details, that he had been picked
on and lured by other individuals who were the real
culprits behind the Carousel fraud.

It was a complicated trial that lasted for four weeks.
The jury listened to turgid details of the mechanics of
Carousel fraud. It was alleged that Silicon Technologies
had supplied STG£1.6 billion worth of computer units.
The scam started slowly with STG£14 million worth of
transactions from September 1997 to February 1998
between Silicon Technologies and a UK firm that went
missing. One of the final series of transactions saw
STG£17 million being traded between Creavan's
company and another UK firm in just two days in early
2002. Almost all the customers the company had dealt
with in the UK subsequently disappeared, each owing
a tax liability to Her Majesty's Revenue Commissioners.
The prosecution counsel said that for a year Creaven
and his companies supplied "vast" consignments of
VAT-free chips to a "motley" array of off-the-shelf
firms. On the face of it, the missing-trader companies
had been set up to sell goods such as underwear, rum
and garden fencing. In reality, according to the
prosecution, the "ramshackle collection" of concerns
"existed only for fraud." David Cocks QC, told the jury

that once the companies had sold the high-value "processing units" to other firms, they disappeared with the VAT they had charged. In the meantime the missing cash had been sent "on instructions" to Creaven's firm.

For his part 'Hollywood' Creaven said that he never once suspected anything amiss, and was "distraught" to find himself in the dock. At times he appeared to break down and took a few moments to compose himself. Under cross examination Creaven was asked: "Now do you understand that the business you built was in fact based on fraudulent activity by persons in the United Kingdom?"

"Yes," came the reply. To a similar question he answered: "I can see that now. Yes, I can see that now."

The fact that his entire empire was based on fraud was pointed out in no uncertain terms. "I can see that now 99 per cent of the people that we dealt with, yes are absolutely missing traders. It was never brought to my attention at any level before this," he said.

Creaven claimed there were other people involved in the fraud and that he had been a victim of their manipulation. The seven women and five men on the jury who tried the month-long case, took eight hours, over two days, to clear him of all charges. As the verdict was returned, he buried his head in his hands and wept. He was not the only one weeping. The ARA had been fighting hard for its survival and badly needed a victory.

Even though they failed to get a conviction against Creavan, the Assets Recovery Agency, pushed by the Irish CAB officers, were determined to get some of the cash back. Despite his acquittal, they threatened to take a civil case against Creaven. This followed his admissions, under oath, that the source of his millions was as a result of missing trader fraud. Despite admitting his money came from fraud, during the criminal trial, he still wanted to hang onto it.

By this stage the UK's Assets Recovery Agency were under serious political pressure to perform and to get a result. It had been a fraught and expensive process to bring the criminal prosecution case which eventually failed. A lawyer working for the ARA, Diane Stanton, led the two-day negotiations to reach a settlement with Creaven. She later spoke to the BBC's *File on Four* about the final deal.

"There were about twelve people on either side. It was a little bit agitated; it had been an extremely long day and considering the settlement took place in September it was actually extremely warm as well, so everybody was feeling a bit groggy from the day. We as a team didn't break till about ten o'clock for something to eat, so everybody had sort of snacks when they could sort of fit them in around the mediation, so people were feeling a bit agitated up to that stage, so when they actually managed to get everything signed and everybody was happy, just total elation that we'd actually done it. Everybody was happy and we were actually going away from the settlement with a signed agreement that we could forward and enforce."

In the deal, Creaven had to pay back STG£18.5 million, but he walked away a free man. He had spent less than a year behind bars while on remand. The original amount which had been stolen was put at STG£240 million, but ARA investigators knew that the total was a lot higher. Although it was the ARA's biggest success, it was hard to portray the deal as anything other than a small victory as the fraudsters had been stripping cash from the Exchequer at an alarming rate. One series of transactions in just seven weeks, between Silcion Technologies and a missing trader, amounted to STG£300 million. Creaven and his company were supposedly shipping more computer components than even the biggest multi-national manufacturers based in Ireland. From Janaury 2001 until June 2002, his company supplied goods to the value of STG£1.6 billion.

In Ireland, the media spotlight was on Creaven when his racehorses were seized to be sold off by the Criminal Assets Bureau. There was a lot of sympathy for respected trainer RJ Osborne who owned five per cent of the Cardinal Syndicate which owned the horses. The other 95 per cent was in 'Hollywood's' hands. One of the horses auctioned off in Ireland by the CAB, 'Latino Magic', had won the McDonagh Handicap at the Galway Races in 2005. Even though he lost some of his prized assets, such as the Marbella villa, Creaven kept his Knightsbridge property and his house in Ennis. Reported comments by the then CAB chief, Felix McKenna, suggested that if the Clare man had stopped stealing sooner and moved his cash out of Ireland in early 2002 he would never have been caught. Such words from an experienced investigator would hardly have soothed 'Hollywood's sense of loss and his bruised ego.

Creavan's was not the only high-profile case to falter in the criminal courts. In a related trial at the same Blackfriars Crown Court, the prosecution of eight men and a woman in relation to a vast STG£100 million VAT fraud, was stopped by the judge. The attempted prosecution came after an investigation known as Operation Vitric. There had been a 40-day pre-trial hearing as the defence argued that Customs had failed to hand over to them all the documentation used by the prosecution. The main target of Operation Vitric was

businessman Neil David Lewis. He had been arrested
in Marbella and subsequently extradited to Britain. The
trial, along with Creaven's, was one of the first
prosecutions to go ahead after UK Customs undertook
a massive internal review. They wanted to prevent VAT
fraud trials collapsing due to Customs' failure to
disclose all evidence to the defence. In Operation Vitric,
despite the disclosure of thousands of pages of
evidence uncovered before the beginning of the
proceedings, more material continued to surface. The
judge said that the system had failed "to produce the
degree of efficient, exhaustive disclosure that a case of
this extreme complexity and massive scale demands."
The cases had collapsed under the weight of the 'paper
monsters'.

The case put into focus just how difficult it can be to
unpick a white collar fraud, committed by clever and
well-organised criminal gangs, with good business
administration skills. It also highlights that the risk
involved is very low for anyone with a criminal
mindset. By the time a Carousel VAT fraudster is
caught, millions have been salted away. At worst, they
face being forced to hand over some of their traceable
assets and spend a few years in an open prison. Once
the unpleasantness of dealing with the authorities is
over, they can retire to the sunny tax haven of their
choice and enjoy the pampered lifestyle of wealthy ex-
pats.

While 'Hollywood' Creaven's pride may have
demanded that he cling to the façade of an international
businessman, Riviera Ray Woolley had no such hang-
ups. When it came down to it, the Englishman had no
qualms about admitting that it was a scam. He didn't
care how he had ensured that he and his family had lifelong financial security. He commented: "You worked

hard seven days a week on-site all your life but now you're sitting pushing a few bits of paper around and making great money. I just thought 'this is great'. Anybody would."

In October 1999, he set up a company, Viltern, which was registered in Ireland with an office in the Harcourt Centre in Dublin's south city centre. It was first registered for VAT in Ireland in January 2001. He listed himself and his wife Bernadette as the only directors. At the time he was working as a pipe welder and lived in a council house in Stoke-on-Trent. The Staffordshire town later became synonymous with VAT fraud. At one point it was claimed in the media to have the highest concentration of mobile phone companies in the UK.

Viltern exported and imported mobile phones from Ireland to Riviera Ray's firms in Britain, one of which was called Roofsmart Limited. Viltern was subsequently described in court as an off-shore company "at the heart of the fraud". Two other businessmen and a solicitor were involved in the fraud with Woolley. He worked with Robert Garner from Stone in Staffordshire and they linked up with a gang which included businessman Duncan Evans and local solicitor, Paul Morris, who helped launder the cash for investment around the world.

The gang bought a bulk shipment of mobile phones from Spain and the Republic of Ireland and then sold them on to another company in the UK but they did not pay the Inland Revenue any VAT. Within just three months in 2000 their company racked up an astonishing STG£24 million in VAT debts to the Revenue. In its entire history Woolley's Roofsmart firm, put in just a solitary VAT return to the taxman – it was for a mere STG£273. Within just six months of trading across the Irish Sea, Riviera Ray's bogus firms had a turnover of

STG£218 million. From January 2000 to February 2001, Woolley went from driving a van, to owning a fleet of stunning cars that included a €156,000 Aston Martin, a convertible Ferrari worth €123,000, a limited edition Bentley Arnage worth €315,000 and a €22,000 Harley Davidson motorbike. As well as his cars Riviera invested in property in Marbella, Spain, including STG£600,000 in El Girasol restaurant. He was eventually arrested at Amsterdam's Schipol Airport following a business trip to Hong Kong and sent back to the UK.

In 2002, he was brought to court where a judge described him as a "skilful and elaborate" fraudster. During sentencing, the judge remarked that Woolley regarded STG£250,000 as "if it were loose change lost down the back of an armchair". Convicted of conspiracy to defraud the public revenue, Riviera Ray was sentenced to nine years in jail at Birmingham Crown Court in 2002. This was a record for tax fraud at the time. He also pleaded guilty to removing the proceeds of crime from British jurisdiction.

British Customs and Excise had spent years trying to track the illegal cash Woolley had spent on top-of-the-range cars, Spanish villas and restaurants with little success. They knew they'd only scraped the surface.

In February 2005 Riviera Ray walked out of an open prison at Sudbury near Uttoxeter, hailed a cab and disappeared from the country. The following month the court ruled that he must repay STG£9.5 million within 13 months or face a further four years in jail. Unsurprisingly, Woolley didn't give himself up in the month allowed by the judge. An international arrest warrant was issued for Woolley and Interpol was notified that he was a fugitive from justice.

The next time he turned up, it was in the five-star Marriot Hotel in Switzerland. He agreed to meet BBC reporter Justin Holwatt who had managed to get him on the phone. Riviera Ray admitted that he had gone on the run to Switzerland where he had been arrested for travelling on a false passport. However, he was released before British authorities could track him down because VAT fraud is not an extraditable offence under Swiss law. Asked about his role in the multi-million pound swindle Riviera Ray tried to claim that he thought his little company, which had a turnover twice that of Manchester United was a legitimate scheme. He commented: "You're looking at everything now with the benefit of hindsight I never had at the time. Looking at it from where I am now, knowing what I know now, yes, there was a fraud."

"Knowing what I knew then, no I didn't realise there was a fraud. I just thought, this is great, anybody would. If you were in my position you would think, 'this is fabulous'. I've got two children and a wife and I've now got security for my family for the rest of my life, that's my way of thinking. Security for my family – this is great; we don't need to worry anymore. It's not taxpayers' money; it's business profit – that's what I say."

Riviera Ray Woolley is still on the run and presumably enjoying the fruits of his ill-gotten gains.

The prospect of attaining such astronomical sums of cash means that the practice of Carousel VAT fraud is not restricted to such former up-standing members of the community as 'Hollywood' Creaven and Riviera Ray. Organised crime gangs and terror groups are well-positioned to make such scams pay well. The owners of legitimate companies can be forced or unwittingly used to take part in bogus Carousel VAT trades with companies controlled by the fraudsters. They are then left to carry the can when the tax inspectors come calling

for their cheque. A book-keeper linked to a number of
missing trader frauds in Glasgow went missing in 2006,
highlighting the involvement of more sinister types of
businessmen than a Stoke-on-Trent plumber.

The cold wet mud of west Dublin building sites is a
world away from jet-setting tours of Caribbean tax-
havens. It's a place where 'Hollywood' Creavan
wouldn't be seen dead and from where Riviera Ray was
so desperate to get away. It is the hard slog of manual
labour where every cent earned is hard-earned.
Whether it is stifling hot or bitterly cold, the work goes
on. There's little job security between projects. Foremen
are under constant pressure to keep the wage costs
down while at the same time they must make sure there
are workers to get the job done. Then there is the whole
problem of managing contractors and sub-contractors
brought in to do their specialist work, whether it is
electrical, plumbing or some other construction skill.
There's a lot of paperwork and rules and regulations
that have to be complied with. Sometimes, to get the job
done it's easier and quicker to skip all the red-tape. For
years the construction business was well-known as a
sector that thrived in the black and grey economy.
Hundreds of builders worked for a good weekly wage
and still got Thursday mornings off to collect their dole
money. Dodging the tax man was part and parcel of the
building game. It happened at every level, from the
major construction giants down to the moonlighting
police officer or teacher building a kitchen extension for
a neighbour. It suited the building firms. They wanted
to able to hire and fire with ease and it suited the
workers who didn't want their names appearing on any
official documents. It was a world where cash was king
and no one was trying to remember exactly where all
the money was going.

By 2000, the Celtic Tiger boom was well underway. The number of projects being undertaken and the number of people employed in the construction industry had broken all records. The number of registered sub-contractors had jumped from 63,000 in 2000 to 93,000 in 2004. In his 2004 reports the Comptroller and Auditor General had highlighted the problems faced by Revenue. The chairman of the Revenue Commissioners is quoted in the report: "The difficulties in tackling non-compliance [in paying tax] in the construction sector are recognised internationally and different jurisdictions have come up with their own responses to the problem."

Early in Ireland's property boom, the Revenue Commissioners in Ireland tightened up the rules on how construction workers and sub-contractors got paid. The way things had been run historically meant that it was all too easy for small contractors to disappear with their earnings at the first sight of the tax man. Revenue put in place tighter regulations over the years to combat the black economy. The system depends on a certificate known as a C2, which is issued to companies taking part in the scheme. An individual, partnership or company can qualify for a C2. It is a personalised card similar to a credit card but with a full face photo and signature of the sub-contractor or the nominated user. Under the C2 certificate system, the main contractors could hold back cash due to a sub-contractor who wasn't registered. In the standard case 35 per cent tax would be automatically deducted from their gross earnings by the main contractor. This was then supposed to be paid to Revenue and it was up to those who were self-employed to claim the tax back themselves. For example Joe the Plumber agrees to do a job for Bill the Builder for €1,000. Joe, however, isn't registered and doesn't have his C2 card, so Bill pays him the agreed fee minus €350 tax. Joe the Plumber then gets his act together and organises to pay his taxes as a sole trader. He is entitled to then claim back the money held by Bill from Revenue. The tax man can be defrauded by Bill the Builder, who disappears without paying the tax, or by a whole range of Joe the Plumbers who claim back tax on fake contracts with Bill's co-operation.

Like the Carousel VAT scam, C2 fraud exploits the fact that the tax authorities allow registered companies to collect taxes on their behalf. Ironically, the C2 was designed to reduce the traditionally high levels of tax evasion in the construction business. Anywhere there is a lot of dull paperwork, rules and regulations there is an opportunity for a fraudster.

In terms of tax fraud, the C2 scam is at the bottom of the rung and someone is always going to get caught. Riviera Ray Woolley was only too happy to get away from building sites and into the more pleasant surrounds of a luxurious office and the comforts that could be bought with his stolen cash. It takes a different animal to work the C2 scam to any effect. When a heavyweight Dublin criminal had learned the niceties of the C2 tax scheme, he quickly set about using his more basic gangland skills to good effect. People don't like to say no to an offer they can't refuse and many were sucked into the fraud. It is quite likely that quite a few individuals were left in no doubt that they had little choice but to take part.

In 2003, Revenue officials had certain construction sites under surveillance, particularly ones involving large amounts of public money. Their purpose was to enforce the rules and cut down on the level of fraud by those not paying their taxes and by others claiming welfare benefits while working. As a result of their work they also uncovered a massive tax fraud. A key participant was the owner of a County Laois based company. The owner had applied for and received a C2 that allowed him to withhold the tax due on money paid out to sub-contractors who were operating as sole traders. Of course, he hadn't actually employed any sub-contractors. The other people involved were then persuaded to pretend to be sub-contractors and claim back the tax, supposedly held by the Laois company, from the government. None of those applying for rebates had actually done any work. The fraudsters behind the scam, like the Carousel scammers, had created a non-existent series of transactions.

One man who was later prosecuted in Dublin District Court for taking part in the scam explained to the Gardaí that he had known the criminal figure from his school days, but he was also someone he feared. The Tallaght man had a genuine tax query at the time when he was approached. The gangster had told him he would sort out his tax affairs and made a false claim using his details. He was told that he would get a cheque that would include money for other people who didn't have bank accounts. The man involved admitted to the Gardaí that he was surprised at the details included on the form in his name because he worked in a supermarket and had never been employed as a building sub-contractor.

The shop worker was one of 120 people uncovered by the investigation into the C2 scam, before his cheque was paid out. The cheques that weren't stopped, however, totalled €1,200,000. The entire fraud had centred on the use of a C2 certificate issued to Portlaoise man, Thomas Hynes. He had been persuaded by another drug dealer to allow him to use his C2 certificate in return for €23,000 in 2001. A copy of the certificate was later found in the drug dealer's possession. Hynes was given a sentence of 240 hours of community service for his role in the fraud. Most of the other people who ended up in court, like Hynes and the shop worker, were described as being "pawns" and not the beneficiaries. Many got a €2,000 share of the average rebate of €8,600. They still had to pay back the full amount to the Revenue Commissioners when the scam was rumbled. The small-time would-be fraudsters ended up being the real victims of the scam. The whole scenario was a house of cards, propped up by a frightening and sinister gangland figure, Sean Dunne.

Originally from St Donagh's Road, Donaghmede, in north Dublin, Sean Dunne was a serious gangster and a highly dangerous thug. His abilities set him a step ahead of many of his contemporaries who didn't quite have his skills when it came to developing their drug dealing business. While other fraudsters used their slick charm and plausible personalities to win people's confidence, Dunne simply forced them to co-operate with implied and overt threats of violence. He described himself as a builder but in reality he had four criminal convictions for assault and theft, but local people, and many in the building trade, knew that he was a serious criminal.

In 2003, there were two attempts on his life. In one, he was blasted in the back and chest by two masked gunmen outside his plush home in Rathoath, County Meath. His injuries were so severe that it was initially thought he would not survive. It took emergency surgery and a long stint in intensive care, to save his life. The would-be assassins were not his only problem at that time. His tax scams and drug dealing activities had attracted the attentions of the Criminal Assets

Bureau, which includes Revenue officers. After checking himself out of hospital he fled to Spain from where he continued to direct his criminal activities in Ireland. However, in September 2004, the 33-year-old career criminal suddenly disappeared without trace. The CAB had issued a tax bill against him for €4 million and there was speculation that he had faked his own death. A site owned by Dunne in Rathoath was sold by the CAB for €755,000 and three of his Donegal properties were sold for €1.1 million. Various reports later claimed that Dunne had fallen foul of former members of the Provisional IRA who had a share in his tax scam. He has never been found.

Another notorious Dublin criminal, Anthony Spratt, was also discovered to have taken part in the C2 fraud. Down the pecking order from Dunne, he set up a small sub-contracting company which he claimed carried out carpentry work for major construction firms. His C2 certificate was used to claim back tax for work that had never been carried out. Spratt had been a member of a particularly violent gang of armed robbers and drug dealers, most of whom have since met with violent or tragic deaths. Spratt committed suicide in March 2005 at the age of 31, while jailed in Mountjoy Prison. In March 2008, the CAB secured a court order freezing €107,800 of his estate.

In some of the Carousel VAT frauds there may be some lingering sense that the proceeds were siphoned off to further some political cause. The reality is that those fraudsters were blinded by greed, dazzled by the sudden and vast financial power at their fingertips. The money was blown on giddy luxuries, such as expensive cars and top end properties. Like kids in a sweet shop, they blew their stolen cash on the trappings of obscene wealth. The tax money they had stolen comes from the same coffers that build hospitals, schools and pays old age pensions. It is not a victimless crime and the money fraudsters, such as Riviera Ray, 'Hollywood' Creaven or Daniel O'Connell, used to satiate their impulses did not, and does not, belong to them.

EIGHT

Farm Fakes

There is a spin-off industry spawned by Europe's Common Agricultural Policy (CAP). It's all about bending or breaking the rules to make money and has very little to do with farming. This black economy runs in parallel and sometimes hand-in-hand with the legitimate face of food production. Like most illicit business enterprises it is a grubby underworld that crosses over into other scams such as fuel laundering and the smuggling of contraband goods such as tobacco. It works on the basis that gangs able to smuggle sheep across the border also have the necessary skills to illegally drive tankers full of laundered fuel. Agricultural-related fraud is endemic to the industry all over Europe. Apart from organised criminal gangs, ordinary farmers have frequently taken advantage of the complex rules and grant-aid programmes to pocket some cash. The fact that the vast majority of CAP-related payments go to a handful of big agri-business conglomerates has caused a sense of injustice among the small farmers. The rich and wealthy get the lion's share of the subsidies making some farmers feel that stealing some money back is simply righting a wrong.

Agricultural fraudsters exist because of the thousands of regulations enacted under the CAP. Imagine a paper jungle that is so big no one really knows where it begins or where they fit into it. Problems really start to crop up when rules get too complicated for anyone to completely understand. This is the case with the Common Agricultural Policy. The thoughts of ordinary EU taxpayers on the CAP rarely get past some half-digested comment heard on the TV or radio. It is a jargonised and impenetrable subject which very few people truly understand. Farmers and their EU cheques have long been the source of jokes and jealously from those who don't live off the land. There is only a vague understanding of why farmers are being paid to leave fields untouched and why vast quantities of unwanted produce are being allowed to accumulate in butter mountains and wine lakes. The only people who are motivated enough to plough through the minutiae of CAP-related schemes and systems are fraudsters looking for a lucrative loophole.

Since its inception in 1959, CAP has been wide open to abuse and false claims and fraud has been endemic at every level. Herds of ghost cattle have long shuffled back and forth across the border between the Republic of Ireland and Northern Ireland. In Italy, claims have been made for dairy cows who produced impossible amounts of milk, with pay-outs proving enormously profitable to farmers and processors. The original inspiration for CAP was based on far loftier ideals. There were indeed laudable intentions behind the ambitious scheme to control agricultural markets. The Treaty of Rome stated that the aim of CAP was to increase productivity, ensure fair living standards for the agricultural community, stabilise markets and to ensure availability of food at reasonable prices. In postwar Europe the end of food shortages was vital to building democratic societies. People were well aware that wonderful ideals, such as peaceful co-existence and communal harmony, don't put bread on the table. The CAP was the cornerstone on which the early European community was built. France and Germany were the

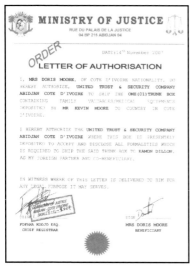

'Dr Konan's' passport
© *Sunday World*

A sample of the type of fake
letter used by the 419ers.
© *Sunday World*

A bogus 'ownership certificate' (© *Sunday World*)

Gardai drive fuel tankers away after a search operation in County Louth.
© *Niall Carson PA*

Thomas 'Slab' Murphy
© *PA*

Customs examine fuel tankers seized from Murphy's
farm. © *Photopress, Belfast*

Counterfeit goods seized by Gardai.
© *Collins Photo Agency*

Richard O'Brien
© *Padraig*
O'Reilly

Sean Garland
Courtesy of BBC Insight

Birdworld, Portlaoise
© *Padraig O'Reilly*

Cornelius Keane
© *Collins Photo Agency*

Jeremiah Hickey
© *Collins Photo Agency*

Thomas Hickey
© *Collins Photo Agency*

Sheep cull, County Louth
© *Paul Faith/PA*

John Walsh
© *Collins Photo Agency*

Brendan O'Brien, Ignite
Leisure
© Padraig O'Reilly

Thomas Burke
© Padraig O'Reilly

Ignite Leisure agents shield 'Ian Dore' from being
photographed.
© Brian McEvoy/Sunday World

Dylan Creavan as shown on his company website.

Sean Dunne
© *Sunday World*

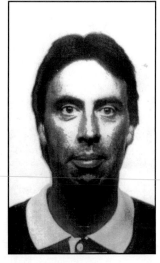

Bernadette Divine

Daniel O'Connell
© *London Metropolitan Police/PA*

key players. The French government insisted on a system of agricultural subsidies in return for a free market in industrial goods. In order to live up to the aims enshrined in the Common Agricultural Policy, governments had to pick up the tab when the food prices dropped below an agreed rate. This would keep markets stable, agricultural communities alive and people fed. Armies of inspectors would tally what was produced, including counting all the sheep and cattle. Chickens were not on the list.

The Common Agricultural Policy went into operation in 1962, but within five years some politicians were already getting worried about the cost. They were right to be worried. The system had been set up in such a way that it encouraged farmers to over-produce. There was a minimum price, so the more farmers produced the more they got paid. The CAP turned normal economics upside down by rewarding suppliers for flooding the market. Farmers who re-invested and got better at over-producing got more cash. Throughout the 1970s and 1980s there was more beef, butter and milk than Europe could eat and enormous reservoirs of unwanted wine: some of it was dumped cheaply into the world markets; some of it was expensively stored. There was a lot of produce and paper work being moved about. There was also a steady flow of money emanating from Brussels, the heart of Europe's bureaucracy. The waste of EU money and food came in for a lot of criticism. Euro-sceptic politicians in various countries found plenty of ammunition to use in the debate against a closer EU. There was also a clamour for reform from outside Europe. Subsidies have a habit of distorting markets. They hit producers in emerging countries very hard. Unwanted European produce was dumped in the world market and political pressure began to build from the rest of world who were sick of EU subsidised food wrecking their agricultural business.

Once upon a time farmers needed useful knowledge about tillage and animal husbandry to be successful. The CAP changed that. Under the EU scheme they needed to become good administrators who knew which forms to fill in and when to send them back. By 2000 spending on the Common Agricultural Policy took up practically half the EU budget. Farmers and producers were getting cheques worth €50 billion a year. There has been a vast array of schemes under which farmers can claim grants and subsidies. Thousands and thousands of EU regulations exist regarding agricultural practice and produce. While there was political pressure from the outside world to change the CAP there was also pressure from within to keep the gravy train going. Farming lobbies have a strong influence in the domestic politics of every member-state. Although reforms might be agreed in one part of the EU, they could provoke protests in another. In Ireland, for instance, successive governments held back from letting various officials do their job, according to some professionals who worked in the agri-business sector. Attempts to expose fraudulent and exaggerated subsidy claims went nowhere or were met with official indifference, such was the political clout then wielded by farming organisations. One veterinarian, who ventured an opinion in 1993 that half the beef in Ireland was tainted with growth promoters such as Angel Dust, was threatened with a boycott of his business. At the time rogue farmers could use drugs to add weight to their cattle, knowing that the beef would go straight into intervention stocks. It would never be released onto the market, thereby avoiding any testing. In the case of Angel Dust, however, the agricultural inspectors were allowed do their job and its use was stamped out within a few years.

In 2003, the level of produce and the rate of subsidy payments were finally separated after years of negotiations between the member states. The idea was to stop rewarding farmers for producing more crops than were needed. European farmers now get a single payment based on the subsidies for which they have previously qualified. The size of the payment is determined by those subsidies received over a three year period, known as 'reference years'. Eventually it is planned that these payments will also be phased out.

The fact remains that it is impossible to count every olive tree in Greece, every vine in France or every lamb in Ireland. Over the years farmers and processors consistently inflated the size of their herds or the annual grain output. The limited capacity for double-checking subsidy claims ensured that the chances of being caught were low enough to make it worth the risk. Things changed, however, in 2001 when the prospect of a devastating epidemic of foot-and-mouth disease threatened Ireland's agricultural economy. In other beef-producing countries such as Argentina or Brazil, foot-and-mouth disease is endemic. The disease doesn't kill the animals and they recover, but they don't put on much weight while they are sick. Both Ireland and the UK trade heavily on their 'disease-free' status. It allows a premium to be charged for their beef and lamb. As a result there are safeguards in place to ensure that any cases of disease are dealt with quickly. Animals showing any signs of carrying certain diseases are quickly destroyed and the farmers are paid the full market price. It is a necessary measure and farmers are compensated to make sure there is a financial motive to declare diseased animals.

When the foot-and-mouth epidemic hit the UK in February 2001, Ireland was shut down. All shipments of animals between the Republic of Ireland and the UK and Northern Ireland were immediately banned. The Gardaí, Customs and Army were called out, in a huge operation, to seal the border with Northern Ireland. Vehicles had to be driven through wheel-washes. Every farmer had to take precautions at their gates to stop the virus from spreading by accidental cross-infection. Livestock allowed to graze on commonage such as the Curragh in County Kildare had to be taken off the land. For the wild goats of the Cooley Peninsula in County Louth it meant a death sentence. Army sharp shooters were brought in to shoot the wily cross-border herbivores. There was some mirth at the idea, considering that for years people believed that British Army soldiers would try to shoot the goats, in case they gave away the positions of comrades engaged in covert surveillance on the mountains. The goats had long experience of being hunted by military Special Forces and were not easy targets. The civilian sheep, which had been free to roam across the mountain border, were also earmarked to be culled. If the future of farming was to be safe-guarded it was in the farmers' interests to ensure that the job was done properly. Compensation would be paid for each culled animal. No one was going to hold back.

As it turned out, after the operation was completed, officials from the Department of Agriculture discovered there were 20 per cent less culled sheep than expected. The foot-and-mouth cull, for the first time, provided an insight into how the farming sector had been systematically making bogus claims under the Common Agricultural Policy for years. The sheep population to be destroyed had been compiled from the number of animals claimed for by the farmers under the subsidy scheme. Farmers had claimed for 37,165 ewe payments at IR£19 a head. After the cull only 30,540 animals could be accounted for. Obviously someone had been over-counting. Subsequent investigation revealed that there were 100 farmers in the area who had made claims for 6,500 sheep that did not exist. Some farmers who did not even own sheep were found to have made claims for payments and they were caught red-handed.

As the foot-and-mouth cull hit the rest of the country what happened in Cooley proved to be symptomatic of the entire sector. Previously sheep farmers on mountains and commonage were given 48 hours notice of inspections to allow time for them to gather their herds. It gave those involved in making fraudulent claims plenty of time to move animals around. As a result of what the cull had revealed in Cooley and the tighter restrictions placed on sheep movements, 7,500 sheep farmers throughout Ireland were penalised for 'irregularities' in their ewe premium applications. The year before the foot-and-mouth epidemic, cash was claimed for 4.49 million ewes. In the aftermath the number of claims fell to 3.8 million, leaving a rather large ghost flock of 600,000 sheep. Foot-and-mouth had provided a hard figure for the size of Ireland's fake flocks. Up to then it had been impossible to quantify the level of fraud when it came to agricultural subsidies. The farming lobby were able to play down the level of bogus claims because no one had any real statistics. When the cull was over, there was no more wriggle room.

The smuggling business that went hand-in-hand with CAP fraud was also hit hard by the foot-and-mouth crisis. Mad Cow disease and scrapie, the sheep version of the infection, had already caused a massive drop in British exports. What was the UK's pain was Ireland's gain. France at the time had banned British meat because of Mad Cow, so there was a strong demand for Irish produce. Sheep that were virtually worthless in the UK and Northern Ireland could command good prices in the Republic of Ireland. Rogue livestock dealers had for years fully exploited the presence of a land border on the island of Ireland. Moving livestock from the UK and passing them off as Irish animals had always been a very profitable scam. During the foot and mouth crisis, such was the threat posed to Irish agriculture from suspected smugglers that the National Bureau of Criminal Investigation were called in to tackle them. Farmers who reported unusually high multiple birth rates for their herd were singled out for inspection. Animals were tested to check their DNA and several farmers were caught trying to pass off smuggled animals as stock from their own herd. By April 2001, hundreds of calves had been found dumped or abandoned in different locations around the country. Obviously the smugglers or their customers had simply dumped livestock on the road and in fields rather than risk getting caught.

One of the first successful prosecutions was brought against a farmer from County Clare, Peter Stritch. He replied to a newspaper ad and bought calves from Northern Ireland for €15 a head. They could be sold in the south for €100. When he was first approached by Gardaí in April 2001 he denied having got any animals from the North. When they came back the following month and questioned him again he confessed. He had imported 150 calves which had been mixed up with his own herd. As a result the entire herd of 287 were slaughtered. The attempted scam lost the farmer

€100,000 in livestock. He was also jailed for four months in November 2002 and fined €10,000.

Stritch's case was described as the biggest case of its kind at the time, but that dubious distinction really went to another man. It was to belong to a more serious smuggler who also came a cropper thanks to foot-and-mouth. John Walsh, a Wicklow native living in Offaly, had a bad reputation as a livestock dealer, going back many years. The 51-year-old looked the part of a stereotypical 'culchie' farmer in his ill-fitting jacket and tie. He wasn't a particularly pleasant character. The hard-faced wheeler and dealer was often aggressive, both in his manner and in his approach to people. He has convictions for cruelty and neglect of animals as well as for assaulting people and failing to pay fines. In early 2001 he was going about his usual business of importing sheep from the UK into Northern Ireland and smuggling them across the border into the Republic. In the south there was a ready market for animals of questionable origin. Walsh was far from being a lone operator. He was part of a wider black market network of corrupt dealers. They survived as fraudsters because of the sheer volume of business and the acceptance within the sector that a certain fraction of that business was going to be fraudulent.

Unluckily for Walsh on February 21, 2001, foot-and-mouth disease broke out in the UK, two days after he had imported a flock of sheep and just as the unprecedented crackdown on livestock smugglers began. Animals from his flock in south Armagh soon became the first cases of the disease to be found on the island of Ireland. Department of Agriculture officials worked furiously to trace the infected flock that were known to have been smuggled in by Walsh. Most of the 390 sheep he brought in from the UK ended up at the

Kepak factory in Athleague, County Roscommon. They had all been slaughtered and processed and it appeared there had been no new infections.

Walsh had fled to the UK when the smuggling racket ground to a complete halt. For awhile he must have felt he was Ireland's most wanted man. The black market dealer eventually came back to Ireland in April 2001 to face the music. He was served with a €363,000 tax demand from the Criminal Assets Bureau.

The following year in January 2002 he was jailed for three months for the illegal importation of animals. No action, however, was taken against anyone working for the Kepak factory in Athleague where Walsh had off-loaded his cargo of smuggled sheep. The smuggler who knew staff at the plant had told them to book in the sheep as belonging to different farmers. Walsh told Gardaí: "Anyone can come along and give a name if he knows the name is on the factory records." Walsh said that he had given a false registration number for the lorry at the plant. He had then used a code provided by someone in the factory to cash four cheques, worth IR£13,097, at the local Allied Irish Bank and made out to innocent farmers for a sterling draft, without having to show identification.

In a statement at the time, a spokesperson for the company explained that no one at the Kepak plant was guilty of any wrong-doing. "The company found nothing that warranted the sacking of any member of the staff. The security man recognised Mr Walsh who told him that he was booking sheep into the plant for other farmers. Mr Walsh had been a regular user of the plant in the year 2000 and there was nothing exceptional in him bringing animals in for other people, even though he was not a big dealer," he said.

The case showed that for those who were ready to

exploit the subsidy and rebate system there was a well-oiled machine in operation. It also exposed the level of tolerance in the food processing industry towards the dodgy dealers who circumvented the usual controls and restrictions. It took an act of God, in the form of the foot-and-mouth crisis, to reveal just how widespread that network had extended throughout the farming community. The authorities were galvanised into action and the cracks through which the rogue traders had operated were squeezed shut.

In the past Walsh had also been suspected of deliberately importing an animal infected with Mad Cow disease so that compensation could be claimed for a culled herd of cattle. A Cork farmer, who went ahead with a similar plan, plugged into the same network of dodgy livestock dealers to which Walsh belonged to acquire an infected animal. Walsh was a high-profile example of a black market livestock dealer and smuggler. He was just one individual following a path already well-worn by rogue traders. Years before the foot-and-mouth crisis exposed the vibrant network of black market smugglers operating in Ireland, there was another infamous case that provided an insight into how far some people would go to steal tax-payers' money.

James Sutton was based near Clonakilty in west Cork where he worked a 90-acre farm. Then aged 45, the father-of-five had mounting debts of IR£700,000 on a holding that was worth half that amount. His business had been plagued by mysterious fires for which he had made insurance claims. An investigation revealed that he lied to Gardaí about a €20,000 tractor which he said had been stolen from his farm. He had then tried but failed to claim €36,000 compensation for the vehicle. He was also accused of deliberately infecting a herd of cattle with TB a year later, again to make a bogus claim for compensation. At best he was a sharp operator who played fast and loose with rules and regulations.

When, in 1996, Sutton owed cash to cattle dealer Andrew Wilson, a plot was hatched to scam compensation payments from the Department of Agriculture to pay off his debts. At the time there was a lot of concern about Mad Cow disease or BSE (Bovine Spongiform Encephalopathy) and its potentially disastrous effects on Ireland's beef trade. The disease has been linked to a human version, Creutzfeldt-Jacob (CJD) disease, which causes terrifying symptoms of agonising pain and dementia before death. In the UK, where the practice of feeding bone meal to cattle had been widespread, Mad Cow disease had taken hold. There had also been a number of high-profile cases of CJD and many countries, including France, had placed a blanket ban on importing British beef products. It had the effect of placing a market premium on disease-free Irish beef, while making British animals almost worthless. For some the simple scam of illegally importing cattle into Ireland from the UK to pass them off as Irish was not enough. Better still to bring in a BSE infected animal to spark a herd cull to get a hefty compensation cheque.

In September 1996, Sutton's latest scam was put into motion. If successful it would make the conspirators IR£75,000 in compensation. He was phoned and told to travel north to Portlaoise to pick up the infected animal. 60 extra animals were also be added to boost the compo payment. While on the road he got another call directing him further north to Cavan. Being so close to the border the west Cork farmer would later claim that he got worried that a paramilitary organisation was behind the operation. Eventually he was directed to a holding pen on a farm where he picked up the herd of cattle which he brought back and introduced into his herd in Cork. The true source of the infected animal or whether paramilitary-connected 'border bandits' were involved in the plot was never established.

While the plan looked good on paper the fraudsters made a number of critical mistakes. They didn't realise the extent to which the Department kept records on the identification of individual animals. To carry off the scam, the infected animal had to be fitted with an ear-tag so it looked like it had grown up as part of Sutton's herd. Under the monitoring system at the time, the tag rather than the individual animal is tracked by the Department. The tags are attached to a calf at birth and stay on the animal for life. It is not a foolproof system as tags can be accidentally torn out or sometimes taken off a dead animal and re-used. The veterinary inspector called in to check the suspect animal at Sutton's farm in October 1996 quickly realised that something was amiss. In the metal barrel of the ear-tag, which is pushed through the ear of the cattle, he found fresh flesh. Such material would have long since degraded if the tag had been attached at birth. Records taken at a previous inspection showed that the animal bearing that tag had been de-horned. The Mad Cow-infected animal still had its horns, so it was obvious that the tag had been recently switched. The infected animal was also found to have just one tag hole in its left ear, while the corresponding tag number files at the Department of Agriculture had a record of two tags on the animal. One of the tags was for identification and the other was a TB reactor tag. With the stakes so high in protecting Ireland's €2 billion disease-free beef industry there was no hesitation in calling in the Gardaí to investigate.

They immediately focussed on finding out how a BSE-infected animal had turned up in Clonakilty out of the blue.

By the time the case came to court in 2000, James Sutton was still trying to deny being part of a conspiracy. After the opening speeches had been made by the lawyers at Cork Circuit Criminal Court, the trial went into legal argument. Two weeks later Sutton pleaded guilty to the main charge of conspiracy and the jury were sent home.

In June 2000, Sutton was jailed for five years. Judge AG Murphy acknowledged that while the case had been "a personal tragedy" for Sutton, he had to impose a jail sentence. "If this fraud had gone undetected, it would have had a devastating effect on the beef industry, eroding the confidence of overseas customers. It would have affected the livelihoods of everyone in Ireland." It was the first time such a case had been successfully prosecuted anywhere in the European Union.

The fraud attempt had sparked a long and detailed investigation by the Gardaí. They unravelled the links between Sutton and the network of unscrupulous livestock dealers who were able to acquire a BSE-infected animal for the fraudsters. The Cork farmer travelled to various markets with the Gardaí to point out the rogue dealers who were prepared to expose Ireland's valuable beef trade to ruin for the sake of a few thousand pounds. Sutton pointed the finger at livestock dealers Bryan Wilson and his son Andrew. They were the people who had acquired the 'mad cow'. At the Wilsons' trial in 2002, Sutton described the fraud attempt as "a dream scheme gone wrong". Both father and son at first denied the charges, but changed their pleas to guilty a week into the trial. Bryan, then aged 57, was given a two year sentence, with one year suspended. He had a number of previous convictions for the illegal movement of animals. His son Andrew described as "a passenger" in the conspiracy, was given a two year suspended sentence.

It had been a long and complex investigation. In Sutton's case there were 200 witnesses and it was expected to have lasted six weeks if he had not shortened events by pleading guilty. As if to highlight the bureaucratic nightmare surrounding attempts to monitor the farming sector, it emerged that Wilson junior had been granted a livestock agent's licence in July 2001. He had applied under a new scheme which had been introduced after the foot-and-mouth crisis.

The Wilsons were not the only rogue dealers to come to grief over the plot. Thomas and Jeremiah Hickey from County Tipperary, also a father and son outfit, were finally brought to trial in 2006, ten years after their attempt to swindle the State out of compensation. Both men were listed as directors of the firm Hickey's Meats and operated as livestock traders. In 2002, they were charged with conspiracy, having been identified as among those who helped to source the infected animal for transfer to James Sutton's farm. There were delays because of Thomas senior's ill-health. He was then aged 72. The trial eventually broke the record for Nenagh Circuit Criminal Court, lasting seven weeks and involving 70 witnesses.

Sutton again gave evidence against the Tipperary men, who both denied the charges. They were linked to the plot, however, by their mobile phone records. The Hickeys went down fighting all the way. The trial was interrupted 44 times for legal submissions as the prosecution case was put to full proof. On one morning of the trial, Jeremiah, the son, stood at the door of the courthouse, staring hard at the jurors as they filed past him one-by-one. Eight jurors complained about his behaviour and he was moved by the time the remaining four had arrived.

When the trial ended the jury of eight woman and four men took four hours to find them guilty. The presiding judge, Miriam Reynolds, was mindful of the potentially huge negative impact that a bogus BSE case could have had on the wider Irish economy when sentencing the pair. She said they were part of "a greedy scam" and they had no regard for their fellow farmers or their country and noted that it had never been established from where the infected animal had been sourced. Thomas was sentenced to three years in jail while his 38-year-old son, Jeremiah, was given a similar sentence.

Despite the sentences, the two men continued their legal battle, first to get bail after lodging an appeal. The appeal was heard in December 2007. The three-judge panel again expressed the opinion that their actions could have had a serious impact on the Irish economy. The Appeal Court backed the decision by the lower court branding the fraud as "most selfish" and commenting that it could have had almost "incalculable consequences". The original convictions and sentences were upheld.

The dealers involved in Sutton's scam were, like John Walsh, part of a black market that thrived on the opportunities created by the combination of land borders and agricultural compensation payments. The fraudsters involved in Sutton's case got caught because they didn't have the right inside knowledge. The fraud unravelled because the Department had more information on individual cattle than the fraudsters had bargained for. As for Walsh, he didn't really know how to cover his tracks beyond the casual wink and nod arrangements that were apparently already in place.

The system of compensating farmers for keeping the national livestock herd disease-free is a necessary expense. The payments protect the commercial edge 'disease-free meat' affords Irish producers. It does, however, sometimes present a temptation to farmers that wouldn't exist in any other commercial sector. For some, it is an incentive to court disaster. In 2000, Cornelius Keane, a 37-year-old farmer from Drimoleague, County Cork had an excellent reputation. He was so good at farming that he had been considered as a candidate for Young Dairy Farmer of the Year. Keane had done a brilliant job building up a small dairy farm of 120 acres which he had taken over in the early 1990s. He had inherited the property from his father which came with a small debt attached. The Cork farmer had never been in trouble in his life.

By January 2000, however, Keane had hit a rough patch. He was in debt to the tune of IR£136,000. A father-of-four, with another child expected, he was under considerable stress. He didn't appear to be well-equipped to deal with the pressure and put off making decisions for as long as possible. Suddenly there was an outbreak of disease on the farm. His dairy herd developed symptoms similar to TB, with large swellings on their backs.

The Department of Agriculture's veterinary inspector for the region was called to Keane's farm in February 2000. He found the dairy herd in "a sad state". The animals were in considerable distress, arching their backs in pain. He would later give evidence that the cattle had: "massive swellings that were half the size of Gaelic footballs on their necks and pus weeping from them." The vet was immediately suspicious as to the true nature of the TB in Keane's herd. He called in the Gardaí and officials from the Department's Special Investigations Unit.

Keane was arrested and immediately admitted that he had injected the animals with slurry shortly before they were due for a routine TB test. He had thought the cattle's skin would swell with lumps similar to cattle with TB. Keane unwittingly made matters worse by injecting each animal with two cubic centimetres of slurry, taken from the floor of the milking parlour. Unfortunately it contained traces of caustic soda which made the injections even more toxic. The farmer had then used a knife to pierce the lumps to try and reduce the swellings.

Keane's plan didn't make economic sense even it had worked. If the inspector had agreed that it was TB, the Department of Agriculture would have had the herd culled and paid him compensation. The young farmer, however, stood to get just IR£21,320, in this eventuality, nowhere near enough to clear his debts. The lump sum grant to compensate for the slaughter of the herd would have amounted to about the same money that he would have earned by the milk produced in a year. As it turned out, the herd were successfully treated, the animals made a full recovery and never contracted TB.

When he was prosecuted at Cork Circuit Court in May 2001 Cornelius Keane admitted to four sample charges. His trial came at the height of the foot-and-mouth scare and as the widespread agricultural smuggling and corruption was in the spotlight. In Keane's defence his lawyer argued that, unlike foot-and-mouth and BSE, TB did not pose a danger to the food chain. Judge AG Murphy, however, took a very dim view of Keane's ham-fisted attempt to defraud the State.

"This man set out to rob his neighbours. This is what he did. The Department does not have any money. It was his neighbours, the people of Ireland who provide the money. This man set out to rob them. It was an outrageous offence of fraud and gross cruelty. This was a man from a farming background. He should have known how to treat animals," said the judge.

Judge Murphy wanted to ban Keane from ever being allowed to farm with animals but admitted he did not have the power to make such an order. "I cannot leave this man away other than with a custodial sentence. The crimes are grave. The message to the farming community would be quite wrong. I think this sort of thing merits seven years in prison."

In the end the judge handed down a three year sentence, acknowledging the effect it would have on his family and the level of desperation which had driven Keane to try such a mad-cap scheme.

The rogue livestock traders and farmers may account for some scams, but they are certainly not the only ones involved in CAP related fraud. Those on the inside have also tried their hand, one way or another, at siphoning off the cash that flows from Brussels. Every Thursday, the EU's Agriculture Directorate sets the level of grain export subsidies for the following week, and its decision can significantly affect world markets. In 2001, the European Anti-Fraud Office, OLAF, announced that someone in the Commission had been tipping off grain dealers about the weekly changes in price subsidies before they were publicly announced. It was claimed the official accepted bribes in return for passing on the commercially sensitive information. Belgian prosecutors later alleged that certain cereal companies were told the prices two hours before they were officially available. Two years later, in October

2003, Belgian authorities arrested two people, one an employee of the European Commission over the alleged fraud. Another six were arrested in France. Prosecutors raided the Commission's office in Brussels and carried out other raids in Belgium, the Netherlands and Paris in an operation involving more than 100 officers.

The fraud is just another example of how a part of the enormous bureaucratic tangle could be unpicked for a fraudulent profit. In a move aimed at reducing fraud, Irish politician Ray MacSharry, during his role as EU Commissioner, had initiated the first attempt to reform the morass of the Common Agricultural Policy. His attempts to rein in the huge spending were known as the MacSharry Reforms and had come into force in 1993 but they hadn't stopped the corruption.

No doubt the EU Commissioner was unimpressed by the actions of his cousin, who conspired with an official in the Irish Department of Agriculture to commit a fraud a few years later. Publican, auctioneer and failed local election candidate, Michael Clarke, had every appearance of an upstanding member of the community. The temptation of EU cash, however, proved too much for him. Clarke's insider in the conspiracy was civil servant Robert Patrick Walsh. Then aged 43 and a father-of-four, Walsh was from the village of Tubbercurry in County Sligo. Part of Walsh's job involved paying out cheques to dairy farmers who were upgrading their operations to fulfil new and stringent European directives on dairy farm standards. Thousands of EU farming directives have been issued and Ireland has been more enthusiastic than most in implementing the new regulations. Various schemes offer grants to encourage farmers to stay compliant with the rules. Walsh claimed that he and another official hatched the plan to pay out cheques under a dairy hygiene improvement scheme to fictitious farmers. They picked that particular scheme simply because it was the most lucrative. Clarke's role in the fraud was to cash the cheques and effectively launder the money for the corrupt civil servant. He would get IR£20,000 for his part in the scam.

The co-conspirators took great care and went to obsessive lengths to maintain secrecy. Details of the plot were discussed during clandestine meetings on remote back roads in the Ox Mountains, Sligo. Nothing would be left to chance. They finally put the plan into operation in the autumn of 1997. The cheques were made out to the fictitious payees. Addresses were necessary for official records so the cheques were posted to local guesthouses where Walsh had previously made bookings in the fabricated names. In one instance, Clarke got one of his barmaids to pick up one of the cheques by offering to pay her IR£1,000 for the simple errand. Whatever spy thriller from which they had concocted the plan obviously didn't feature an alert guesthouse owner who wasn't keen on suspect envelopes arriving at her address. In December 1997, the landlady got suspicious about a Tom Anderson. He had cancelled his visit and then phoned her looking for mail. Two junk mail envelopes had arrived and when the barmaid called to collect them, pretending to be 'Tom Anderson's' daughter, she found the Gardaí waiting. She told the officers everything she knew about the scam.

The next day the Department cheque, which had never actually reached the guesthouse, was intercepted at Tubbercurry Post Office. The investigation found that three other suspect cheques had been paid out and cashed by the fraudsters, to amounts totalling IR£65,000.

In 2001, Walsh and Clarke were initially charged with the fraud plot which centred on five cheques, worth a total of IR£178,388. When they appeared in court the media were waiting for them. It had already been reported on the national news that a first cousin of a former EU Commissioner was facing fraud charges. The two were remanded on bail.

At his trial in October 2001, Walsh admitted to conspiring to steal a cheque worth IR£26,900 that was made payable to Mary Anderson. Phone records indicated that Walsh had made the calls posing as Tom Anderson from his own mobile phone and from a public phone close to his house. 13 other charges of theft and larceny were withdrawn by the State and Walsh became the main prosecution witness against Clarke.

Clarke's trial took place the following January in 2002. Walsh named Clarke as a co-conspirator along with another senior Department of Agriculture official whom he said had helped him mastermind the scam. Clarke was eventually prosecuted for handling four stolen government cheques worth IR£128,885 and conspiring to steal the IR£26,900 cheque. He denied the charges.

After a six day trial the jury found him guilty of handling two of the stolen cheques which had been made out to fictitious dairy farmers 'Thomas McDonagh' and a 'Brian Kilgariff'. He was acquitted of handling two other cheques but found guilty of conspiracy to steal Mary Anderson's cheque along with Walsh. Clarke was jailed for two years while Walsh was fined IR£30,000 for his part.

At the sentencing hearing in March 2002, Judge Anthony Kennedy was surprised to learn that Walsh had been kept on half pay by the Department since his arrest in October 1998. He had also been granted free legal aid to fight his case. "Why it has taken all this time without the Department firing him is a mystery," said the judge. No one else was prosecuted with the fraud despite Walsh's claim in court of another official being involved.

Keeping track of grant payments, milk quotas, headage payments, set aside grants, intervention payments, not to mention wayward civil servants, is a massive headache for the bureaucracy. But their problems are not just confined to dry land. Whatever chances inspectors have of counting lambs and calves, the prospect of counting the fish in the sea poses an even greater challenge. The European Union's fishery policy, however, means that the mandarins in Brussels seem to have committed to doing just that. Dwindling fish stocks have forced the European Union to enforce quotas for each of their member states' fishing fleets. The rules, regulations and how they are enforced, however, differ from country to country. They also depend on the type of fishing operation and the species being caught for the commercial market.

Like the Common Agricultural Policy, the fisheries policy with all its rules and regulations is wide open to abuse and fraud. For fishermen, it came down to a very simple thing: how could they sell off catches of fish that were over and above the agreed quotas? The fish became known as 'black fish' and like smuggled livestock, black fish became an underground trade that ran in parallel with the legitimate trade. Processors and the authorities turned a blind eye in the drive for profits. There was also a vacuum created by the absence of any political will to restructure the industry. Politicians knew that many fishing communities believed that their interests were sold out in favour of the farmers when Ireland first entered the Common Market in 1970s. On top of that the Irish authorities seemed to be more enthusiastic than other countries when it came to enforcement, while at the same time foreign fishing boats were tolerated in Irish waters. On a local level there was an understanding that if controls became more stringent, it would certainly spell the end of some traditional fishing communities. There was another similarity with CAP in that there was a strong sense of injustice among those at the bottom of the pile, who ran small operations. Big producers had bigger boats that could stay at sea for longer and in harsher weather. Smaller boats had to take their chances when the weather allowed. If a boat failed to catch its quota one week it would be lost. The rules meant that a boat couldn't make up for a bad week by landing a double load the next week. There is no love lost between Irish fishing communities and EU bureaucrats.

The landing of illegal catches was known to exist for years. Every so often a skipper of a boat might be fined or even jailed for over-fishing. The full extent of the inherent fraud within the industry didn't really become apparent, however, until a fisherman from Donegal blew the whistle on the endemic nature of the black market in fish. Pat Cannon had been a lifelong fisherman, based in Killybegs. The County Donegal town is at the core of Ireland's fishing industry. Over 200,000 people depend on it for their livelihood. Cannon had spent years wrangling with the system to set up his own legitimate business. In 1981 he applied for a licence for his own boat. His application was turned down, but he decided to appeal the decision. He was eventually granted a licence in 1986, but was unable to put a trawler into the water until 1989, by which time the rules had changed again. He decided to sue the State and the High Court ruled that the Department had delayed dealing with his application and awarded him costs and damages. It had been an uphill struggle for Cannon, one in which other players seemed to be working to a different set of rules or even outside of the rules he had been told to adhere to.

In July 2004, Cannon wrote a letter to the Minster for the Marine in which he claimed that the Killybegs fishermen had blatantly disregarded European fish quota rules. He wrote: "I have documentary evidence in my possession which proves that, practically on a daily basis, the tonnage of fish being caught far exceeds the allowable catch as laid down by the quotas. I have in my possession documents including receipts, log-sheets, etc., which have been altered and falsified so as to give the impression that everything is in order and in accordance with quotas." Cannon also alleged that government officials were colluding with fraudulent claims. He later met with a Department official but refused to hand over his documentary evidence. In October that year, after no action had apparently been taken Pat Cannon then wrote to the European Commission and the Norwegian government about his allegations.

The allegations became public in October 2004 and caused an immediate furore. The rumour mill among the fishing industry, particularly in Donegal went into overdrove. Questions were asked over Cannon's motivation and if the entire row had a political basis. Pat Cannon told an RTÉ news reporter at the time that he was standing up for himself and all of the small fishermen in Ireland who were being neglected. He denied that his actions in reporting his allegations to Irish and European authorities were motivated by a vendetta or a personal grudge. The Donegal man said that if things went on the way they were going, then there would be no fish left in Irish waters in a few years.

This time there was an immediate response. The new Minister for the Marine, Noel Dempsey, requested a Garda investigation to be carried out. The EU Commission indicated that they would await the results of the investigation. Only a few months before, in May that year, the European Court of Justice Advocate General had recommended the French government be fined €115 million for failing to police illegal fishing. The fishing industry in Britain, Spain and Portugal were also under active investigation by the Commission. In this political climate, Cannon's allegations had to be taken seriously.

Detectives turned up at Pat Cannon's door to find that he had lodged his documentary evidence with his Dublin solicitor. The following month, on November 18, officers from the National Bureau of Criminal Investigation raided several addresses connected with the fishing industry in Donegal, Galway, Cork and Kerry. Targets included in the dawn raids were fishing vessels, fishing agents, co-ops, company offices and private homes. The officers seized documentation and computers during the operation. The most extensive searches were carried out in Killybegs, the State's largest fishing port, where all the local fish processing factories were visited. Four trawler owners were later charged with under-reporting catches. They were sent for trial in early 2007 as a result of the investigation started by Cannon's whistle blowing.

In the meantime, following the raids in 2004, boat captains went to Scotland and Norway to land their illegal catches. Over the next two years investigators found more irregularities in reporting fish catches. Systemic false declarations by Irish boats were discovered in Scotland where illegal catches of mackerel and monkfish were landed. The apparent routine landing of catches of black fish forced the Irish government and the EU Commission to take action. In June 2006, with the threat of a €40 million EU fine hanging over the government, specialist Gardaí were trained to work alongside sea fisheries' officers employed by the Department of the Marine. Ireland then had to re-negotiate its fishing quotas based on the estimates of the black catches. The mackerel quota for 2007 was reduced as a result. The illegal catches were simply taken out of future quotas for all Irish fishermen.

There were a further series of searches, unconnected to Cannon's allegations, at four western fishing ports in July 2007 as the crackdown on the industry continued. Unfortunately the threats facing the future of the Irish fishing community increased in 2008 as the rocketing price of oil forced most owners to tie up their boats. At the same time it was estimated that the EU imports €1.1 billion worth of illegally caught fish and fish-products every year. It seems the only way to make a living from fishing is by flouting the law.

The fraud within the fishing industry showed how attempts to control a market, or in this case the stock of fish, can create incentives to defraud the system. When one gate is shut, another can open. For instance the EU paid a subsidy to suppliers of live cattle for export at a rate of €230 per animal. The subsidy only applied if the cattle were shipped to certain designated countries. In 2004, it emerged that 90 per cent of all live cattle exports went to Lebanon. In other words 226,000 cattle were shipped to a country with a population of 3.2 million people, which didn't have the slaughtering capacity to handle such numbers. Ireland accounted for 30,000 cattle destined for Lebanon. It was clear that animals being documented as being exported to Lebanon were obviously going somewhere else in the Middle East and the subsidy was being pocketed by the suppliers.

Fraud can take all sorts of shapes and forms. Farm fraud shows that it can grow legs as well. Black fish and ghost sheep, like the mythical unicorns, exist in a shadowy world of half-truths, created by the imaginations of con-artists. In the paperwork jungle of the Common Agricultural Policy, con-artists have discovered little niches that can be quietly exploited. It was made possible the creation of complex systems and barriers designed to regulate the production and supply of food. The system is being streamlined and reformed, slowly but surely, but every new rule or regulation can create another loophole for a fraudster to squeeze through. The specialist knowledge needed to navigate through the system works in favour of the fraudster. Their bogus claims and scams can stay hidden unless they are uncovered by an accident such as an outbreak of disease or the fraudster's own incompetence. Without a doubt, the best frauds that have exploited the CAP have passed though the system undetected. Someone somewhere is living life on the hog thanks to cheques from Brussels – safe in the knowledge that they'll never be caught.

NINE

Pyramids of Sand

There is an air of tense excitement among the people gathered in a hotel meeting room. Attractive young men and women animatedly chat with great enthusiasm, shaking hands, patting backs, as they calmly work the room. Slowly but surely they build up a feeling of obvious excitement and the sense of anticipation in the crowd. It is very hard to resist the seductive sensation of being part of a collective positive experience. Among the acolytes there is talk of life-changing decisions. In hushed tones it is mentioned how life would be different if only they had seen the light sooner but now they know, things will never be the same again. When the overhead projector is turned on the show really begins. Confirmed followers and newcomers alike are dazzled with the inner-secrets that have been there all along, if only the ignorant had known where to look. But now help is hand. To be truly rich and happy all it takes is to believe, to ignore the doomsayers and to step into the light. An outsider looking in could be forgiven for mistaking the meeting as a religious cult on the verge of making a great new revelation. The reality is somewhat different. The meeting is designed to entice new members into a precarious financial scheme known as a pyramid.

A well-organised outfit known as Ignite Leisure were on the prowl in Ireland in 2005 for new recruits to their holiday company. A similar operation known as OMI Club had been operating in the UK the previous year. It ran out of steam as the supply of fresh faces withered up and disappeared. On a Sunday afternoon at a west Dublin hotel in April the sales people from Ignite Leisure turned out in force, dressed in their best suits. They welcomed the potential new recruits with plenty of warm handshakes and back slapping. The location of the meeting had only been released the day before to the invited guests. In the meeting room James Brown's *I Feel Good* blared out loud enough to make a full conversation uncomfortable. The track changed to Gabrielle's *Dreams Can Come True* then to the Abba classic *Money, Money, Money*. Throughout 2005, at its peak, the organisers were hosting at least three such meetings a week, packed with 50 or 60 new recruits.

A man finally stood up to address the crowd. Frankie Lawler, who lived in a pleasant bungalow in south Kildare at the time, started the sales pitch. "Do you want to be the kind of person who reads the food or the price list first from the menu?" he asked, not unlike a holiday rep trying to work up some enthusiasm among a bus load of tourists. Strategically placed plants in the audience gave Frankie the excited answer he wanted to hear. Straight away he declared that it was not a pyramid scheme because the investors were buying membership of Ignite Leisure – a discount holiday club. Print-outs of internet pages with the company's holiday information were then handed out. They were very basic fakes but with the audience already well warmed up the company's Director Ian Dore was introduced.

The mumbling 'Ian Dore' with a Manchester accent, even forgot his own name as he told the audience of his financial success through Ignite Leisure. "Martin Luther King said hope makes the world go round. This business lets people dream again. The reason why I enjoy what I do is I work with people with smiles on their faces. Ours is the perfect business model. All you need is people and a hotel room."

His patter lacked Lawler's enthusiasm, probably a reflection of his own comfortable position at the top of the pyramid. Prospective members were told that for their €2,500 investment, and by selling one membership a month for the next ten months, they would receive €159,000. The final two months of the year would be spent holidaying in the Bahamas, according to 'Dore': "After two months doing nothing you can ring your agents from the lilo in the pool to find out how your business is doing. So you've got one hand on the phone and the other hand on whatever you like. You discover that you have made a fortune for doing nothing. Not a bad little earner to run alongside something else you already do," he told the gathering.

The doors remained shut and the heat built up as the sales pitch went on and on. People were receptive, even keen to get on board. They happily signed up with the firm. Dore and Lawler repeated their favourite catch phrases to the audience, hamming up the benefits of the scheme. They insisted on a need for secrecy to maintain Ignite Leisure's "closed user group" and to safeguard its financial security. The meeting itself was carefully controlled. People are first approached by junior agents and given just a tantalising hint of what the meeting is about. The inviters are warned to say as little as possible, to leave the real spiel to the senior boys. It costs €2,500, the initial investment, to become an Ignite Leisure Junior Agent or 'professional inviter'. Once a junior inviter completes a first sale of €2,500 to a new member they get €350 back. On a second €2,500 sale they get another €350 back and they are promoted to 'senior agent'. This also entitles them to a commission on whatever sales the two latest recruits manage to bring into the fold. As a senior agent the member is entitled to €850 of each new €2,500 sale as well as €350 from sales made by their juniors. According to their chart, a person who makes their way to the top of the pile can walk away with a total of €159,900. How long that takes depends on the rate of growth of the pyramid.

Another senior agent was then introduced as Brendan O'Brien. He instructed new recruits: "You need to find a person's 'hot button'. Target people who work unsociable hours, people with more than one job." O'Brien was clear that these are the people who obviously dream of a get-rich-quick scheme.

Potential new recruits at the meeting who showed any reluctance to join up came under pressure. One Ignite Leisure salesman came out with the logic-defying line: "If you don't have €2,500, then borrow it from someone who does and give it to us. If you didn't have it to begin with and you don't have it now, then what's the problem?" Others were cajoled and asked to explain their fears about the scheme. Anyone feeling unsure that they would get their money back would be introduced to new converts, enthusing about how they had already made their investment back. For some it was nearly easier to sign up just to get out of the stuffy room and to escape the crude attempts at brainwashing.

By the end of the event 45 people agreed to sign up and to hand over €2,500 in cash by the following Wednesday. For the main organisers it was a tidy income of €112,000 for just one evening's work. By the end of the evening Dore, Lawler and O'Brien had done well.

One of those people whose 'hot button' got pressed was 55-year-old carpenter Tommy Burke from Bray,

County Wicklow. He had suffered a series of tragic events in his life. First, one son, 21-year-old Tristan, had died suddenly and in tragic circumstances. The year before his other son, 17-year-old Stephen, had succumbed to a brain haemorrhage which had left him paralysed and unable to speak before dying in 2004. In 2000, Tommy's elderly mother had died after falling into the sea. It was a trying time for Burke who had given up work to care for his stricken boy. Separated from his wife, he lived alone in a one-bedroomed council flat. Broke, in poor health and a recovering alcoholic, Tommy Burke could hardly have been more vulnerable. He had kept the cremated remains of his two sons to help with the grieving process. "It was my intention all along to give them a proper burial when I had the money," he said.

Just as he was at his lowest ebb, Tommy was approached in April 2005 by a couple whom he knew well. They knew that Tommy had just left hospital where he had undergone heart surgery. As he sat in a local café close to his flat, the pair asked him how he was recovering from the surgery. "I knew them well and they knew me equally well. They knew everything about me through their mother who I grew up with. That's why I went into it. They would have known of the loss of my sons and the fact that I did not have the money for their burial."

The couple didn't hang about and got straight to the point. Tommy's battered spirits soared when he heard what they had to say. "These just arrived to me at a restaurant and said 'Tommy, do you want a quick way of making money?' I just looked at them 'are you mad or what' but they said 'no this really works. It's a holiday club,'" he recalled.

They knew he was a plum ripe for the picking.

"When you are after going through the mill, you have that bit of naivety. You're vulnerable. He was driving a BMW and she was in a big car. They knew I was in AA and that I had good friends, some of which would have been wealthy."

The younger man had a history in sales and telemarketing. Tommy was in no condition to see through his slick patter and was easy prey for the pitch. The man's partner was, using Tommy's description, a sexy woman who knew how to attract the right kind of attention to get her customers. Tommy was made to feel as if this fabulous young couple were about to do him a favour that would turn his life around. "That's the way they worked. It's not my type of thing to stroke anybody, so when I seen these people coming along I couldn't believe it. They were so masterful in selling it. They believed in what they were doing. They knew the goals were high and there was big money involved in this thing. I only found afterwards they were into other pyramid schemes. They did know what was going on. They told me they were making money out of it. It was as simple as 'come and see and see what you think.'"

He went to a meeting organised by the Ignite Leisure outfit at the Great Southern Hotel near Dublin Airport. Tommy thinks there could have been between 400 and 500 people at the event. Bowled over by the energy of the evening, he admits he was putty in their hands. "The whole glamour of the thing, the music and then the presentation, it was in a top hotel. Everyone was dressed in their shirt and ties and pinstripe suits. The music took off and they showed pictures of the exotic holidays," he said. Glamorous models mixed and mingled during the short breaks between the different presentations. They did their best to make everyone feel at ease and as if they were the centre of attention.

The senior salespeople, the main organisers of the scheme, turned on the charm. They worked hard to blow away any lingering doubts and to stoke up the enthusiasm of their victims. "They had about eight fellas with them, who they had brought in to show how to do the big presentations. What they did then was produce people who had been away on holidays. The guy that was giving the big talk on Ignite Leisure, he was dressed in the suit. He looked the part," said Tommy.

With the benefit of hindsight he recalls the man as being somewhat "sleazy". "He looked like a bouncer on a door. He looked like a tough nut but a charmer, one of those guys, a real smoothie. My gut was telling me there was something bloody wrong here. At the time I think, I was so confused I thought this was a Godsend. You'd be going along with it in your head that this isn't a scam even though your gut would be telling you that it is. He went into this charming spiel of how he started off in business."

The high pressure sales pitches were almost too much for Tommy to resist but it was the apparent success of the organisers that finally swung Tommy into believing he had a good chance of making money out of the scheme. "These guys made a fortune out of it. I saw loads of people sign up to it. What made me sign up was that I started believing in the people who brought me in. I thought that they wouldn't lie to me because I knew their mother well, I grew up with their mother. I thought there's no way they would do that. I come from an ordinary working class estate and that sort of stuff never went on. It's the last thing you think would happen to you."

The Ignite Leisure professionals handed him the form to sign and a few days later he handed over the

€2,500 in cash, after taking out a bank loan he could ill-afford.

The plum had been picked.

After all the love-bombing from the couple who inveigled him into Ignite Leisure, Tommy felt slightly rejected once he'd paid out his €2,500. "The penny dropped the following week. They were so smooth when they were out to get me at the start and then it dropped off. They brought a Chinese woman in and just took the money off her. They were to collect her the following week, but they weren't even interested in bringing her in to show her how to make her money back. I noticed they were cold and ruthless bastards. They have necks like leather to be truthful about it. It was like they were two strokers, giving you a spiel. They could go through all this without blinking an eye. He rang me one night to say he was just back from Euro Disney and he'd made €14,000 out of Ignite Leisure while he was away."

In the meantime, Tommy had been contemplating encouraging his own friends and acquaintances to join up. "I brought a friend of mine in [to a meeting] and her boyfriend. They were very interested. She rang me and told me she was interested and had five other people, which meant I would have made a couple a grand that night. I got a bit nervous then because my gut was telling me it was wrong. I could have done with the money, but I thought 'I'm going to lose friends over money'," said Tommy.

With his common sense doubts getting harder to ignore, Tommy decided to approach the main organiser after one of the meetings: "I went to see yer man Ian [Dore] when they were doing the gig. I asked him to show me their insurance details as a holiday company. He nearly dropped and that's when it blew it out of the water for me. I rang my friend and told her I wasn't getting her involved. I was lucky in the end that I didn't have anything like that on my conscience."

The couple who enticed Tommy into the scheme lost a lot of friends including Tommy's daughter. There were rumours locally they had been threatened by other investors who got caught out. "There were two other chaps from my area that were stung as well. One of them was just getting married. We went to a solicitor about it, but it would have been too much bother for €2,500. After we were caught by it no one really wanted to talk about it." Three years later Tommy was still paying off the €2,500, commenting: "Anything I make now, I earn hard."

Tommy's gut feeling had been right all along.

* * * *

A pyramid scheme is a financial device that is always doomed to fail, no matter what bells and whistles are added through the slick sales patter of those pushing the scheme. The pyramid scheme, also known as Ponzi schemes in the United States, is a fraudulent way of making money. They are scams. In an example of a pyramid scheme a new member, let's call him Bob, is asked to invest €1,000. Bob then goes on to recruit four new members, bringing another €4,000 into the scheme. As the junior, Bob keeps €1,000, getting his investment back, and his recruiter gets €3,000. Those four new members also go on to each recruit another four more members. Bob's four recruits bring in a total of 16 new people, which means that Bob, his recruits and their recruits have now invested €21,000. Bob receives €12,000, of which he keeps €3,000 without having had to get involved in any more recruiting. Bob has now made a profit of €3,000. If the latest batch of recruits do their job then another 124 new investors pay €1,000 to join up. Bob's initial €1,000 has now created a pot of money worth €145,000 from just four layers of investors. From this fourth round of recruitment started by Bob, he keeps €9,000 and hands over €27,000 to his recruiter. Bob's €1,000 investment has now made him a €12,000 profit. A fifth round of recruitment brings in another €496,000 to the scheme, of which Bob gets to keep €27,000, bringing his total profit to €36,000.

To be continually successful the scam requires an infinite stream of new recruits. Pyramid schemes are so called because of the structure in which investors make up several layers of increasingly fewer investors. Bob's initial investment bought him a place at the bottom. The structure rises from the layers of new members to a single beneficiary at the top, in this case Bob's recruiter, who makes €144,000 from the section started by Bob. There are three others like Bob, so his recruiter's total take is now €576,000. It may sound great, but there is a major flaw. Consider that for Bob's €36,000 profit, a total of 496 people had to join the scheme. A pyramid scheme in which each junior member has to recruit ten new people would involve the entire population of the planet, in just ten levels. It works out at ten billion people. Even a scheme that required recruits to each bring in just four new members, would surpass the population of Ireland after ten levels. The initial members make a handsome profit, but the supply of new recruits quickly runs out. The only way someone can make money from a pyramid scheme is to defraud other people by persuading them into handing over money. The 'late' new recruits are promised the same healthy financial return that first sucked in their recruiters, when it is impossible for them to get anything back. If everyone is to be successful, the recruiting of new members has to go on forever. It is mathematically impossible for a pyramid scheme to succeed.

Even though common sense would appear to dictate that pyramid schemes are pointless, they are still hugely popular. It comes down to greed and people loving the fantasy of a get-rich-quick scheme. The con-artists who work hard at setting up schemes, and in fact do most of the recruiting themselves, prey on their victims' delusion and wishful thinking. According to them, people who don't get involved are fools and asking too many questions about how the scheme works is rude or unfriendly. Offering the lure of quick cash and using high-pressure sales techniques is all that a con-artist of below average talent actually needs to make big amounts of cash. Besides, everyone who is persuaded to join believes they are nowhere near the bottom of the pyramid.

The first task of a con-artist selling a pyramid scheme is to persuade his new recruits that it isn't a pyramid and to disguise the true and improbable nature of the financial structure behind the scheme. Ignite Leisure dressed itself up as being some kind of tourism company selling cut-price holidays. Other pyramid scams describe themselves as gifting schemes with titles such as Women Empowering Women, Liberty, The Money Tree, Infinity and so on. It is obviously easier to sell schemes if a con-artist can first disguise their bogus nature.

In the US, pyramid schemes are also known as Ponzi schemes because of one Charles Ponzi, a charismatic salesman with a tenuous grip on reality. In 1920, the Italian immigrant persuaded investors to hand over cash on the promise of healthy financial returns from a scheme trading in international postal reply coupons. Such coupons were bought by customers and sent abroad to allow a recipient to buy stamps in their own country. Ponzi realised that redeemed US coupons could be bought in Italy at a cheaper price than in the US. He organised to buy and re-import the coupons to the US where they could be re-sold for a profit. Basically, it was a form of arbitrage, buying low and selling high. The initial investors received their payments, making it look like they had bought into a fabulous scheme. Ponzi got friends and associates to back his venture, offering a 50 per cent return on their investment in an incredible 45 days. He started his own company, the Securities Exchange Company, to promote the enterprise. Ponzi claimed the profit on these transactions, after expenses and exchange rates, was in excess of 400 per cent. Some people invested and were paid off as promised. The word spread and investment came in at an ever-increasing rate. By July that year he was making millions. People were mortgaging their homes and investing their life savings. Ponzi lived luxuriously in a mansion with air conditioning and a heated swimming pool. He was a hero among the Italian community in the US, cheered wherever he went as the financial frenzy he had created went from strength to strength. Ponzi appeared to be bringing in cash at an incredible rate.

In reality Ponzi was mostly pocketing the money and using cash from fresh investors to make dividend payments. As long as money kept flowing in, existing investors could be paid with the newly-invested money, but the debts were soon building up. Things finally unravelled when a financial analyst, writing in a newspaper, pointed out that to cover the investments made with Ponzi's Securities Exchange Company,

160,000,000 postal reply coupons would have to be in circulation while just 27,000 actually existed. The authorities shut him down and began criminal proceedings against him.

Ponzi's scheme was essentially a pyramid scheme that needed an infinite supply of new investors to keep going. It was doomed to fail from the very beginning. Even after his conviction and jailing, Ponzi remained a hero to many of his 'investors', even to those who lost their life savings. On his release, such was his charisma that there were people still seeking him out to invest cash.

It would be naïve to think that pyramid schemes are anything other than schemes devised by professional fraudsters who get out early, leaving the hapless amateurs to deal with the mess. One such professional is Gabriel Francis MacEnroe. The jetset 63-year-old, with Irish citizenship, purported to have made a career as a financial deal maker. With a home in London and offices in Saint Gallen, Switzerland, MacEnroe was no slouch when it came to pushing his credentials. He had two companies Commercial Capital Finance in Switzerland and Commercial Capital Enterprises in Lichenstein. Flitting between clients all over the world, his home in London and office in Saint Gallen, MacEnroe liked to give the impression of being a top-level financial fixer. Internet searches reveal lengthy articles about MacEnroe which he could well have written himself. They included his involvement in some controversial schemes. One project he was involved in resulted in the collapse of a bank in Grenada which implicated the island's Prime Minister. Investors in the First International Bank of Grenada had been promised a 300 per cent return on their cash. The plot read like a tacky thriller in which the bank's main asset tools, a dodgy share certificate and a ruby, were fleeced from their true owners. This all added to the air of mystery with which MacEnroe likes to surround himself. Fact and fiction are mixed together for a potent cocktail that could leave the unwary with a serious hangover.

With this type of background it came as no surprise when MacEnroe became involved with an investment scheme being pushed by a husband and wife team in the United States. Throughout 1999 until early 2000, Virgil and Charlotte Womack worked hard at selling investment bonds for their companies Alliance Trust and Chemical Trust. They told investors they had offices in Georgia, Arizona, Alabama and Florida. They promised 25 per cent annual returns, on minimum $10,000 investments. The Womacks, through a network of 300 salespeople, told the investors their money would be put into high-yield government securities and property development projects. Hundreds of victims, many of them retirees living in South Carolina and Florida, handed over cash. The fraudsters had targeted elderly people, successfully stealing a massive $52 million dollars in a ruthless scam. When the scheme imploded the Womacks and other conspirators were arrested and indicted. In return for a more lenient sentence the Womacks co-operated with the FBI with the result that nearly half the stolen millions were recovered.

The Feds, however, hadn't given up on getting the rest of the money back. Twin bothers, Frederick and David Morgenstern, were discovered to have laundered the money through cheque cashing outlets controlled by a Miami-based Mafia family. The cash in turn was lodged in various international accounts, with the help of MacEnroe's companies. That was not MacEnroe's only link to the scheme. One of the victims stung by the Womacks was contacted by the bogus investment banker, who promised to help him retrieve his cash. The man contacted the FBI who then, using wire-taps, spent three months listening to MacEnroe at work as he attempted to set up the victim for a second fall. MacEnroe showed himself to be a slick and persuasive salesman with a cut-throat mentality. He promised the man a no-risk investment scheme that could yield an incredible 1,500 per cent return.

In subsequent court documents, FBI Special Agent Paul Jacobs outlined how they built the case against MacEnroe. The would-be victim and an undercover agent pulled off a sting on the fraudster by pretending they had $60 million to invest. To encourage them to invest David Morgenstern did his best to convince the target that the government's case against the Womacks' companies was bogus. He claimed that the cash was in the Bahamas earning ten per cent interest per month. In September 2000, Morgernstern told the man he would have to travel to Switzerland to meet Gabriel MacEnroe – the man who would handle the deal. He described MacEnroe as one of just five traders in the world who handled such specialised investment deals. In a move to create another layer of fog, MacEnroe then sent a fax to their target in which he said: "Please also be advised we do not allow, nor are we permitted to use, outside parties to negotiate or advise clients on what we do. Thus, the introductory party is going to see you to purely facilitate communications between us and establish a better understanding. He knows this, but I do have to mention this to you. He is not involved with us except as an introductory party. I am not in any way diminishing his role. He will be rewarded for his work. I trust this is acceptable to you." The idea was to plant the notion that MacEnroe and Morgenstern were not working together.

An undercover FBI agent, introduced by the would-be victim, then set up a meeting with MacEnroe and Morgenstern. When the agent expressed some concerns about the safety of the investment, he was told huffily by Morgenstern it was a privilege to be able to do business with someone of MacEnroe's calibre. The con-men constantly worked to build up MacEnroe's image as a world class financier, with connections at the highest levels. At the first meeting on October 16, MacEnroe promised the would-be investor that his money would see 400 per cent returns in the first year. He stated that his commission would be paid by the US Treasury Department and the Federal Reserve. MacEnroe told the investor that he could meet with the "approving officials" in Switzerland following the transactions. There followed more phone calls in the course of which MacEnroe promised the man he would bring documents that would show the location of the Chemical Trust money as well.

On October 30 MacEnroe met the target and the undercover agent and told them the investment would make between five and seven per cent per week, earning them $20 million in just six to eight weeks. The FBI later said that during this time MacEnroe made wild and various claims about the pedigree of his financial acumen and banking contacts. His ridiculous claims rolled easily from his lips, one after the other, as he was clearly convinced that he had his victim already on the hook. Among the spurious claims was that he worked with the US National Treasury, he was a "trustee" of the Central Intelligence Agency and he worked for the FBI, as did his father. He claimed that the Federal Reserve Bank would frequently enter into negotiations with him and his associates regarding investments. MacEnroe said that the high-yield scheme into which the target would be investing his $60 million involved a 52-satellite project for the National Security Agency in the United States. Later, in his affidavit, Special Agent Paul Jacobs, who ran the investigation, said: "MacEnroe further represented that the person actually handling the proposed investment was contracted with the Federal Reserve, that MacEnroe was associated with the NSA and that he had previously handled placement of investments for the CIA. He also stated that he was a financial advisor to the Vatican. MacEnroe further stated that there would be a "world tax exemption" for all profits generated from the proposed investment."

If MacEnroe was to be believed, it was a deal that was almost too good to be true. The Feds presumably kept a straight face when they were confronted with such boastful and outrageous lies.

MacEnroe was arrested there and then at the apartment complex in Myrtle Beach, Florida. The next day he appeared in court where bail was initially set at a hefty $800,000. MacEnroe's lawyers highlighted his high blood pressure and other medical problems. A doctor was ordered to the jail to treat him. Within a week the bail bond was reduced to a more manageable $200,000. When it was paid in cash he was released.

Two and a half years later, in June 2003, the bail bond was forfeited when MacEnroe failed to show for a court appearance in South Carolina. A warrant was also issued for his arrest and MacEnroe became a fugitive from the law-enforcement machinery of the United States.

In 2004, MacEnroe was back spinning stories, this time to the Irish newspaper *The Sunday Tribune*. He claimed he was completely innocent of the charges and that he had been on the verge of signing a plea-bargain deal before he left the US. He blamed the US authorities for reneging on that deal, by issuing the arrest warrant when he was too ill to travel.

"The reason why I didn't go back for the hearing was because I was seriously ill. The US authorities didn't accept that and so they issued a bench warrant for my arrest," he said.

He claimed he had never heard of the Womacks or their scam. He added he had been introduced to Morgenstern in 1998 and he agreed to do business with the American in 2000 when his references checked out. "I had no idea what he was really up to," he said in the interview. Money had been transferred to his company by Morgenstern but nothing like the $10 or $20 million that David Morgenstern had told the FBI. Even though, according to MacEnroe, bank records proved the statement to be false, he said the Feds decided to pursue him anyway. As for the Womacks' victim, MacEnroe claimed that he had been used by Morgenstern in an attempt to steal more money.

His story didn't cut any ice with the Feds. Two Assistant United States Attorneys from the Southern District of Florida, J Brian McCormick and Robert J Lehner, continued to pursue the case. In May 2007 they finally succeeded in extraditing MacEnroe from Switzerland. He appeared in West Palm Beach Federal Court in November, where he admitted charges relating to conspiracy to launder money and wire fraud. Court documents stated that he had received $2.8 million through the pyramid scheme operated by the Womacks and their network.

In January 2008, he was jailed for five years and five months for his role in laundering the proceeds of the massive pyramid scheme. A straight-forward investigation had cut through his tissue of lies and incredible claims and landed him right where he belonged.

MacEnroe's elaborate scheme and the Ignite Leisure scam point to the obvious fact that pyramid schemes are set in motion by professional criminals. In Ireland, the early pyramid schemes during the 1970s and 1980s took the form of product sales. While they didn't appear to be so obviously fraudulent, the schemes were clearly of a dubious ethical nature. Goods such as perfume, kitchen ware or books were bought and paid for up-front by new members. Once someone had sold enough products or recruited enough new investors they moved up the chain. By the time people realised the goods were useless or had already been over-sold, the scheme collapsed and they were stuck with dozens of boxes of unwanted goods. The outright fraudulent pyramid schemes also have an inglorious history in Ireland. Many scams have been imported from the UK which in turn had been imported from the US. In the United Kingdom pyramid selling schemes were outlawed in 1976 and in Ireland legislation was enacted in 1980. Despite this, throughout the 1990s and 2000s, there has been one scheme after another for which people have fallen.

Trading schemes, also known as multi-level marketing, are not illegal. They are a legal form of business, although ethically dodgy, in which people can earn money by selling the schemes' goods or services, usually from home. New recruits can earn extra commission by persuading others to join the scheme and from the sales made by people they've recruited. It's quite common to see handwritten notes posted in shops with something like: "Do you want to earn €3,000 a month part-time?" These schemes become illegal when their real purpose is to generate money by recruiting new participants. To the lay person it is a grey area that the fraudsters exploit with expert aplomb. The fact that Ireland's economy boomed thanks to a huge hike in property prices made more people ready for high-risk investment vehicles. Ten years of rising prices gave Irish investors a sense of not being able to lose.

One such scheme spread throughout Ireland like a particularly nasty 'flu bug. There were outbreaks among different areas and among different social sets. Known as Women Empowering Women (WEW), it was a scheme that sold itself, as the name implies, on being a support network for women. For an initial investment of IR£3,000 a member would receive IR£24,000 in a week, when they had brought in six new converts. Each new entrant had their name written into a chart. At the next meeting, to which they then brought six new recruits they moved to another level on the chart. The chart, not surprisingly, was in the shape of an inverted pyramid. When the wheels come off the pyramid scheme wagon, people can get very upset. Usually gullible participants have brought their own friends and family to join the scheme. It adds to the emotional fall-out when the schemes go bust.

The WEW was going strong in August 2001. Promotional leaflets promised women: "new ways of providing emotional support and financial gain in all our lives." A lady living in the upmarket suburb of Blackrock, County Dublin, was hosting one of the meetings at which new recruits would hand over their cash gifts. It was the second meeting that week. At the centre of the room was a crystal bowl full of cash. This would be handed over to the member next in line for their reward. The little ceremony, and the sight of the cash, would help push the new recruits in the drive for more members and quell any lingering doubts. A pleasant glass of wine also helped ease the process. After all, this was the Celtic Tiger sisterhood clubbing together to make money.

That evening on August 3, 2001, 70 women were taking part in meetings at the house. Some uninvited guests, however, suddenly turned up. There was chaos as three masked men burst into the house, one firing a shot from an air rifle. Another threatened the women with a handgun, while the third brandished a sledge-hammer. It was easy pickings to snatch the bowl of cash, containing IR£20,000 from the terrified women. The robbers piled into a Mitsubishi jeep and careered across a park area to make their escape. Behind them pandemonium broke out as the women hid behinds cars or tried to flee the area.

No one was ever charged with the robbery but it gave plenty of unwelcome publicity to the scheme. It was never clear whether the raiders were opportunist thieves from the criminal underworld or were thugs working for a disillusioned investor. The converts still trying to push the scheme worked quickly to repair the damage to keep the flow of new recruits coming in. As a result the name was changed to the suitably benign 'The Eternal Gifting Circle.'

There was one court case as result of Women Empowering Women. A brother and sister tried to sue former friends who had persuaded them to invest in the scheme. Flight attendant Rose Snedker and her brother Dermot, sued Linda Laird and her friend Hazel Johnson for breach of contract and misrepresentation after they had invested IR£4,500(€5,713) in the scheme. As they explained, at first things appeared rosy, with promises that they would make IR£45,000 in just two months. The introductory meetings were positive affairs with plenty of wine flowing and the sales pitch highlighting how it would take 37 years to make the same returns through a conventional bank. The Snedkers, from Templeogue Road, Dublin, became quickly disillusioned. They had yet to make any profit from their investment by the time their friend Ms Laird had made €26,000 from her investment. The Snedkers blamed Ms Laird for not putting enough effort into setting up recruiting meetings. They decided to use the courts to bring their former friends to book. Rose Snedker said in court that she had been unaware of any negative publicity about the gifting scheme and that it was likened to a pyramid scheme, with an inevitable collapse. She appeared to be convinced of the scheme's money-making capacity. She and her brother claimed they could have made their promised returns but Ms Laird had neglected to hold the scheduled meetings. When they asked for their IR£4,500 back, instead they got the run-around.

Lawyers for the defence claimed that the Snedkers had simply failed to find new participants and wanted to give up. In her own evidence, Ms Laird claimed that an estimated 4,000 to 6,000 people were involved in the scheme. It was vital, she said, to get into it as early as possible.

Judge Michael O'Leary said the Snedkers failed to prove there was any contract between themselves and the main beneficiary in the scheme. He ruled that a gifting certificate signed for Ms Laird did not represent a binding contract. The judge went on to state what should have been blindingly obvious from the start; that the scheme involved people coming in at the lowest tier and gifting money to others on the basis that contributions would come in from a "never-ceasing flow of new entrants". It was clearly unsustainable.

"Nemesis was an in-built feature of the scheme from the start. An early minority would win, but a large majority would always lose," he said. He also ruled that the case did not come within the scope of the 1980 Pyramid Selling Act, accepting that WEW was a 'gifting' scheme.

The judge had made the point that the Snedkers had failed to understand. Pyramid schemes, even ones called gifting schemes, can't and don't work. While a version of the scheme manages to avoid being illegal, it still remains outside the normal practices of legitimate business. In bringing their case to court, the Snedkers were still claiming that they could have got their expected investment. This seems to suggest that they were still under the illusion that a pyramid scheme could work. It was a hard lesson for the Snedkers to learn, but one that didn't seem to register with other people. Within six months, in May 2003, there were reports of another gifting scheme doing the rounds in Leinster, amongst equestrian enthusiasts. Known as Circles or The Network it promised an enticing 700 per cent return. The promo gushed: "There is no reason why this network should ever stop if people follow these simple guidelines. Money is energy and energy is continual. Keep it flowing!" No reason at all, apart from there not being enough people on the planet.

Another scheme involved 300 people and is thought to have generated €1.3 million. Such cash pales into comparison with the estimated €90 million supposedly generated throughout Cork and Kerry in 2005 by the Liberty scheme. It was another gifting scam that spread like wildfire, with the early entrants reaping huge benefits. A slick Power Point presentation was used to help persuade participants who seemed only too eager to get involved. Local pillars of the community including lawyers, business people and even police officers joined up. At one of many meetings, the would-be converts were given the usual sales pitch. The emphasis was on how the scheme would make an eight-fold return on their investment. In a quiet part of a suburban Cork city pub in 2006, two Liberty zealots made their sales bid. Unlike Ignite Leisure, it wasn't the typical high-pressure sales environment. Instead they relied on emphasising a sense of community. All Liberty needed to work was the trust of everyone in 'the family' working hard together as a team. The man leading the meeting used only a nickname, Cracker, and he claimed to run a small chain of retail outlets. The small lean man, with sandy hair spoke with an air of quiet confidence. Cracker was also very persuasive. He said he had made €320,000 from his investments, some of which he had used to buy property in Spain. Another player in the scheme smugly spoke of having a share in every level, such was the pace of income. They were very good at giving the impression that only a chosen few would be lucky enough to get a chance to buy their way into the scheme.

The Liberty System, the small meeting was told, originated in Africa and was brought to the US by a Canadian nun, before a German entrepreneur started it in Europe. "Liberty = Freedom, running successfully in Germany for eight years" read the presentation. The Liberty System is:

NOT a pyramid system.

NOT a snowball effect system.

NOT a type of lottery."

The word 'not' was printed in bold red letters. The presentation went on to show a diagram of a pyramid system, consisting of five layers of circles in the shape of a pyramid. Next was the same diagram upside down with the explanation: "The Liberty Chart works like this."

Surprisingly the low-key sales approach seemed to work, judging by the numbers in Cork and Kerry who enrolled in the get-rich-quick scheme. Entrants bought a position on the pyramid by buying a 'money ball' or a share of a ball worth €20,000. There were eight such balls on the bottom level of the chart, adding up to €160,000. That money was, in theory, handed over to the members or owners of the ball at the top of the pyramid, representing a €140,000 profit for that person or group. Once a ball reached the number one position it had to drop out. The two balls just below the top then became the top of two new pyramids or 'charts'. The initial layer of eight balls, also split into two each forming the second layer of the two new pyramids. Work then started on filling up the new eight-ball layers. Those previously involved in the top position could re-enter again by buying in for a new €20,000 investment.

According to the people pushing the Liberty System, to join a chart a new entrant would hand over the money in Germany, where under local laws it counts as being tax-free. "It's about lots of money and lots of trust," reads the presentation. "When the eight-ball entry level is full, we travel to Munich to present the money. After every money presentation, each person moves up one level in the chart until they reach the money position. You can go in under whatever name you want, it doesn't make any difference as it is completely anonymous. The only time you use your actual name is on the documentation that accompanies the money presentation."

New recruits are reassured that even if they have problems recruiting people to the eight-ball level their "team" will help them. Of course there are the usual warnings about letting the unconverted know too much about the scheme. Information meetings are by invitation only "in order to prevent Joe Public from attending." The presentation warns that only word of mouth is allowed to advertise the scheme. The aura of secrecy feeds into the sense that participants are getting an opportunity that most people will never even know about. It also means that the scheme is perfectly suited for running a straight-forward con. The four-ball and two-ball levels are filled with fictional investors to encourage gullible victims to join the eight-ball level.

Although, by early 2006, the Liberty System was clearly on its last legs thanks to a lot of negative publicity, it was claimed there were still plenty of "healthy charts" for newcomers to buy into. Despite the emphasis on trust and the importance of making tax-free payments in Germany, 'Cracker' was able to offer a share of a four-level ball.

"All that stuff about Germany is bullshit. You can buy straight into level four if you want and hand over the cash in Ireland. You only have to hand over the cash in Germany if you are starting at the eight-ball level. If you still want to start at the eight-ball I can organise someone to hand over the cash for you," he said.

As with all pyramid schemes the Liberty System crashed with typical results. In the town of Clonakilty, one woman seen as an organiser, was frog-marched to an ATM by a mob of disgruntled investors. There was a stand-off at a hotel in Bandon where a meeting had been scheduled after it emerged all the beneficiaries were members of the same family. The Gardaí were called in to investigate the scheme and some of the revenge attacks sparked by the ensuing controversy. A truck and heavy machinery were damaged in one arson attack as a result of the fallout. There were even rumours that an entry level €1,000-a-ball version of the scheme had been started among schoolchildren. In February 2007, it emerged that officers had sent a file to the Director of Public Prosecutions as a result of their investigations into the Liberty scheme and its subsequent fallout. No prosecutions have gone ahead.

Despite the furore over the Liberty Scheme no one faced a prosecution. Similarly, Woman Empowering Women was deemed by a District Court judge not to fall under the 1980 Pyramid Selling Act. It highlights the difficulty with the law when people decide, of their own free will, to hand over their money to a fraudulent or a doomed financial scheme. There is no law protecting people from their own gullibility. There also always seems to be enough ambiguity about the legality of 'contracts' to sow doubts in the minds of the disgruntled participants in such schemes. By the time they finally persuade themselves that they have been the victim of a con, it is too late or too expensive to do anything about it.

Pyramid schemes appear to spread like a social virus. The origins of each scheme are always unclear as they flower and then wither in one geographic or demographic locale after the other. In Cork it was difficult to pin down the source of the pyramid outbreak which resulted in the Liberty Scheme. With Ignite Leisure, there appeared to be a hard core of organised professionals pushing the scheme. Compared to the antics of the shifty thugs from Ignite Leisure, MacEnroe was sheer class. It takes as much effort to tell a big lie as it does to tell a small one. MacEnroe clearly went for broke and told some really big ones. Playing the role of an international financier is probably more fun that trying to sell a share of a 'money ball' in west Cork. When it comes down it, however,

MacEnroe and 'Cracker' are basically just liars and cheats who'll tell gullible or greedy people what they want to hear. The victims in such cases, the pensioners robbed by the Womacks or Tommy targeted by his old neighbour's kids, are left with an uncertain future. The nest egg is gone or they are saddled with a debt they'll struggle to pay off. The con-artist in the pyramid schemes dazzle their prospective 'clients' with technicalities and promises of outlandish returns. They have such skill that many people will continue to fall for the schemes.

TEN

The Counterfeiters

Illicit goods, fakes and forgeries are a multi-billion dollar global industry. Bogus products are available everywhere and anything that can be faked probably has been by this stage. In back street operations cheap alcohol is poured into bottles with fake, but expertly printed, brand labels. Handbags, jewellery, sunglasses, shoes, jeans and 'designer' T-shirts produced by the black market are widely sold. There are also imitations that are obviously counterfeit but the buyer seems happy to take the cheaper option. There is always a demand for illicit goods whether it is just to dodge taxes, supply a low-cost product or to get around some other local restrictions. For example, in 2003, Irish soccer fans who travelled to Tehran, Iran, for a World Cup qualifier match found people willing to bring them to illicit booze parties. The fans enjoyed the thrill of drinking out-of-date cans of lager in a Muslim country notorious for its hard-line religious police. Profound political, social and commercial revolutions such as the fall of Communism, the globalisation of world markets, the internet, the lowering of currency restrictions and better communications, have all contributed to a boom in the underworld of piracy and forgery. The same dodgy designer watches hawked by street-sellers in New York can be found in Asian-owned shops on the Canary Islands. Fake digital video cameras are made in factories that have licit and illicit production lines running in tandem. Fraudsters have evolved from cottage industry artisans to global entrepreneurs.

In February 2007, Operation Diabolo was launched by the European Anti-Fraud Office (OLAF). The joint operation, involving various custom agencies, seized 67 shipping containers which had originated from Asian ports. The haul provided a disturbing snapshot of the scale of the trans-national trade in counterfeit goods. It included 135 million counterfeit-branded cigarettes, and 557,000 other counterfeit products such as textiles, furniture, suitcases, mobile phone accessories, footwear, electronics, toys, sunglasses and football shirts. It took the co-operation of customs officers from 27 EU member states, as well as help from the authorities in Israel and Egypt, to organise the operation.

The scope for forgery and trade in illicit goods is unlimited. Condoms, prescription drugs, budgies and even herbs have been faked. In 2006, OLAF had previously launched an investigation into the smuggling of garlic into Europe. Grown cheaply in China it was then shipped to Europe. En route, the garlic was re-labelled as local produce. This way the producers don't have to pay a 9.2 per cent tax or the specific tariff of €1,200 per tonne. Considering that 20 tonnes of garlic can be loaded into a shipping container, the smuggler can make a substantial profit of €24,000 per load. OLAF officials estimated garlic smuggling was costing the EU taxpayer €60 million a year.

The illicit industry of fakes and forgeries is full of highly professional corporate criminals who sell bogus goods throughout markets and retail outlets worldwide, but there is of course, still room for the one-man cowboy operator. The 'white vans' piling on and off the ferries between Ireland, Britain and continental Europe shift a lot of dodgy goods. Millions of euro worth of tobacco and cigarettes are smuggled this way. Once they reach Ireland they are sold on through street vendors and black market networks. All the little vans plying back and forth can generate a large volume of traffic. One man who made regular trips across the water in his trusty Transit was businessman Richard O'Brien. Around 2005, his main energies were focussed on his Birdworld shop in Portlaoise in the Irish midlands. Situated in a housing estate, the shop had a ramshackle appearance. At best it could be described as having an 'earthy' feel. On any given day a visitor could hear the birds singing furiously. To the untutored eye it looked no different from any other pet shop, despite being a little down-at-heel. To those in the know, however, there were signs that all was not as it should be. The drinking water had a blue hue, a sign of the antibiotics fed to the finches, parrots and canaries to keep them free of infection. Some of the birds showed signs of distress, fluttering non-stop in their cages. Others had leg-rings that were loose and would sometimes fall off. O'Brien was relatively new to the business, but had connections all over Ireland. He regularly traded with other pet supplies stores, selling pet birds to them for the retail trade. The unkempt pet shop owner, wholesaler and bus driver was a frequent visitor to Belgium, a smuggler's paradise because of the low tax-rate on tobacco. One day in Kent, as O'Brien rolled off the ferry at Dover port, he was stopped. If the Customs and Excises officers had expected a van crammed with booze or cigarettes, then they were in for a surprise. Instead of the usual tax-dodging booty, they found hundreds of song birds. The van was packed full of the birds and also contained pet rodents, some of which had escaped from their boxes and were running around.

"It was a van literally stuffed full of animals. Some were in crates; some were running loose in the van.

There were parrots, mice, gerbils, finches and starlings, to name but a few," said an officer.

Trading Standards officials took over and sent O'Brien to an animal reception centre in Heathrow where a rest period for the little creatures was enforced. A fine of STG£3,760 was imposed on O'Brien for the prohibited landing of animals and the transport of animals in a manner likely to cause injury.

Strange as it may seem, O'Brien was in effect trading in fake birds. The birds he passed off as being born and bred in captivity were in fact bought without any certification or paperwork at open air markets in Belgium. The Sunday morning markets at Antwerp and Brussels are famous among bird lovers. It was there that O'Brien bought the vast majority of his feathered cargo. The traded birds are bred in farms in countries such as the Czech Republic, Romania and Bulgaria. Many others were wild-birds captured in North Africa and the Middle East for sale in the pet trade. The birds are shipped from countries where there have been confirmed cases of the Avian Flu virus, H5N1. Oblivious to the potential health risks, O'Brien tapped into the well-established network of dealers who were only too happy to supply the right kind of paperwork for the wrong kind of birds. The certificates are supposed to relate to a number on the birds' leg-rings. The tiny leg-rings were loose, however, because they were fitted when the birds were fully grown. Birds bred in captivity have the rings fitted within days of hatching and there is no danger of them falling off as the bird grows. The chances of every single bird being checked by customs are extremely slim. In case of a cursory check one certificate for ten birds with the same leg-ring number is more than enough. The rogue dealers have also worked on ways to fit the leg ring, to make it look as if it was done when the bird was a chick.

Trapping wild birds is a cruel practice but there is a strong economic reason for doing it. Goldfinches, prized as song birds and plucked from the air for free, can be sold in Belgium for €40. It's a lot cheaper to buy a van load of canaries, with fake paperwork, than it is to breed them. It doesn't take as much skill or time either. The trappers use 'mist' nets, which have a fine mesh that a bird in flight won't see. Once caught, the birds can struggle and injure themselves in the net. Even when caged, a wild bird will throw itself against the bars in a desperate attempt to fly away. Another tactic used by the trappers is to spread rat-glue on birds' favourite perches. The birds become stuck fast and are easily caught. Only about ten per cent of birds caught in this fashion actually survive to reach a customer.

Customs officials, busy with cigarette bootleggers, and agricultural inspectors, holding back the tide of illegally imported calves can be forgiven for not prioritising the bird trade. O'Brien found a niche in the market and was determined to make it pay. By the end of 2005 he was making monthly trips to Belgium. One member of the bird-breeding industry suggested O'Brien could be making as much as €25,000 on each shipment. He was also making money on the outward trip. On one of several visits to Birdworld, inspectors from the National Parks and Wildlife Service found Irish wild birds that had been illegally caught. Just as there is a demand for canaries in Ireland, abroad native-Irish birds are easily sold. Attempts had been made to fit leg-rings to the wild Irish finches the inspectors found in Birdworld. For his trouble O'Brien was taken to court and fined €1,000. A rather more exotic discovery was a Macaw. This endangered species, also found on his tatty premises, is a rare and beautiful bird. It is so under threat that the only place licensed to legally keep it in Ireland is Dublin Zoo.

Regardless of the attention from the National Parks and Wildlife Service inspectors, O'Brien carried on. A crate of canaries delivered through Dublin Airport was stopped and inspected in January 2006. Destined for O'Brien's shop, it was found to contain the carcass of a dead bird amongst those still alive. The remains were sent for testing, but were too decomposed. Samples were also taken from five other birds. In the meantime O'Brien, despite being exposed as an unscrupulous dealer, was given the suspect shipment and told to keep the birds in quarantine. At the height of the fears about Avian Flu reaching Ireland, a couple of dead swans in Wicklow made the evening news. There was also plenty of media coverage about the dangers of a cross-over virus to humans and the devastation that could be caused by a SARS epidemic. The government was criticised for not stockpiling any supplies of the anti-flu drug Tamiflu. O'Brien's dodgy canaries, however, didn't seem to attract a great deal of interest.

12 days later the samples from the five other birds proved negative for the Avian Flu virus. Even though the authorities were warned in advance of one shipment organised by O'Brien, it sailed through Rosslare Port without an obstacle. The hit-and-miss nature of customs work, when it comes to keeping unwanted deliveries out of the country, couldn't have been more apparent. At a time when owners of free-range fowl were being told to keep them indoors and away from wild birds, O'Brien's dodgy business continued unmolested.

The potential danger posed by cowboy dealers like O'Brien was made apparent in the UK. One of the few cases of Avian Flu in the country was traced back to an aviary in Essex. Pegasus Birds was run by a man who was a convicted fraudster and had been exposed on a TV show as a rogue trader. He traded in the same type of exotic birds found in Birdworld. O'Brien's Birdworld and Pegasus Birds are perfect examples of the organic nature of the global trade in illicit goods. The illegal trapper, whether in an Irish bog or in a Moroccan river valley, are part of the same system. The 'white vans' move back and forth over a journey that can span thousands of miles. O'Brien didn't have to go too far, from Ireland to Belgium but those few miles are enough to make the connection between the western-most shores of Europe to the steppe plains that run from central Europe to China. There is a demand for illicit imports everywhere. Like the garlic shipped from China, once the leg-ring was changed a wild-caught bird was turned into a captive-bred bird and it became fully legal and ready for re-sale.

In Ireland there are markets, just like the bird bazaar in Belgium, where there are plenty of illicit goods on sale. Most Sunday mornings there are a series of markets dotted all over Ireland. Shoppers who are early enough, and unscrupulous enough, can get a good deal from dodgy traders on obviously stolen material. Power tools and tradesmen's equipment are the best bargains, with the understanding that no questions are asked. Lawnmowers, most likely liberated from a suburban garden shed, are another good seller in early spring. Trade from the white vans is brisk. A lot of the stalls will have legitimate goods such as cheap imported clothes, T-shirts, plastic and electric goods. Others will have fake designer clothes, ranging from Armani suits to Fred Perry T-shirts, as well as counterfeit Gucci or Louis Vuitton designer bags. At the weekend markets there is also a heavy trade in the latest Hollywood film releases. Blockbuster movies that haven't even opened in European cinemas can be bought for as a little as €3 a DVD. Anyone with a reasonable computer and an internet connection can download a bootleg copy of a new movie. Even so, there is still a vibrant trade for pirate DVDs. People are too lazy to download a movie that can be bought so cheaply. Despite the shabby appearance, this is a trade in which professional operators have a huge influence. They pay thousands to steal early review copies or to film the big-screen version at a preview showing. Within hours, the same movies can be on sale all over the world. The counterfeit pirates work hard at their trade.

In February 2007, a raid at a market in Drogheda netted the Gardaí counterfeit DVDs that would have sold for €100,000. The stalls had simply been abandoned by the traders once the raid had started. The Drogheda traders had even made an effort to pass off the fakes as the genuine article as they came complete with good quality covers. These raids are now so commonplace as to be routine.

Gardaí, working with the anti-copyright theft organisation INFACT, seized another 20,000 illegal copies of movies in April 2008. In the house, near Balbriggan in north County Dublin, DVD-burning equipment was also discovered. It was clear that this was an illegal operation being run at a commercial level. The size of the haul and the type of equipment made it one of the largest counterfeiting factories exposed so far in Ireland. Gardaí estimated that the value of counterfeit DVDs recovered was about €500,000. There were also 90 DVD burners found in the house, some of which were able to copy ten discs at a time. The equipment was valued at close to €500,000 as well, totalling an overall haul of €1 million. There had obviously been a significant investment on the part of pirates, assuming that the equipment hadn't been stolen. The Balbriggan factory was probably supplying markets within a short driving distance. One nearby market had come to the attention of local Gardaí. They made seizures of smuggled cigarettes and counterfeit DVDs nearly every weekend. Such seizures could probably be made every week at markets all over Ireland if the Gardaí had the resources to do it.

The Balbriggan factory is just one illustration of how well-organised and professional the pirating criminals have become. The scale of the DVD copying and counterfeit clothing business in North Dublin was obvious from another Garda operation just a month earlier in March 2008. The officers from the Criminal Assets Bureau targeted the activities of one 15-man gang. In a series of raids, in one weekend, officers seized goods that would have retailed for €3 million. They searched 23 premises around Dublin in the operation aimed at disrupting their black market trade. The gang, based in south inner-city Dublin specialised in the sale and distribution of many kinds of bootleg goods including clothes, sportswear, jewellery and other fashion accessories. The haul of dodgy goods included fake Lacoste, Armani and Nike products, as well as footwear, sunglasses and DVDs. Considering that €5 million worth of counterfeit goods were seized in the whole of 2007, the haul was a massive seizure. The Gardaí had to hire a warehouse specifically to store all the illicit goods. The rule of thumb applied to drug smuggling is that just ten per cent of shipments are seized. If the same criteria is to be applied, then the seizures in March and April 2008 suggest counterfeiting and bootlegging is an industry of significant financial worth.

Pirating movies is just one revenue stream for criminal organisations. They can also make their money from fuel laundering, drug-running, people trafficking and producing fake brand-name booze. Gardaí who seized a cache of counterfeit DVDs in Louth in December 2000 were left in no doubt about the criminal capabilities of the people they were dealing with. A mobile shop on the road was found to contain thousands of counterfeit DVDs which, just 12 days before Christmas Day, were destined for people's Christmas stockings. Customs called in the Gardaí to seize the goods under the Copyright Act, as they were worth about €120,000. Three unarmed Gardaí were left to watch the haul of illicit goods at Carrickeena, not far from the village of Jonesboro across the border.

Six hours later two rockets were fired into the air, close to the mobile shop. Six or seven men dressed in camouflage and wearing balaclava masks then blocked the road on both sides. One man carried a handgun, another a rifle and others were armed with metal bars. The Gardaí couldn't put up any resistance. They had no choice but to watch as the gang connected the trailer to a jeep and made off over the border with their mobile shop. The effrontery of the raiders left the police in no doubt that they were dealing with the border bandits, who were probably members of the dissident republican group the Real IRA. At the time Garda sources claimed that counterfeit DVDs were sold to raise funds for the paramilitary group.

Those DVDs were most likely sold by stall holders at the Sunday market in Jonesboro. Located in south Armagh the market was in an area that had long been controlled by the Provisional IRA. During the Troubles security forces from either side of the border would have faced huge difficulties trying to police the trade in counterfeit goods. The border bandits running the trade have been part and parcel of the Provisional IRA's organisation for 30 years. They have developed counterfeiting and smuggling to the highest levels of proficiency. The type of operation broken up in Balbriggan in 2008 could trace its origins to those developed by the border bandits working in the security of no-go areas. The gangs in south Armagh, north Louth and Monaghan are every bit as good at their jobs as criminal organisations anywhere else in the world. Customs in Northern Ireland in July 2006 estimated the trade to be worth at least STG£270 million a year. The same year a report by the House of Commons Northern Ireland Affairs committee stated that the police in Northern Ireland were seizing more fake goods than the other 43 police forces in Britain combined. The sale of fake goods was, and still is, big business.

The fuel smuggling trade also became very big business in Ireland's border area, flourishing from the early 1990s. By 2002, it was estimated that the sale of illegal fuel in Northern Ireland had cost the UK Exchequer the equivalent of €29 million a month in lost revenue. At its most simple the fraud works by filling a tanker at a distributor in the Republic of Ireland and then driving it, illegally, across the border. The excise paid on a tanker-load in the south is €13,000. In Northern Ireland, where the duty is considerably higher, it would be equivalent to €29,000. The smugglers pocket the difference. But there is also a dirty side to the business. Diesel intended for agricultural or industrial use has an even lower tax-rate, making it cheaper for use in off-road vehicles and machines. By 2008, the

unmarked diesel known as 'fuel oil' retailed at around
€1.40 per litre while marked diesel, known as 'gas oil'
sold for €1 per litre. To curb the use of fuel in road
vehicles that is meant for heating homes, running
generators and farm machinery, an easily detectable
chemical marker is added to it. The unmarked diesel is
free of the visible dye. The smugglers, however, simply
set up crude diesel-laundering plants to get rid of the
chemical marker. Marked diesel is pumped through a
series of tanks. Kitty litter is used to soak up the
markers and the diesel is then 'washed' with sulphuric
acid. The product is basically a counterfeit, tax-free fuel.
Since 2005, 18 such laundering plants have been broken
up by Excise officials on both sides of the border. At the
same time 60 per cent of legitimate retailers in Northern
Ireland went bust. They were unable to compete with
the cut price, bootleg fuel on sale. The smugglers even
went as far as counterfeiting fuel tanker vehicles. One
tanker, complete with the livery of a legitimate international oil business, was being followed by Customs
officials. When they rang the driver to discover his
destination, they realised that the real truck was in a
completely different location. Customs officers have
discovered bogus tankers on more than one occasion.

The people who control a stake in the fuel
laundering business have made a lot of money. One of
these 'businessmen' is Eamon Devlin. In the early 2000s
Devlin looked the part of the successful border
businessman. Originally from Culloville, on the
northern side of the border, he is a native of the border
bandit heartland. His house, 'The Rath', on the Ardee
Road outside Dundalk is a splendid head-turner. He
owns a string of spectacularly successful racehorses
and hasn't been shy in attending champagne-guzzling
occasions to celebrate their victories. One of his horses,

Ansar, owned by his wife Kay, won the Galway Plate. Few people in such social circles knew the full extent of his role in the cross-border fuel laundering racket. Throughout the 1990s Devlin was responsible for supplying 2.4 million gallons of laundered diesel to filling stations throughout Northern Ireland. Devlin was regarded as one of the Mr Bigs when it came to the cross-border fuel-laundering rackets. He came to wider notice during the trial of John Hunter in Belfast in 2002. Regarded as Devlin's partner, the operation was estimated to have cost the UK taxpayer STG£6 million. This was in just an eight month period between July 1997 and May 1998. At the time the 50-year-old Shell-station owner knew Devlin through the business. In 1997 Hunter had become bankrupt and was battling alcoholism. According to Hunter's defence barrister, when Devlin made his client an offer: "it was the best day of his life." Devlin offered him a financial lifeline and a connection to the flow of illegal diesel controlled by the border bandits. At the time, diesel was nearly 20 per cent cheaper in the Irish Republic than in Northern Ireland. Hunter built up a client base that included at least 40 petrol stations where Devlin's laundered diesel and smuggled petrol was sold. The pair is thought to have moved at least 30 million litres of fuel during this period. Hunter admitted he made STG£120,000 from the scam but the prosecution lawyer at his trial stated: "there must be a lingering suspicion that the amount which he pocketed was substantially in excess of that."

Hunter was jailed for two and a half years. Devlin, although named in court, had managed to stay out of reach of the Northern Ireland authorities. Behind the scenes, however, there were efforts being made by the authorities to force Devlin to face the music in Northern Ireland. In August 2007 Devlin finally appeared before the High Court in Dublin on an arrest warrant. The supporting documents stated that he was wanted for not paying STG£10 million in tax. Devlin was remanded on foot of his own surety of €40,000 and an independent surety of €20,000. His lawyers argued a technical point over the European Arrest Warrant regarding the implications of a tick in a box on one of the accompanying documents. They also claimed that the warrant was not issued until April 2007, ten years after the alleged failure to pay his taxes. Such a delay would prejudice his chance of a fair trial it was argued. They also pointed to the fact that in 2000 Devlin had a liver transplant and raised the prospect that even a mild infection could be enough to kill him. Considering his deteriorating medical condition, the effect of the delay was even more 'oppressive' on Devlin.

In February 2008, Mr Justice Michael Peart upheld the request for extradition to Northern Ireland. He also granted leave to appeal to the Supreme Court. To this day, Eamon Devlin remains living in the Republic of Ireland.

Like Devlin, Thomas 'Slab' Murphy was another of the border bandits, but he was more than just a smuggler. As a senior member of the Provisional IRA, and eventually Chief of Staff of the organisation, he was an influential and dangerous figure. He came to public prominence after he tried to sue the *Sunday Times* for libel. They had printed an article in 1985 in which he was named as an IRA commander. He lost the 11-year legal battle in 1998 and costs were awarded against him. 'Slab' Murphy has never paid the STG£600,000 bill.

The bachelor farmer's high status within the IRA was built on his capabilities as a smuggler. His success was helped hugely by virtue of the fact that his farm property straddled the border at Ballybinaby,

Hackballscross. He could move from one jurisdiction to the other while staying in his own farmyard. Murphy ran the area close to his farm with an iron fist. Other smugglers using Larkin's Road, which crossed the border at his front gate, had to pay for the privilege. Nothing went on without his knowledge and approval. It would have been impossible for the likes of Eamon Devlin to operate without deference to Murphy. A BBC documentary team who attempted to film Murphy's farmhouse in 2004 were chased by two car loads of men. The pursuit of the journalists went on until they reached the safety of a Garda station near Castleblaney. They were later escorted back across the border by the Gardaí, from where they safely returned back to Belfast. The BBC team estimated Slab Murphy was worth about €50 million. This placed him at number nine in an Underworld Rich List they were compiling at the time.

While security forces on both sides of the border were aware of the smuggling and fuel laundering activities, there was little they could do. Throughout the Troubles the northern side was an absolute no-go area for the British Army and the police, never mind customs offices or tax officials. 'Slab' Murphy, the paramilitary struggle and the fundraising efforts through illicit trade, were directly connected. From the mid-1990s, however, as the peace process paid dividends in Northern Ireland, there was increased political pressure to roll up the criminal activities that had funded the IRA for years. Following the Provos' ceasefire 'Slab' Murphy opted to side with the dissidents, one of the few senior members to do so.

When police and customs finally raided his premises in March, 2006, they discovered an efficient operation. In the kitchen of his farmhouse his half-eaten breakfast sat on the table but 'Slab' was nowhere to be found. The officers had expected to find evidence of a fuel laundering operation and they weren't disappointed. Two fuel tank systems were connected by a pipe that crossed the border. Although the tanks were in separate jurisdictions they were housed in the same outhouse, built on Murphy's land. It made it almost impossible to detect the fuel smuggling. Of the 18 laundering plants discovered by the Gardaí close to the border, this one was the most sophisticated. The police also found €1 million worth of cash and cheques, some hidden in a plastic bag, on the property. The Criminal Assets Bureau (CAB) won a High Court order to give them control of the cheques and cash. Also discovered were six oil tankers used to ferry the laundered fuel around Ireland, 30,000 smuggled cigarettes and 8,000 litres of laundered fuel. Crucially, while 'Slab' Murphy avoided arrest, the authorities found several documents which they claim provided the financial details of the massive fuel laundering operation.

In May 2006, the CAB was back in the High Court seeking €5.3 million from 'Slab' Murphy after an initial assessment of his assets. In documents supplied to the courts Detective Chief Supt Felix McKenna said the CAB had been investigating Murphy and his operation for some considerable time. He said Murphy and his two brothers, Frank and Patrick Murphy had for the past 20 years been involved in the oil distribution industry, oil smuggling and money-laundering activities. His evidence was based on the information gleaned from the documents found during the raid in March, 2006.

The intensive probe into 'Slab' Murphy's finances continued. A year later, the 58-year-old farmer was arrested in dramatic fashion by members of the Emergency Response Unit who stopped his car near his

Louth home. He was charged with nine counts of failing to make tax returns from 1997 to 2004.

On November 8, 2007 Murphy appeared at Ardee District Court where he was bailed after lodging €20,000 with the court. His trial was later set for hearing in the non-jury Special Criminal Court, a decision the County Louth farmer challenged in the High Court. After losing that challenge in January 2008, his lawyers sought to overturn the decision in the Supreme Court. His case, like that of Eamon Devlin's, remains on the court list but can't be heard until the back-logged Supreme Court makes a ruling on the legality of its referral to the Special Criminal Court.

Thomas 'Slab' Murphy was a key figurehead in the Provisional IRA and later within the dissident Republican movement. Sean Garland, however, had legendary status. He was an IRA gunslinger in the 1950s, when there was almost no popular support for the organisation. As a raw recruit he was ordered to infiltrate the British Army to get weapons. He successfully carried out his mission, establishing his reputation. He then became involved in planning, and participating in, IRA operations from 1955 to 1956. His actions in one particular raid became part of Republican lore.

On New Year's Day 1956 he led a squad of 14 IRA men to attack the police station at Brookeborough in County Fermanagh. But the high-risk plan didn't work and two of the attackers, Sean South and Fergal O'Hanlon, were shot dead by the police. Even though wounded by bullets, Garland braved the gunfire to rescue a dying comrade. The gun battle was later enshrined in song *Sean South of Garryowen*, made famous by The Wolfe Tones.

There could be no doubting Garland's devotion to the cause. His political beliefs landed him in jail on both sides of the border. When the IRA spilt in the late 1960s into traditional and Marxist factions, he followed the left-wing thinking. He became one of the leaders of what became known as the Official IRA. Although it announced a ceasefire in 1972, it remained embroiled in a number of lethal feuds with figures from the Provisional IRA and other splinter groups. Garland himself was shot and badly injured by one such splinter group in 1975. He was attacked by a gunman close to his Ballymun home in Dublin. The Irish National Liberation Army claimed responsibility for the shooting. The Official IRA continued to exist for years and raised funds by running drinking clubs in Northern Ireland. They were also involved in forgery and robberies. Forgery was justified not only as a way of making cash, but also as a way to undermine the economy of the oppressor. Garland was elected General Secretary of Official Sinn Fein in 1977 which later changed its name to the Workers Party. He remained General Secretary of the party until he was elected President in 2000. One of the fundamental beliefs within the Workers Party had been complete opposition to the foreign policy of the United States. They stated it has: "inflicted great suffering, repression and untold deaths."

Despite his varied and colourful career as both an IRA commander and politician, there was another strand to his life. During the 1990s the legendary IRA man had become tied up with a near mythical forgery scam known as the 'superdollar'. The forged dollars were given this name because their quality was at such a high level. Only a forensic expert could tell the fake money from real dollars. The counterfeit $100 notes, with Benjamin Franklin's perfect portrait, were a serious cause for concern. They had the potential to de-stabilise the dollar. As it is virtually the standard currency against which other currencies are measured for value, this could have a global effect.

At a Congressional hearing into the phenomenon of superdollars in 2006, Deputy Assistant Treasury Secretary Daniel Glaser commented: "A little bit of counterfeit currency of very high quality can go a very long way". It can cause "people to lose their faith in the dollar, which is extremely important to the United States to maintain."

The superdollars were traded at a price lower than face value. The money, however, would eventually be used by people at its full value, unaware that the note was a forgery. In 1989 the first superdollars had been detected in circulation in the Philippines. Concern about the potential appearance of the superdollar in Ireland during the early 1990s led banks to decline to exchange $100 notes. In a bid to frustrate the forgers, the US government had introduced changes to the notes in 1996. The intricate new safeguards had included an enhanced embedded security thread, a security watermark, changed micro-printing and the use of an optically variable ink. The old $100 dollar notes became known as 'small head' and the new ones as 'big heads', because of a change to President Franklin's portrait. But by the late 1990s counterfeit big-head superdollars started appearing in circulation. It hadn't taken the highly sophisticated forgery operation very long to counteract the new security measures. So far, the US government has seized about $50 million worth of the fake notes. Most are so good they are only detected when they reach the Federal Reserve.

Garland's role in the superdollar scam was uncovered following a huge investigation. Police in Birmingham, in the United Kingdom first launched Operation Mali in 1998 when samples of the superdollars appeared in the city. They had been detected after a man tried to pass them through a city centre travel agency. Until then superdollars had been passing unnoticed through the banking system in the UK. Although prosecuted, the man was acquitted. At his trial he claimed that he had won them in a poker game. As a result of the case, detectives from the National Crime Squad began an undercover sting operation. Two officers, known only as Jono and Mike, posing as American criminals involved in cigarette smuggling, infiltrated a UK gang suspected of supplying the forgeries. They discovered the gang were involved in the wholesale selling of the fake notes to various buyers. The conspiracy was very carefully structured and organised. The individuals involved used code words such as 'paperwork' or 'jackets' when referring to the forgeries. The conspirators used secure communications wherever possible and carried out meetings when they were on legitimate trips abroad. One of the co-conspirators had extensive business interests in Europe and Russia, while Garland's role as Secretary General of the Workers Party involved regular meetings with fellow socialists around the world. The UK police operation with the aid of Interpol and the Russian police tracked couriers working for the Birmingham-based network all over Europe. In January 1999, the British officers took part in a secret surveillance operation in Moscow. With their Russian colleagues, they watched as the conspirators met their contacts among the Moscow criminal underworld. Also under surveillance was Sean Garland who made a number of visits to the North Korean embassy in the Russian capital.

The hoped-for deal didn't go ahead on that trip but the following month undercover officers obtained a fake, big-head superdollar bill. It was so good that it had to be sent to forensic experts in Washington to determine, beyond all doubt, that it was indeed a fake. Jono and Mike had hit a rich seam of intelligence. As well as discovering the involvement of Garland and therefore the Official IRA, they also identified another vital member of the operation. This key conspirator was David Levin, a Russian citizen who had worked for the KGB before moving to the UK. He maintained contacts with the Russian Mafia and was able to organise visas and passports for other members of the network. Levin enjoyed the high life, driving a Jaguar and Mercedes. He had bought both cars with cash. The undercover cops met him a number of times in the UK, keen to set up a deal to purchase a consignment of superdollars. In July, 1999, the gang were again followed to Moscow by the investigators.

It had been a slow business to gather intelligence on the group and to piece together the various bits of the jigsaw. Acting on information passed on by the Operation Mali agents, the German Police seized $250,000 worth of fake dollars at the border with the Czech Republic in May 2002. The following month, working on information that $100,000 in genuine currency was about to be sent to the Official IRA, the UK police decided to act. They were determined to prevent any chance of the cash falling into the hands of Irish republican paramilitaries. Three men involved in the plot to import superdollars were arrested at a pub and Levin was arrested some days later. The network used by Garland had been smashed.

It later emerged that the forgery gang had smuggled and laundered an estimated $30 million worth of fake notes across the world of which $5 million was distributed in the UK. In 2002, Levin was jailed for nine years for conspiracy to import superdollars. His appeal against a confiscation order for STG£789,000 was thrown out after the court heard that he had made STG£1 million from the forgeries. His arrest and conviction was seen as a major blow against the network. However, the authorities were convinced that the main players had managed to get away. Also prosecuted for their role in the network were Mark Adderley and Terence Silcock. Both men were part of the Birmingham gang that distributed the notes sourced in Russia by Levin and Garland. Adderley, then aged 45, was jailed for four years at Worcester Crown Court. He was described in court as being a runner for Levin. Silcock got seven years for his part which involved smuggling consignments of the fake notes from Dublin to Birmingham. He could conceal up to €250,000 worth of superdollars in a long coat while making the crossing by ferry. Two other men who faced charges were acquitted of committing any offence. Another man, Alan Jones, who worked with Silcock, went on the run when the first arrests were made in 2000. In 2005 he gave himself up to police and was sentenced to three years jail for making at least seven smuggling trips, over 18 months between Dublin and Birmingham.

In June 2004, a documentary by the BBC's *Panorama* team highlighted Sean Garland's major role in the scam to import fake dollars into the UK through Ireland. It included footage of the conspirators in Moscow taken by the joint British and Russian police operation. They were also given access to the Moscow police logs cataloguing the Workers Party General Secretary's, Sean Garland, visiting the North Korean embassy in the city. A North Korean defector was interviewed and described the forgery operation: "We bought the best equipment and the best ink, but we also had the very best people."

The TV exposé was followed in September by a Grand Jury indictment sought by the United States Attorney General's Office. Garland was named as one of the conspirators in the plot. The Americans claimed that the fake notes were being manufactured in North Korea with the full support of their government. This claim was believed to have been supported by the testimony of high-level defectors, presumably including the same one who had given the interview to the BBC. In his role as General Secretary of the Workers Party, Garland would meet with officials from various former communist countries, including North Korea. The US indictment against Garland claimed that he travelled to Poland in October 1997 to buy superdollars from the North Koreans. They claimed that Garland, also known as 'The Man in the Hat', was part of a network who continued to buy superdollars until July 2000. By buying the forgeries direct from the source the conspirators stood to make more money. The forgeries were smuggled to Moscow in diplomatic bags and distributed from the North Korean embassy. The Attorney General's Office claimed the group did their best to disguise North Korea as the source by letting others know that the forgeries were coming from Russia. The Grand Jury indictment made it clear that Garland was viewed as a key figure in the network that included criminals based in the UK, Russia, Latvia and other countries.

In October 2005, at the age of 71, Garland was arrested on foot of the extradition warrant from the US, issued by the Secret Service. He was picked up at 10 pm as he attended the annual general meeting of the Workers Party in Belfast. The following day he appeared at Belfast County Court where he sought bail. There were objections from the Crown lawyer to the application.

"We would say in simple terms that the defendant would have a strong incentive to flee back to the Republic of Ireland," said the barrister for the Crown. Garland's lawyer responded that his client had a suitable address in Northern Ireland where he could stay with a life long friend and that he "strenuously protests his innocence".

Bail was granted on condition that three independent sureties of STG£10,000 were put up and he stay at the provided address in County Down. Those conditions were varied the following month to allow him to travel home to Navan for medical treatment.

When Garland failed to appear at the next court hearing on December 1, 2005 a warrant was issued for his arrest. The Official IRA man stated that he would challenge any extradition attempts. He claimed that the US wanted to get him because of the Workers Party stance opposing America's foreign policy. So far the US government have failed to have Garland extradited from the Republic of Ireland.

Like the superdollar, the best kind of fakes are the ones that look like the real thing. These can be passed off at the full price, maximising profits for the master forgers. The preference forgers have for copying large bank notes is also evident at a local level. In Ireland, many petrol stations and convenience stores feature signs warning customers that €100 notes won't be accepted. At ATMs €50 notes are the largest denomination issued because retailers don't want to lose out to a fake €100 note. This precaution is a source of annoyance for many tourists from countries where €100 notes are regularly used. However, most years it is the €20 and €50 notes which make up two thirds of the detected forgeries. In 2007, there was €35.6 million worth of forged notes withdrawn from circulation in the EU. Currency is the target of the most professional crime gangs who specialise in fraud. It takes serious investment and expertise to produce good quality forged currency. A successful operation also takes the street-level hustler, on the bottom rung of the ladder, willing to put his neck on the line to float €5,000 worth of fake notes. The plot to launder superdollars in the UK and Ireland was unravelled from the bottom up when they were first discovered at the Birmingham travel agency.

After currency, the most faked items are designer clothes and fashion accessories, which can also be easily produced, shipped and distributed around the world. It is clear that different crime gangs specialise in disparate areas. Some, who move laundered diesel, might also run guns, while those who produce fake money may also deal in drugs. It is a prime example of free-market economics at work. Fuel laundering has been developed into an art form by the Irish border bandits and is a mixture of big business and small-time entrepreneurs. Every step of the way is a separate franchise. Other criminal groups, however, specialise in their own areas of expertise. Just as Chinese garlic smuggling provides a lucrative niche for the specialist smuggler, so too does the trade in counterfeit medicines. Unlike forged currency, pirated movies and bogus watches, however, this type of fraud can kill people.

A popular choice for the medicine fakers is Viagra, the drug designed to combat male impotence. It commands a good price and customers will probably be too embarrassed to complain about its failure to work. A plethora of websites purport to offer cut-price Viagra for sale. Enterprising Irish hustlers happily buy the tablets in full knowledge they are fake with a view to selling them direct to local customers. But the buyers should be careful. In one extreme case reported by the Europe Federation of Pharmaceutical Industries and Association in 2008, a batch of counterfeit Viagra contained too much of its active ingredient, sildenafil, putting users at risk of a heart attack.

In 2007, the European Union seized four million packages of fake drugs at its borders. The World Health Organisation estimates the global market in counterfeit drugs to be worth €40 billion annually and is set to rise to €70 billion by 2010. While tales of dodgy Viagra may provoke a few sniggers, bogus medicines can pose a serious health risk. In one of the worst counterfeit medicine cases around 2,500 people died in Niger in 1995 when over 50,000 people were given fake vaccines to prevent meningitis. The vaccines had been supplied in good faith, but were later proved to be sophisticated fakes with no active ingredient. Between 1995 and 1998 it is estimated that 119 children died in Haiti and India after being treated with a cough syrup that contained diethylene glycol, an industrial solvent toxin normally used to make anti-freeze. The World Health Organisation suggests that ten per cent of all medicines in circulation are fakes. In developed countries, that figure drops to just one per cent but climbs to 30 per cent in poorer countries.

In August 2007, there was a health scare in Ireland. It was sparked by 1,100 tubes of fake toothpaste which had found their way into Irish shops. The bogus Sensodyne toothpaste contained diethylene glycol, the same poison that killed children in Haiti and India. It has the potential to cause renal failure if it is ingested in big enough amounts. The chemical is used by counterfeiters who want to make toothpaste for a fraction of the cost of the real thing. The batch of bogus toothpaste, identifiable by Arabic writing on the tube, had turned up earlier in the year in the UK at car boot sales and open-air markets. The UK's medical council issued an alert although there were no arrests or charges brought against anyone for selling the toothpaste. An Irish wholesaler bought it in and distributed consignments in good faith to 70 small pharmacies around Ireland until it was recalled. Two years earlier another distributor had been fined €5,000 for putting counterfeit condoms on the market. The Irish Medicines Board had issued a warning after it emerged that 500,000 fake Durex condoms, some with holes, had been sold in Ireland over a ten month period. Both cases highlighted the danger posed by cowboys who are prepared to doctor products for the health and medical markets if it will earn them some easy money. However, there is also a temptation for some legitimate firms to maximise profits and get an edge over the competition by passing off fakes as the real thing.

When American entrepreneur Joseph Patrick Smith Jr arrived in Ireland to set up business, he was greeted with open arms. His plan was to source and broker aircraft parts to clients all over the world. It was just the type of industry that the Irish government wanted to encourage. The 60-year-old brash American business man was an experienced and confident operator who had developed connections all over the world. Plans to site the new industry in Shannon added to the American's appeal. The new firm would add weight to Shannon Airport's claim to be an aviation industry hub.

Smyth Aerospace Manufacturing started business in April 1997. The company was family run, Joseph being helped by his two sons, Joseph Patrick Smith III and

Thomas Edward Smith. They advertised and sold aircraft parts though the Inventory Locator Service, a computer database used internationally by commercial companies and individuals to trade aircraft spares. The items advertised by the Smiths were listed as being 'Original Equipment Manufacturer' parts, in other words they were brand new. The then Minister for Enterprise and Employment, Richard Bruton, officially welcomed Smyth Aerospace Manufacturing to Ireland. The Shannon Development Company awarded the firm €150,000 of grants. Another 25 investors were found through the Business Expansion Scheme, raising €250,000 in capital.

As business developed, customers submitted their requests for quotes to the company office, either in Arizona or Shannon. When a customer ordered a part they were asked to pre-pay by sending a cheque or wiring money to its Allied Irish Bank account. Then the items would be shipped from Ireland to the customer. The first two years of business for Smyth Aerospace Manufacturing went very well, exploiting a lucrative niche. Its biggest customers were the United States Air Force and other air forces around the world, including NASA and the Irish Air Corps. Bolivia, Burma, Australia and Turkey were some of the countries listed on the firm's website, which stated that they "offered worldwide sales and engineering". Parts were also supplied to commercial airlines for Boeing 747 and 737 passenger aircrafts. Although it kept an office in Arizona for the convenience of its US clients, the firm's real business took place within the Shannon duty-free zone. By 1999, the company was generating an annual turnover of $4.5 million and employed 20 people.

Unfortunately things were not as straight-forward as they seemed. In the US a number of bogus parts had been found in some aircraft. As a result Operation Phoenix had been launched in 1998. The undercover operation, started by the FBI with the Air Force Office of Special Investigations and the Defence Criminal Investigative Service, set out to identify the sellers of the bogus aircraft parts. The trail led to Shannon and to Smyth Aerospace Manufacturing. Smith was probably already on a list of suspects having been convicted for selling bogus parts in Arizona in 1992. Any background checks carried out on Smith by the Irish authorities had failed to turn up his criminal conviction and they were happy to hand over grand-aid. Jailed for 15 months in the US in 1992, Smith had simply upped sticks and set up business in Ireland to avoid the unwanted publicity. As a result of Operation Phoenix launched in 1998, Smith was back on the investigators' radar. Undercover agents targeted the company's sales operation, ordering parts most likely to have been refurbished or re-labelled as being new and unused. Several parts, labelled as new, were bought during an undercover operation that involved US military agents. When the investigators then passed them to the original manufacturers for inspection they were able to establish that the parts were either previously used or were fakes. The parts were for use in the US Air Force T-37 Tweet and T-38 Talon jet trainer aircraft, the NASA aircraft fleet and the commercial Lear Jet. In some cases the parts could have made Smith 1000 per cent profit, after being simply repainted and re-packaged. It was discovered that from the very beginning Smyth Aerospace Manufacturing had been shipping bogus parts to its customers.

In the United States, where the aviation industry is far more developed than anywhere else in the world, the issue of counterfeit aircraft parts is a serious problem. The US National Transportation Safety Board has found unapproved parts were "causal factors" in numerous accidents and emergency landings with airlines, small private planes, cargo carriers, crop-dusters and helicopters. The Federal Aviation Administration estimated that 166 accidents or serious mishaps between May 1973 and April 1993 were due to bogus parts. Between 1992 and 1999 more than 350 cases involving unauthorised parts were prosecuted in the USA. The problem of counterfeit aircraft parts is not solely confined to the United States. Faults in minor parts were blamed for the crash of a Danish airliner just after take-off from Oslo in 1989. All 55 people on board were killed. Air accident investigators found the aircraft had broken up in the air. The tail fin was found some distance from the rest of the wreckage. The nuts and bolts that had secured it to the fuselage were made from ordinary steel rather than the necessary specially hardened and heat-treated steel. Needless to say the FBI and the military agencies were taking the case involving Smith's company very seriously. By October 2000 they had enough evidence from their undercover investigation to act and the Gardaí were called in to assist them.

On October 6, 2000, Smyth Aerospace Manufacturing's premises in Shannon was raided along with 11 other premises in the Shannon and Limerick regions. Gardaí took a consignment of parts from a warehouse owned by the company. These were then shipped to Lakenheath, an RAF base in England, and transported from there to the FBI headquarters in Phoenix, Arizona, by the US Air Force. Samples were sent for forensic testing. The tests confirmed that the parts were counterfeit.

In the aftermath of the raid, Smith stripped the company of whatever assets he could lay his hands on.

At that stage, while the counterfeit parts had yet to be confirmed as being bogus, there was no reason for Smith's arrest in Ireland. A shipment of stock was transferred to the UK and $1 million was paid out to the company's directors, Smith and his sons, of which $700,000 went directly to Smith. Although Smyth Aerospace Manufacturing continued to trade, its turnover collapsed from $4.5 million to just $830,000. It finally went into liquidation, leaving a number of creditors and the 26 investors from the Business Expansion Scheme out of pocket.

In the official indictment later filed by the United States Attorney's Office from Phoenix, Arizona, it was asserted that Smith had created false certificates and documents for the aircraft he sold, passing them off as new. Smith's sons, who were based in the US, were arrested and quizzed by the FBI. The case against them was watertight. They admitted that the company had set up separate phone lines and a new postal address in Shannon to hide the illegal trade in bogus aircraft parts. They agreed a deal with US prosecutors and they pleaded guilty to the charges. In return the brothers agreed that they could be called to testify against their father in any future prosecution. Joseph Patrick Smith III, then aged 43, of Phoenix, and Thomas Edward Smith (39), of Rockville, Maryland were each sentenced to five years probation and ordered to pay $24,722 in restitution to the US government. They agreed to waive their right to appeal and their five year sentences were suspended at a Federal Court hearing in Arizona.

Joseph Patrick Smith Jr, however, had left Ireland and kept a low profile, possibly in France where he is thought to have owned property. Although he did contest the liquidator's report in the High Court in 2005, he did not turn up in person. He denied claims that he had transferred cash and stock from Smyth Aerospace, but the court ruled against him and barred him from acting as a company director for five years.

Luckily enough none of the bogus parts supplied by Smith's firm are known to have contributed to any air accidents. For a while the Irish Air Corps fleet of Cessna aircraft was grounded, however, when it emerged spare parts bought from a contractor had been supplied by Smyth Aerospace Manufacturing.

United States Attorney, Paul K Charlton, who took the case against Smyth Aerospace, highlighted the dangers posed by cowboy dealers who compromise air safety: "These aircraft parts could have been used on a variety of highly sophisticated aircraft, flown by some of the nation's finest military pilots. This scheme of selling parts of questionable quality not only defrauded the government but potentially could have put these dedicated pilots' lives at risk."

Patrick Joseph Smith Jr denied being involved in fraud, but remains a fugitive from the US Justice Department.

Whether it is fake budgies or bogus Lear jet engine parts, the likes of O'Brien and Smith managed to blur the lines between illicit and licit trade. They created a commercial edge by playing outside the rules of the games. Their corner-cutting, in the chase for profits, could have had potentially disastrous effects. One fraudster could have introduced the Avian Flu virus to Ireland and the other could have caused an Astronaut's jet to fall out of the sky. Counterfeiting is not just an economic crime. In some cases it can pose a real physical threat. Garlic smuggling may sound harmless but in the era of genetic modifications and the use of dangerous pesticides any food product that strays beyond proper controls could develop into a health risk. A hole in a counterfeit condom could have a personal cost for an individual that might feel like their equivalent to a plane crash. As evidenced by the toxic sludge left behind by fuel laundering operations, counterfeiters seem happy to ignore the potential costs of social responsibility. The border bandits started out as politically motivated black-marketeers but their operations were as much about a guerrilla-style economic war as they were about funding the struggle.

In the end, the flow of illicit money proves to be a torrent too strong for any of the fraudsters to simply turn off – even if they wanted to. So long as the rivers of black market money flows it would be as well to remember the adage; buyer beware.

More Books from Merlin Publishing

Available from all good bookshops

THE OUTSIDERS – EAMON DILLON

Exposing the Secretive World of Ireland's Travellers
ISBN: 978-1903582-67-1 €12.99

The Outsiders uncovers the secretive world of Irish travellers, where prejudice, crime and a burning loyalty to family, clan, and tradition, have made the community ignore external influences.

Eamon Dillon investigates Irish travellers and their worldwide drive to succeed – a hunger that has taken some traveller gangs into the realms of fraud, illegal boxing, home invasions, armed robbery and drug-dealing.

From Bejing to London, Dillon reveals illegal operations by successful Irish travellers, such as the Rathkeale millionaire traveller-traders, the Texan con-artists and the cowboy builders that besiege UK home-owners. These travellers have conquered racism and physical hardship to become modern day pavee princes.

Dillon also exposes another side to life as an Irish traveller, where traveller-on-traveller crime is a major problem and murderous feuds can claim the lives of innocent travellers.

Of an estimated 50,000 Irish travellers worldwide, some will always refuse to bend to the rules of society because they are – the Outsiders.

CRIME WARS – PAUL WILLIAMS

ISBN: 978-1903582-83-1 €14.99

Crime Wars is a terrifying depiction of Ireland's flourishing crime culture. Paul Williams tells the horrifying story of the Canal Butcher, Mark Desmond, suspected of the double murder of two young drug mules in January 2000. He talks about the life and times of gang boss Martin "Marlo" Hyland and his role in numerous murders and reveals the dangerous crime spree of the Finglas Gang, which included armed robberies, drug trafficking and murder.

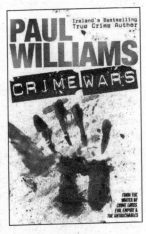

Williams relates the story of impressionable teenager Joseph 'Joey the Lip' O'Callaghan, enslaved by heroin dealer Martin Kenny, describes the life of Christy Griffin, the self-styled Tony Soprano, and of the border-based gang which specialised in drug trafficking worth tens of millions of euro. He talks about the ongoing Crumlin/Drimnagh feud, the story behind a plot to smuggle 20 million worth of heroin into Ireland, the terrifying actions of hitman Shay Wildes and the murder of Sean Dunne, drug trafficker and IRA racketeer.

Crime Wars is essential reading to understand the battle raging on Irish streets.

NEVER SUCK A DEAD MAN'S HAND – DANA KOLLMANN

True Life Experiences of an American Crime Scene Investigator

ISBN: 978-1903582-86-2 €12.99

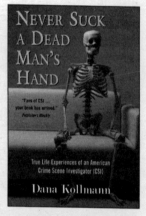

Step past the flashing police lights and enter the world of a real crime scene with this unflinching account of life as an American Crime Scene Investigator (CSI).

Whether talking about rigor mortis or the art of finger-printing a stiff corpse on the side of the road, Dana Kollmann details her unvarnished experiences as a CSI for the Baltimore County Police Department. She recounts stories that the cops and the CSIs usually leave in the field, bringing the sights, smells, and sounds of a crime scene alive as never before. Kollmann's gritty forensic facts explain what really goes on behind the scenes.

Never Suck a Dead Man's Hand takes you into the strange world on the other side of the crime scene tape and gives you an eye-opening and unforgettable perspective on the day-to-day life of a CSI.

THE COMPLEX – JOHN DUIGNAN with NICOLA TALLANT

An Insider Exposes the covert World of the Church of Scientology
ISBN: 978-1903582-84-8 €12.99

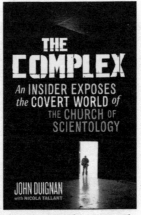

For the first time ever, a former high-ranking Scientology member is lifting the lid on life inside the Church. In *The Complex* John Duignan reveals the true story behind the 'religion' that has ensnared a who's who list of celebrities and convinced thousands of ordinary people to join up.

Celebrities like Tom Cruise and John Travolta may give a friendly public face to the Church of Scientology but behind the scenes Duignan reveals how an insatiable money-making, and power hungry, machine is driving the Church ever forward, crushing every critic in its wake. He exposes the fanatical paramilitary group, known as the Sea Org, that lies at the heart of the so-called Church.

In *The Complex* he looks back on the 22 years he served in the Church's secret army – the hours of sleep deprivation, brain-washing and intense 'religious counselling' he endured, as he was moulded into a soldier of the Church. He talks about the Church's military training programme and the punishments meted out to anyone who transgresses, including children.

The beliefs of the Church of Scientology might sound like something from a science-fiction book but *The Complex* reveals that their growing power base is a shocking fact.

THE IRISH SCISSOR SISTERS
– MICK McCAFFREY
**The Inside Story of the Torso in the Canal Investigation
and the Gruesome Homicide of Farah Noor**
ISBN: 978-1903582-72-5 12.99

On March 20, 2005, Charlotte Mulhall slashed a four-inch gash in Farah Swaleh Noor's throat. She cut her mother's lover again and again with the razor-sharp blade, while her sister Linda hit him about 10 times with the hammer. They then spent hours hacking his body into eight pieces, before dumping his butchered remains in the Royal Canal, Dublin.

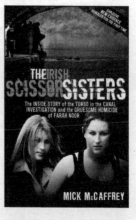

Christened the 'Scissor Sisters' by the media, their names are now synonymous with violence and brutality but what really happened that night? What part did Kathleen, their 'mam', play and where is she now? Did John, their tragic father, help to dismember Farah's remains? And what about the victim – why did Farah carry knives and like to burn himself?

Using witness statements and the Mulhalls' own words, McCaffrey reconstructs the horrific murder in graphic detail, investigating the motives of all the people involved. He gets inside the minds of the women who carried out this unspeakable crime and depicts the intensive Garda hunt that led to the conviction of two of the most notorious killers in Ireland's history.

The Irish Scissor Sisters examines the appalling crime that sent shockwaves through Irish society. It is the definitive account of a sickening murder that should never be forgotten.